# FAVORITE BRAND NAME

# PASTA

# COLLECTION

PUBLICATIONS INTERNATIONAL, LTD.

ISBN: 1-56173-670-8

Library of Congress Catalog Card Number: 92-64238

**Pictured on front cover:** *Top row, left:* Layered Pasta Ricotta Pie *(page 96), Center:* Smoked Turkey & Pepper Pasta Salad *(page 37), Right:* Tortellini with Three-Cheese Tuna Sauce *(page 140). Bottom row, left:* Shrimp Fettuccine *(page 187), Center:* Quick Country Minestrone *(page 40), Right:* Spicy Ravioli and Cheese *(page 190).*

**Pictured on back cover:** *Top row, left:* Tortellini Primavera *(page 151), Center:* Saucy Shrimp over Chinese Noodle Cakes *(page 165), Right:* Vegetable 'n Chicken Alfredo *(page 98). Bottom row, left:* Ham Pasta Primavera *(page 117), Center:* Lasagna Italiano *(page 59), Right:* Beef & Pasta Salad *(page 45).*

8  7  6  5  4  3  2  1

Manufactured in U.S.A.

Microwave ovens vary in wattage and power output; cooking times given with microwave directions in this book may need to be adjusted. Consult manufacturer's instructions for suitable microwave-safe cooking dishes.

# Contents

# PASTA TECHNIQUES

Welcome to the wonderful world of pasta! With over 150 different varieties available, pasta ranks as one of America's most popular and versatile foods. Discover endless combinations of savory sauces and unique pasta shapes with this unbelievable collection of recipes from over 50 of your favorite brand name companies. Following are some helpful tips and techniques to ensure recipe success each and every time.

## PASTA FACTS

• Most pasta products can be classified as either long goods (spaghetti), short goods (macaroni), specialty products (shells and bow ties) or egg noodles (pasta made with eggs). Egg noodles contain some cholesterol while non-egg pastas are cholesterol free.

• Pasta in its dry, uncooked form can be stored almost indefinitely in a cool, dry place. Fresh pasta will last several weeks in the refrigerator or can also be frozen for up to one month.

## TIME-SAVING TIPS

• Plan on preparing an extra batch of your favorite pasta soup or sauce. Simply pour into serving-size freezer containers and freeze. Thaw and reheat for a last-minute dinner or heartwarming lunch.

• Lasagna, manicotti and stuffed shells are perfect dishes to prepare and then freeze for another time. Try freezing these casseroles in single-serving portions for days when everyone is eating at different times. Simply cook in the microwave or conventional oven.

## COOKING PASTA

For every pound of dry pasta, bring 4 to 6 quarts of water to a full, rolling boil. Add 2 teaspoons salt, if desired. Gradually add pasta, allowing water to return to a boil. The boiling water helps circulate the pasta so that it cooks evenly. Stir frequently to prevent the pasta from sticking to the pot. Begin testing for doneness after 5 minutes of cooking. Pasta that is "al dente"— meaning "to the tooth"—is tender, yet firm. Draining the pasta as soon as it is done will stop the cooking action and help prevent over-cooked pasta. Rinsing is necessary only if the recipe specifies to do so. For best results, serve the pasta within minutes of leaving the pot. If the pasta is to be used in a dish that requires further cooking, such as a casserole, undercook it slightly.

As you page through this tantalizing recipe collection, you'll discover creative new ways to perk up your pasta with satisfying recipes perfect for any meal occasion.

4

Rings

Rotini

Bow ties

Gnocchi

Wagon wheels

Ziti

Rigatoni

Ravioli

Egg noodles

Elbow macaroni

Shells

Tortellini

Salad macaroni

Mostaccioli

Spaghetti

Vermicelli

Fusilli

Ramen noodles

Couscous

Orzo

Twistee noodles

Radiatore

Alphabets

Linguine

Angel hair

Fun shapes

Fettuccine

Manicotti

Lasagna

Chinese noodles

# SAVORY SOUPS AND SALADS

## Italian Pasta Salad

3 cups (8 ounces) tri-color rotini,
  cooked and drained
1 cup (4 ounces) KRAFT® 100% Grated
  Parmesan Cheese
1 bottle (8 ounces) KRAFT® House
  Italian Dressing
2 cups broccoli flowerets
½ cup chopped red pepper
½ cup red onion slices
½ cup pitted ripe olive slices

• Mix together ingredients in large bowl
until well blended. Chill.

*Makes 8 cups*

**Prep time:** 15 minutes

## Bow Tie Salad

1 package (10 ounces) bow tie pasta,
  cooked and drained
1 DOLE® Red Bell Pepper, seeded,
  slivered
2 cups DOLE® Broccoli florettes
1 cup DOLE® Cauliflower florettes
1 clove garlic, minced
½ cup rice vinegar
¼ cup vegetable oil
2 tablespoons teriyaki sauce
1 tablespoon sesame seeds, toasted
2 teaspoons sesame oil
¼ teaspoon red pepper flakes

• Combine all ingredients; mix lightly.
Cover and refrigerate overnight.

*Makes 10 servings*

**Prep time:** 15 minutes
**Cook time:** 10 minutes
**Chill time:** Overnight

## Robusto Ravioli Soup

1 pound Italian sausage, casing
  removed
8 cups water
8 teaspoons HERB-OX® Instant
  Chicken Bouillon *or* 8 chicken
  bouillon cubes
1 package (9 ounces) fresh mini
  cheese ravioli
2 cups assorted vegetables (broccoli,
  carrots, tomatoes), cut into bite-
  size pieces
2 tablespoons DURKEE® RedHot
  Cayenne Pepper Sauce
½ teaspoon DURKEE® Garlic Powder

In Dutch oven over medium-high heat,
brown sausage; drain. Add water; bring
to a boil. Reduce heat to medium. Stir in
instant chicken bouillon and ravioli;
simmer 5 minutes. Stir in remaining
ingredients. Simmer, covered, 10
minutes or until vegetables are tender,
stirring occasionally.

*Makes 8 servings*

# Tortellini Asparagus Salad

*This hearty salad is perfect as either a side dish or main dish.*

2 packages (9 ounces *each*) cheese-filled tortellini, cooked and drained
1 pound fresh asparagus, cut into ½-inch pieces
2 cups tightly packed fresh spinach leaves, torn into bite-size pieces
1 cup finely chopped red pepper
¼ cup red wine vinegar
2 tablespoons olive *or* vegetable oil
1½ teaspoons lemon juice
1 teaspoon sugar
1 teaspoon LAWRY'S® Garlic Salt

*Tortellini Asparagus Salad*

Place asparagus on steamer rack; place in deep pot with 1 inch boiling water. Cover and steam 10 minutes. Remove and set aside. Steam spinach in same pot about 45 seconds or until just wilted. In large bowl, combine asparagus, spinach, red pepper and tortellini; mix lightly. In small bowl, combine vinegar, oil, lemon juice, sugar and Garlic Salt; blend well. Pour over tortellini mixture; toss to coat.

*Makes 4 servings*

**Hints:** 1½ cups broccoli flowerettes can be substituted for asparagus. Chopped pimientos can be substituted for red pepper.

**Microwave:** Place asparagus and spinach in microwave-safe bowl; sprinkle with small amount of water. Cover with plastic wrap, venting one corner. Microwave on HIGH 2 minutes to steam vegetables. In large bowl, combine asparagus mixture, red pepper and tortellini; mix lightly. In small bowl, combine vinegar, oil, lemon juice, sugar and Garlic Salt; blend well. Pour over tortellini mixture; toss to coat.

**Presentation:** Serve with fresh bread.

# Creamy Macaroni and Cheese

8 ounces spiral macaroni (rotini), cooked and drained
1 cup (4 ounces) grated Parmesan cheese
1 green pepper, chopped
1 cup chopped green onions with tops
1 cup sliced radishes
¼ cup chopped fresh parsley
1 cup prepared HIDDEN VALLEY RANCH® Original Ranch® Salad Dressing
2 tomatoes, cut into thin wedges

In large bowl, combine macaroni, cheese, peppers, onions, radishes and parsley. Stir in salad dressing. Top with tomato wedges.      *Makes 6 to 8 servings*

## Quick Beef Soup

1½ pounds lean ground beef
1 cup chopped onion
2 cloves garlic, minced
1 can (28 ounces) tomatoes, cut up, undrained
6 cups water
6 beef bouillon cubes
¼ teaspoon pepper
½ cup orzo, uncooked
1½ cups frozen mixed vegetables (peas, carrots and corn)

Brown beef with onion and garlic in large saucepan over medium-high heat, stirring occasionally to separate beef; drain.

Place tomatoes in blender or food processor; cover and process until smooth. Add to beef mixture with water, bouillon cubes and pepper. Bring to a boil; reduce heat to low. Simmer, uncovered, 20 minutes, stirring occasionally. Add orzo and mixed vegetables. Simmer an additional 15 minutes, stirring occasionally. Serve with French bread, if desired.

*Makes 6 servings*

*Favorite recipe from* **North Dakota Beef Commission**

## Teddy Tuna Salad

2 cups MUELLER'S® Super Shapes Teddy Bear pasta (*or* any other Super Shapes), cooked and drained
⅔ cup HELLMAN'S® or BEST FOODS® Real Mayonnaise
1 tablespoon lemon juice
¼ cup milk
½ cup sliced celery
¼ cup sliced green onions with tops
⅛ teaspoon pepper
1 can (6 ounces) tuna, drained and flaked

In large bowl, combine mayonnaise, lemon juice and milk. Add celery, onions, pepper, tuna and pasta; toss to coat.

*Makes 4 servings*

## Fresh Apricot-Pasta Salad

2½ cups California fresh apricots (about 1 pound), cut into sixths, divided
2 tablespoons white wine vinegar
¼ cup olive oil
1 tablespoon chopped fresh basil leaves *or* 1 teaspoon dried basil leaves, crushed
Salt and fresh ground black pepper
2 cups cooked spiral-shaped pasta (fusilli)
2 small zucchini, julienned
1 whole chicken breast, cooked, skinned, boned and shredded
1 red pepper, julienned

Place ½ cup apricots and vinegar in food processor or blender container; cover. Process until smooth. Gradually add oil, while processing, until dressing thickens. Stir in basil. Season with salt and black pepper to taste; set aside. Combine remaining 2 cups apricots, pasta, zucchini, chicken and red pepper in large bowl. Add dressing; toss to coat.

*Makes 6 servings*

*Favorite recipe from* **California Apricot Advisory Board**

*Quick Beef Soup*

## Bella Pasta Salad

6 ounces MUELLER'S® Rosettes™,
    cooked and drained
8 ounces mozzarella cheese *or* smoked
    mozzarella cheese, cut into 2-inch
    strips
1 cup cherry tomatoes, quartered
1 yellow pepper, cut into 2-inch strips
1 zucchini, cut into 2-inch strips
½ cup MAZOLA® Corn Oil
3 tablespoons white wine vinegar
2 tablespoons chopped fresh basil
    leaves
1 clove garlic, minced
1 teaspoon salt
½ teaspoon black pepper

In large bowl, combine pasta, cheese,
tomatoes, yellow pepper and zucchini;
mix lightly. In small bowl, stir corn oil,
vinegar, basil, garlic, salt and black
pepper until well mixed. Pour over pasta
and vegetables; toss lightly to coat.
Cover; refrigerate several hours.

*Makes 12 servings*

## Pistachio Pesto Vegetable Pasta Salad

1 package (8 ounces) mostaccioli,
    uncooked
2 cups julienne-cut DOLE® Carrots
2 cups sliced DOLE® Celery
2 cloves garlic
2 bunches DOLE® Spinach (2 cups)
½ cup roasted DOLE® Pistachios
½ cup water
⅓ cup (1½ ounces) grated Parmesan
    cheese
3 tablespoons dried basil leaves,
    crushed
2 tablespoons olive oil
¼ teaspoon salt

• Cook pasta according to package
directions, adding carrots and celery to
pasta during last 30 seconds of cooking;
drain.

• In food processor or blender container,
combine garlic, spinach, pistachios,
water, Parmesan cheese, basil, oil and
salt. Process until spinach is medium to
finely chopped.

• In large bowl, combine pasta mixture
and pesto; toss to coat.

*Makes 6 servings*

**Prep time:** 10 minutes
**Cook time:** 15 minutes

## Waldorf Chicken Salad

2 cups chopped cooked chicken *or*
    turkey
1 cup CREAMETTE® Medium
    Macaroni Shells, cooked and
    drained
2 cups coarsely chopped all-purpose
    apples
4 ounces mild cheddar cheese, cubed
    (about 1 cup)
¾ cup sliced celery
½ cup mayonnaise *or* salad dressing
½ cup chopped pecans
¼ cup applesauce
2 teaspoons WYLER'S® or STEERO®
    Chicken-Flavor Instant Bouillon

In large bowl, combine all ingredients;
mix lightly. Cover; chill. Garnish as
desired. Refrigerate leftovers.

*Makes 4 to 6 servings*

*Pasta and Walnut Fruit Salad*

## Pasta and Walnut Fruit Salad

8 ounces medium shell macaroni, cooked and drained
1 container (8 ounces) plain nonfat yogurt
¼ cup frozen orange juice concentrate, thawed
1 can (15 ounces) mandarin oranges, drained
1 cup seedless red grapes, halved
1 cup seedless green grapes, halved
1 apple, cored and chopped
½ cup sliced celery
½ cup walnut halves

In large bowl, blend yogurt and orange juice concentrate. Add shells and remaining ingredients; toss to coat. Cover; refrigerate.

*Makes 6 to 8 servings*

*Favorite recipe from* **Walnut Marketing Board**

## Turkey 'n Spaghetti Summer Salad

10 ounces spaghetti, cooked and drained
1 medium zucchini, thinly sliced
2 cups chopped cooked turkey
1 can (8 ounces) cut green beans, drained
18 cherry tomatoes, halved
⅓ cup sliced pitted ripe olives
2 medium green onions with tops, chopped
¼ cup (1 ounce) grated Parmesan cheese
1 teaspoon salt
⅔ cup olive oil
¼ cup white wine vinegar
2 tablespoons water
1 package (0.6 ounce) Italian salad dressing mix

In small saucepan over medium-high heat, bring small amount of water to a boil. Add zucchini. Reduce heat to low; simmer just until zucchini is crisp-tender. Drain and rinse in cold water.

In large bowl, combine spaghetti, zucchini, turkey, beans, tomatoes, olives and onions; mix lightly. Sprinkle with Parmesan cheese and salt. In small jar or cruet, combine oil, vinegar, water and salad dressing mix; shake until well blended. Pour over spaghetti mixture; toss lightly to coat. Refrigerate several hours or overnight to blend flavors.

*Makes 6 to 8 servings*

*Favorite recipe from* **California Poultry Industry Federation**

## Chicken Noodle Soup

1 can (46 fluid ounces) COLLEGE
    INN® Chicken Broth
½ pound boneless skinless chicken,
    cut into bite-size pieces
1½ cups medium egg noodles,
    uncooked
1 cup sliced carrots
½ cup chopped onion
⅓ cup sliced celery
1 teaspoon dill weed
¼ teaspoon pepper

In large saucepan, combine all
ingredients. Bring to a boil over
medium-high heat. Reduce heat to low;
simmer 20 minutes or until chicken is no
longer pink in center and noodles are
tender, stirring occasionally.
*Makes 8 servings*

## Dijon Asparagus Chicken Salad

1 cup HELLMANN'S® or BEST
    FOODS® Real Mayonnaise
2 tablespoons Dijon-style mustard
2 tablespoons lemon juice
1 teaspoon salt
½ teaspoon black pepper
6 ounces MEULLER'S® Twist Trio®,
    cooked and drained
1 pound skinless boneless chicken
    breasts, cooked and chopped
1 package (10 ounces) frozen
    asparagus spears, thawed and cut
    into 2-inch pieces
1 red pepper, cut into 1-inch pieces

In large bowl, combine mayonnaise,
mustard, lemon juice, salt and black
pepper; mix well. Add remaining
ingredients; mix lightly. Cover;
refrigerate. *Makes 6 servings*

*Chicken Noodle Soup*

## Pasta Cheddar Cheese Salad

1 container (15 ounces) SARGENTO®
    Ricotta Cheese*
1 large cucumber, peeled, seeded and
    cut into chunks
1 green onion with top, cut into 1-inch
    pieces
6 to 8 sprigs fresh parsley, stems
    removed
1 clove garlic, peeled
½ teaspoon salt
½ teaspoon white pepper
4 cups (1 pound) pasta spirals *or*
    twists
2 small green *or* red peppers, cut into
    ½-inch pieces
1 cup (4 ounces) SARGENTO® Classic
    Supreme Shredded Cheddar
    Cheese

Fit food processor with steel cutting
blade. Add Ricotta cheese, cucumber,
onion, parsley, garlic, salt and white
pepper; cover. Process until well
combined. Pour into large bowl.

Cook pasta according to package
directions; drain. Immediately add hot
pasta to bowl with dressing mixture. Stir
to thoroughly coat pasta. Add green
peppers and Cheddar cheese; mix
lightly. Season with additional salt and
white pepper to taste, if desired. Serve
immediately or cover and refrigerate up
to 3 days. For maximum flavor, bring to
room temperature before serving; toss
lightly. *Makes 8 servings*

*SARGENTO® Old Fashioned Ricotta,
Part Skim Ricotta *or* Light Ricotta can be
used.

**Variation:** For a heartier salad, add
chunks of cooked sausage, ham or roast
beef.

*Italian Vegetable Soup*

In large kettle or Dutch oven, brown sausage with onion and garlic over medium-high heat; drain. Add water, carrots, tomatoes, bouillon, Italian seasoning and pepper; bring to a boil. Reduce heat to low; cover and simmer 30 minutes, stirring occasionally. Add zucchini, beans and rotini. Simmer an additional 15 to 20 minutes or until rotini is tender, stirring occasionally. Garnish as desired. Refrigerate leftovers.

*Makes 6 to 8 servings, about 2½ quarts*

## Italian Vegetable Soup

1 pound Italian sausage, casing removed
2 cups chopped onion
2 cloves garlic, minced
7 cups water
4 medium carrots, peeled and sliced
1 can (28 ounces) whole tomatoes, cut up, undrained
2 tablespoons WYLER'S® or STEERO® Beef-Flavor Instant Bouillon or 6 Beef-Flavor Bouillon Cubes
1 teaspoon Italian seasoning
¼ teaspoon pepper
1½ cups coarsely chopped zucchini
1 can (15 ounces) garbanzo beans, drained
1 cup CREAMETTE® Rotini or CREAMETTES® Elbow Macaroni

## Tuna Ramen Noodle Salad

½ (3-ounce) package Oriental-flavor ramen noodle soup mix
1 can (3¼ ounces) STARKIST® Tuna, drained and flaked
½ cup julienne cucumber
½ cup julienne green *or* red pepper
½ cup sliced water chestnuts, cut in half

Dressing:

2 tablespoons rice *or* white vinegar
2 teaspoons sesame oil
1 teaspoon peanut butter
⅛ teaspoon crushed red pepper

Cook ramen noodles according to package directions. Drain broth, reserving, if desired, to use as a clear soup for another meal. In medium bowl, toss noodles with tuna, cucumber, green pepper and water chestnuts.

For Dressing, in small shaker jar, combine vinegar, oil, peanut butter and crushed red pepper. Cover and shake until well blended. Add to noodle mixture; toss to coat. Serve immediately.

*Makes 1 serving*

**Prep time:** 15 minutes

## Chicken Salad Deluxe

1¼ cups prepared buttermilk salad
    dressing
½ cup mayonnaise
3 tablespoons half-and-half
1¾ teaspoons Beau Monde seasoning
1 teaspoon salt
½ teaspoon pepper
1 package (12 ounces) slivered
    almonds
10 ounces 100% semolina medium shell
    macaroni, cooked and drained
5 whole chicken breasts (about
    2 pounds), cooked, skinned,
    boned and cubed
3 cups chopped celery
2½ cups seedless green grapes, cut
    lengthwise into halves
2 cans (2.25 ounces *each*) sliced water
    chestnuts, drained
½ cup chopped onion

*Chicken Salad Deluxe*

Combine salad dressing, mayonnaise, half-and-half, seasoning, salt and pepper in small bowl; blend well. Cover; refrigerate overnight to blend flavors.

Reserve 1 tablespoon almonds for garnish. Combine remaining almonds, shells, chicken, celery, grapes, water chestnuts and onion in large bowl. Add dressing mixture; toss gently to coat. Serve on lettuce, if desired. Garnish with reserved almonds. Serve with cantaloupe and starfruit slices, if desired. *Makes 20 servings*

*Favorite recipe from* **North Dakota Wheat Commission**

## Confetti Pasta Salad

1 cup HELLMAN'S® or BEST
    FOODS® Real, Light *or*
    Cholesterol Free Reduced Calorie
    Mayonnaise
3 tablespoons cider vinegar
2 tablespoons sugar
1 tablespoon milk
1½ teaspoons dry mustard
1 teaspoon salt
8 ounces twist *or* spiral pasta, cooked
    and drained
2 cups finely shredded red cabbage
1 cup coarsely shredded carrots
1 medium green pepper, cut into thin
    strips

In large bowl, combine mayonnaise, vinegar, sugar, milk, dry mustard and salt; mix well. Add pasta, cabbage, carrots and green pepper; mix lightly. Cover; chill. *Makes 6 servings*

## Thai Chicken Fettuccine Salad

6 ounces fettuccine, cooked and
　　drained
1 cup PACE® Picante Sauce
¼ cup chunky peanut butter
2 tablespoons honey
2 tablespoons orange juice
1 teaspoon soy sauce
½ teaspoon ground ginger
2 tablespoons vegetable oil
3 chicken breast halves (about
　　12 ounces), skinned, boned and
　　cut into 1-inch pieces
　　Lettuce *or* savoy cabbage leaves,
　　optional
¼ cup coarsely chopped fresh cilantro
¼ cup peanut halves
¼ cup thin red pepper strips, cut into
　　halves

Combine picante sauce, peanut butter,
honey, orange juice, soy sauce and
ginger in small saucepan. Cook and stir
over low heat until well blended. Place
fettuccine in large bowl. Reserve ¼ cup
picante sauce mixture; pour remaining
mixture over fettuccine. Toss gently to
coat.

Heat oil in large skillet over medium-
high heat. Add chicken; cook and stir
until chicken is browned and no longer
pink in center, about 5 minutes. Add
reserved picante sauce mixture; mix
well. Place fettuccine on lettuce-covered
platter; top with chicken mixture.
Sprinkle with cilantro, peanut halves
and pepper strips. Refrigerate to cool to
room temperature. Serve with additional
picante sauce if desired. Garnish as
desired.　　　　　*Makes 4 servings*

## Warm Pasta and Spinach Salad

7 ounces MUELLER'S® Pasta Swirls®,
　　cooked and drained
1 package (10 ounces) fresh spinach,
　　washed, stems removed and torn
　　into bite-size pieces
8 ounces mushrooms, sliced
1 medium red onion, sliced
6 uncooked bacon slices, coarsely
　　chopped
1 tablespoon cornstarch
1 tablespoon sugar
1 teaspoon salt
½ teaspoon pepper
1 cup HELLMANN'S® or BEST
　　FOODS® Real Mayonnaise
1 cup water
⅓ cup cider vinegar

In large serving bowl, combine pasta,
spinach, mushrooms and onion; toss
lightly. Set aside. In medium skillet,
cook bacon over medium-high heat until
crisp. Remove with slotted spoon. Pour
off all but 2 tablespoons drippings. In
small bowl, combine cornstarch, sugar,
salt and pepper. With wire whisk, stir
cornstarch mixture into drippings in
skillet until well blended. Stir in
mayonnaise. Gradually stir in water and
vinegar. Bring mixture to a boil over
medium heat, stirring constantly. Boil 1
minute. Pour over spinach mixture. Add
bacon; mix lightly. Serve immediately.
　　　　　*Makes 8 to 10 servings*

*Thai Chicken Fettuccine Salad*

*Minestrone-Style Stew*

## Minestrone-Style Stew

1¾ pounds beef round steak, ¾ inch
    thick
1 tablespoon dried Italian seasoning
½ teaspoon pepper
2 tablespoons olive oil
1 large onion, chopped
2 large cloves garlic, minced
1 can (10¾ ounces) condensed beef
    broth
½ cup water
1 cup sliced carrots
¾ cup small shell macaroni,* uncooked
1 can (14½ ounces) whole peeled
    tomatoes, cut up, undrained
1 package (10 ounces) frozen Italian
    green beans
1 medium zucchini, sliced
3 tablespoons grated Parmesan cheese

Cut beef round steak into 1-inch pieces. Sprinkle with Italian seasoning and pepper. Heat oil in Dutch oven over medium-high heat. Add steak; cook and stir until evenly browned. Add onion and garlic; cook and stir until tender. Pour off drippings. Add broth and water. Bring to a boil; reduce heat to low. Cover tightly and simmer 1 to 1½ hours or until beef is tender, stirring occasionally. Add carrots and macaroni; simmer, uncovered, an additional 20 minutes. Stir in tomatoes, green beans and zucchini; simmer, uncovered, an additional 10 minutes or until vegetables are crisp-tender. Sprinkle individual servings with Parmesan cheese.

*Makes 6 servings*

**Prep time:** 30 minutes
**Cook time:** 1½ to 2 hours

*Elbow macaroni may be substituted. Add to stew with tomatoes.

*Favorite recipe from **National Live Stock and Meat Board***

# Pineapple Party Pasta Salad

1 can (20 ounces) DOLE® Crushed
    Pineapple in Syrup, undrained*
1 package (1 pound) spaghetti, cooked
    and drained
1 can (13 ounces) solid white tuna,
    drained and broken into chunks
12 cherry tomatoes, halved
1½ cups DOLE® Broccoli florettes
1 cup sliced DOLE® Celery
½ cup sliced DOLE® Green Onions
    with tops
½ cup DOLE® Slivered Almonds,
    toasted

Dressing:
1 cup mayonnaise
⅓ cup cider vinegar
3 tablespoons reserved pineapple
    syrup
1 tablespoon sugar
1 clove garlic, minced
½ teaspoon celery seed
½ teaspoon rosemary, crushed

• Drain pineapple; reserve 3 tablespoons syrup for dressing.

• Combine pineapple, spaghetti, tuna, tomatoes, broccoli, celery, onions and almonds; mix lightly.

• Combine ingredients for Dressing. Pour over salad; toss lightly to coat. Refrigerate.  *Makes 10 to 12 servings*

**Prep time:** 20 minutes
*Use pineapple packed in juice, if desired.

# Pasta and Bean Salad

*Convenient canned beans and artichoke hearts tossed with a tart Italian dressing make this an easy and tasty salad.*

½ cup PROGRESSO® Olive Oil
3 tablespoons PROGRESSO® Red
    Wine Vinegar
¼ cup (1 ounce) PROGRESSO® Grated
    Parmesan Cheese
¾ teaspoon Italian seasoning
½ teaspoon salt
¼ teaspoon sugar
¼ teaspoon dry mustard
¼ teaspoon ground black pepper
⅛ teaspoon cayenne pepper
1 clove garlic, minced
8 ounces ziti pasta, cooked and
    drained
1 can (10½ ounces) PROGRESSO®
    Chick Peas, drained
1 can (10½ ounces) PROGRESSO® Red
    Kidney Beans, drained
1 jar (6 ounces) PROGRESSO®
    Marinated Artichoke Hearts,
    drained and cut into chunks
2 stalks celery, chopped
2 medium tomatoes, cut into wedges

1. For dressing, whisk together olive oil, vinegar, Parmesan cheese, Italian seasoning, salt, sugar, mustard, peppers and garlic.

2. In large bowl, combine remaining ingredients.

3. Pour dressing over salad; toss gently to coat.

4. Refrigerate 2 hours or overnight.
*Makes 8 servings*

**Prep time:** 25 minutes
**Chill time:** 2 hours

*Tortellini Soup*

## Tortellini Soup

1 tablespoon margarine
2 cloves garlic, minced
2 cans (13¾ fluid ounces *each*)
    COLLEGE INN® Chicken *or* Beef
    Broth
1 package (8 ounces) fresh *or* frozen
    cheese-filled tortellini, thawed
1 can (14½ ounces) stewed tomatoes,
    cut up, undrained
1 package (10 ounces) fresh *or* frozen
    spinach, thawed
    Grated Parmesan cheese

In large saucepan, melt margarine over medium-high heat. Add garlic; cook and stir 2 to 3 minutes or until lightly browned. Add broth and tortellini; bring to a boil. Reduce heat to low; simmer 10 minutes, stirring occasionally. Add tomatoes and spinach; simmer an additional 5 minutes. Top individual servings with Parmesan cheese.

*Makes 6 servings*

## Spring Pasta Salad

8 ounces twistee egg noodles, cooked
    and drained
1 can (20 ounces) DOLE® Pineapple
    Chunks in Juice, undrained
1 large clove garlic, minced
1 cup olive oil
½ cup white vinegar
    Juice from 1 DOLE® Lemon
2 teaspoons prepared mustard
2 teaspoons Worcestershire sauce
1 teaspoon salt
    Dash pepper
8 ounces DOLE® Asparagus, cut into
    bite-size pieces, blanched
2 DOLE® Carrots, julienne-cut,
    blanched
1 cup frozen peas, thawed
½ cup sliced DOLE® Green Onions
    with tops
⅓ cup chopped fresh parsley
3 whole chicken breasts, cooked,
    skinned, boned and shredded

• Drain pineapple, reserving juice.

• Whisk together 1 tablespoon reserved pineapple juice, garlic, oil, vinegar, 2 tablespoons lemon juice, mustard, Worcestershire sauce, salt and pepper.

• Combine noodles, vegetables, parsley, chicken and pineapple in large bowl. Add dressing; toss to coat. Cover; refrigerate 3 hours. *Makes 8 servings*

**Prep time:** 20 minutes
**Chill time:** 3 hours

## Aegean Pasta Salad

1 cup HELLMANN'S® or BEST
    FOODS® Real Mayonnaise
⅓ cup milk
¼ cup lemon juice
¾ cup finely chopped fresh mint leaves
½ cup finely chopped fresh parsley
½ cup (2 ounces) crumbled feta cheese
1 teaspoon salt
½ teaspoon pepper
7 ounces MUELLER'S® Pasta Curls™,
    cooked and drained
2 medium tomatoes, seeded and
    chopped
1 medium cucumber, seeded and
    chopped
1 cup sliced pitted ripe olives
3 green onions with tops, sliced

In large bowl, combine mayonnaise,
milk, lemon juice, mint, parsley, feta
cheese, salt and pepper; mix well. Add
remaining ingredients; toss to coat.
Cover; refrigerate.

*Makes 8 to 12 servings*

*Aegean Pasta Salad*

## Ham & Artichoke Pasta Salad

1 cup SARGENTO® Old Fashioned
    Ricotta, Part Skim Ricotta or Light
    Ricotta Cheese
1 cup unflavored yogurt
1 teaspoon dried tarragon leaves,
    crushed
½ teaspoon salt
    Freshly ground black pepper, to
    taste
1 jar (6 ounces) marinated artichoke
    hearts, undrained
2 cups cubed lean ham
1 package (12 ounces) pasta bows or
    wheels
¼ cup (1 ounce) SARGENTO® Grated
    Parmesan, Parmesan and Romano
    or Italian-Style Grated Cheese

In large serving bowl, stir together
Ricotta cheese, yogurt, tarragon, salt and
pepper. Remove artichoke hearts from
jar. Pour marinade from artichokes into
Ricotta cheese mixture; mix well. Cut
artichoke hearts into bite-size pieces.
Add to Ricotta cheese mixture with
ham; toss well to combine. (Cover and
refrigerate up to 2 hours, if desired.)
Cook pasta according to package
directions. Immediately add hot pasta to
Ricotta cheese mixture; stir to combine.
Stir in grated cheese. Serve immediately.

*Makes 8 servings*

# Creamy Shell Soup

4 cups water
3 to 4 chicken pieces
1 cup chopped onion
¼ cup chopped celery
¼ cup chopped fresh parsley *or*
    1 tablespoon dried parsley flakes
1 bay leaf
1 teaspoon salt
¼ teaspoon white pepper
2 medium potatoes, chopped
4 to 5 green onions with tops, sliced
3 chicken bouillon cubes
½ teaspoon seasoned salt
½ teaspoon poultry seasoning
4 cups milk
2 cups medium shell macaroni,
    cooked and drained
¼ cup butter *or* margarine
¼ cup all-purpose flour

Combine water, chicken, chopped onion, celery, parsley, bay leaf, salt and pepper in Dutch oven. Bring to a boil over medium-high heat. Reduce heat to low; simmer until chicken is no longer pink in center. Remove bay leaf; discard. Remove chicken; cool. Remove skin and bones from chicken. Coarsely chop chicken; set aside.

Add potatoes, green onions, bouillon cubes and seasonings to broth. Bring to a boil over medium-high heat. Reduce heat to low; simmer 15 minutes or until potatoes are tender, stirring occasionally. Add milk, macaroni and chicken; return to a simmer.

Melt butter in small saucepan over medium heat. Add flour; cook until mixture begins to brown, stirring constantly. Add to soup; blend well. Reduce heat to low; simmer 20 minutes, stirring occasionally. Garnish as desired.

*Makes 8 servings*

*Favorite recipe from* **North Dakota Wheat Commission**

*Creamy Shell Soup*

# Linguine Summer Salad

3 tablespoons white wine vinegar
1 tablespoon Dijon-style mustard
1 tablespoon chopped fresh parsley
1 teaspoon dried basil leaves, crushed
    Freshly ground black pepper, to
    taste
½ cup olive oil
8 ounces linguine, cooked and drained
4 ounces prosciutto, ham *or* salami,
    cut into julienne strips
1 cup chopped cucumber, peeled and
    seeded, optional
¾ cup sliced radishes
½ cup sliced pitted ripe olives
1 green onion with top, thinly sliced
1½ cups (6 ounces) SARGENTO® Fancy
    Supreme Shredded Low Moisture
    Part-Skim Mozzarella Cheese
½ cup (2 ounces) SARGENTO® Fancy
    Supreme Shredded Parmesan
    Cheese

Combine vinegar, mustard, parsley, basil and pepper in large bowl. Gradually add oil, whisking until smooth and thickened. Add linguine, prosciutto, cucumber, radishes, olives and onion; toss to combine. Add cheeses; mix lightly. Serve immediately or cover and refrigerate. For maximum flavor, remove from refrigerator 30 minutes before serving; toss gently.

*Makes 8 servings*

**Note:** If desired, about ¾ cup prepared Italian dressing may be substituted for homemade herb dressing.

*Salmon Macaroni Salad*

## Salmon Macaroni Salad

1 package (7 ounces) *or* 2 cups
CREAMETTE® Salad Macaroni
Shells, cooked and drained
2 hard-cooked eggs, chopped
1 can (7¾ ounces) salmon, drained,
deboned and flaked
1 cup mayonnaise *or* salad dressing
¾ cup finely chopped celery
¼ cup chopped green pepper
1 jar (2 ounces) sliced pimiento,
drained
2 tablespoons REALEMON® Lemon
Juice from Concentrate
2 tablespoons sweet pickle relish
4 teaspoons WYLER's® or STEERO®
Chicken-Flavor Instant Bouillon

In large bowl, combine all ingredients;
mix lightly. Cover; chill. Stir before
serving. Serve on lettuce, if desired.
Garnish as desired. Refrigerate leftovers.
*Makes 4 to 6 servings*

## Beefed-Up Mostaccioli Salad

3 cups Mostaccioli *or* your favorite
medium pasta shape, cooked and
drained
½ cup vegetable oil
¼ cup red *or* white wine vinegar
2 tablespoons grated Romano cheese
2 cloves garlic, minced
1 teaspoon Dijon-style mustard
1 teaspoon salt
1 teaspoon dried oregano leaves,
crushed
¼ teaspoon freshly ground black
pepper
1 pound cooked roast beef, julienned
1 package (9 ounces) frozen green
beans, thawed
1¾ cups chopped tomatoes
¼ cup chopped green onions with tops

In large bowl, combine oil, vinegar,
Romano cheese, garlic, mustard, salt,
oregano and pepper; blend well. Add
mostaccioli and remaining ingredients;
toss lightly to coat. Refrigerate 4 hours
or overnight before serving.
*Makes 4 to 6 servings*

*Favorite recipe from* **National Pasta Association**

## Oceanside Pasta Salad

½ cup MIRACLE WHIP® Salad
Dressing
¼ cup Italian dressing
¼ cup (1 ounce) grated Parmesan
cheese
2 tablespoons lemon juice
1 package (8 ounces) LOUIS KEMP®
CRAB DELIGHTS® Chunks
8 ounces rotini, cooked and drained
1 cup broccoli flowerets, partially
cooked
6 cherry tomatoes, halved *or*
1 medium tomato, chopped
½ green pepper, chopped
2 green onions with tops, sliced

• Mix dressings, Parmesan cheese and
lemon juice in large bowl.

• Add remaining ingredients; toss
lightly. *Makes 4 main-dish servings*

# Pantry Soup

    2 teaspoons olive oil
½ pound boneless skinless chicken,
        cubed, optional
    2 cans (14½ ounces *each*)
        CONTADINA® Pasta Ready
        Tomatoes, undrained
¾ cup chicken broth
¾ cup water
    1 can (8¾ ounces) garbanzo beans,
        undrained
    1 can (8¾ ounces) kidney beans,
        undrained
    1 package (16 ounces) frozen mixed
        vegetables
½ cup pasta (rotini *or* rotelle), cooked
        and drained
    2 teaspoons lemon juice

Heat oil in 5-quart saucepan over
medium-high heat. Add chicken; cook
and stir 3 to 4 minutes or until no longer
pink in center. Stir in tomatoes, broth,
water and beans; cover. Bring to a boil.
Add vegetables and pasta; return to a
boil. Reduce heat to medium; cover.
Simmer 3 minutes or until vegetables
are tender. Stir in lemon juice; serve
with condiments, if desired.

*Makes 6 to 8 servings*

**Optional condiments:** Croutons,
shredded Parmesan cheese, chopped
fresh basil *or* parsley.

# Asian Noodle Salad

    4 ounces vermicelli, cooked and
        drained
    1 large DOLE® Fresh Pineapple
        Sweet Soy Dressing (recipe follows)
    1 can (8 ounces) water chestnuts,
        drained
    2 cups bean sprouts
    1 DOLE® Red Bell Pepper, seeded,
        slivered
    1 cup chopped unpeeled cucumber
½ cup chopped DOLE® Green Onions
        with tops

• Twist crown from pineapple. Cut
pineapple in half lengthwise with knife.
Cut fruit from shells. Trim off core; cut
fruit into chunks. Set aside 2 cups fruit;
reserve remainder for another use.

• Combine vermicelli and Sweet Soy
Dressing in large bowl; toss to coat.
Cool.

• Add 2 cups reserved pineapple and
remaining ingredients; mix lightly.

*Makes 4 servings*

## Sweet Soy Dressing

¼ cup white wine vinegar
    3 tablespoons sugar
    2 tablespoons vegetable oil
    2 tablespoons sesame seeds, toasted
    1 tablespoon soy sauce
    1 teaspoon minced fresh ginger
    1 clove garlic, minced

Combine all ingredients in small bowl;
whisk until well blended.

**Prep time:** 15 minutes
**Cook time:** 10 minutes

*Pantry Soup*

## Jade Dynasty Pasta Salad

*Flavors of the Orient enhance this pasta salad.*

8 ounces spiral pasta, cooked and drained
1½ cups shredded cooked chicken
2 medium carrots, shredded
1 cup fresh Chinese pea pods
½ cup thinly sliced green onions with tops
½ cup julienne-cut red pepper
   Jade Dynasty Dressing (recipe follows)
3 tablespoons chopped toasted almonds

In large bowl, combine all ingredients except almonds; mix lightly. Refrigerate 30 minutes to allow flavors to blend. Add almonds; toss lightly just before serving. *Makes 4 servings*

### Jade Dynasty Dressing

½ cup vegetable oil
¼ cup rice vinegar
1 tablespoon soy sauce
2 teaspoons minced fresh ginger
¾ teaspoon LAWRY'S® Seasoned Pepper
½ teaspoon LAWRY'S® Seasoned Salt
½ teaspoon sugar

In container with stopper or lid, combine all ingredients; shake to blend well. *Makes ¾ cup*

**Presentation:** Serve as a main-dish salad and accompany with fortune or almond cookies for dessert.

*Jade Dynasty Pasta Salad*

## Ham Tortellini Salad

1 package (7 or 8 ounces) cheese-filled spinach tortellini
3 cups (12 ounces) ARMOUR® Lower Salt Ham, cut into ¾-inch cubes
½ cup sliced green onions with tops
10 cherry tomatoes, cut in half
1 cup bottled low sodium, creamy buttermilk *or* reduced calorie zesty Italian salad dressing
   Leaf lettuce *or* butterhead lettuce, washed and drained
¼ cup finely chopped red pepper

Cook tortellini according to package directions, omitting salt; drain and run under cold water to cool. Combine all ingredients *except* leaf lettuce and red pepper in large bowl; mix lightly to coat. Serve on lettuce-lined salad plates. Sprinkle with red pepper. Serve immediately. *Makes 6 to 8 servings*

# Italian Wedding Soup

*The pasta adds a light, creamy body to the broth, and contrasts deliciously with the savory meatballs.*

1 egg, slightly beaten
1 pound ground beef
1 cup PROGRESSO® Italian Style
    Bread Crumbs
2 teaspoons Worcestershire sauce
1 teaspoon garlic powder
2 tablespoons PROGRESSO® Olive
    Oil
5 cups chicken broth
1 cup water
1½ cups pastina *or* any miniature pasta
1 package (10 ounces) frozen chopped
    spinach, cooked according to
    package directions, drained

1. In large bowl, combine egg, ground beef, bread crumbs, Worcestershire sauce and garlic powder; mix well.

2. Shape meatballs using 1 rounded teaspoon meat mixture for each meatball.

3. In large skillet, heat olive oil over medium-high heat. Add meatballs; cook 5 to 7 minutes or to desired doneness, turning frequently to brown all sides. Drain; set aside.

4. In large saucepan, bring chicken broth and water to a boil over medium-high heat. Reduce heat to low. Add meatballs, pastina and spinach; cover. Simmer 10 minutes, stirring occasionally.
*Makes 8 servings*

**Prep time:** 30 minutes
**Cook time:** 20 minutes

# Spicy Grape Pasta Salad

*Try this impressive combination of grapes, chicken, vegetables and pasta, tossed with a spicy oriental dressing, for your next dinner party. Refrigerate any leftovers and enjoy them for lunch the following day.*

8 ounces angel hair pasta, cooked and
    drained
    Spicy Oriental Dressing (recipe
    follows), divided
2 cups julienne cooked chicken
1½ cups California seedless grapes
1 cup cut asparagus*
1 cup julienne red peppers
½ cup diagonally sliced celery
¼ cup sliced green onions with tops
2 tablespoons chopped cilantro *or*
    fresh basil leaves

Combine hot pasta with ¼ cup Spicy Oriental Dressing; cool to room temperature. Add remaining ¼ cup dressing and all remaining ingredients; toss lightly. *Makes 6 to 8 servings*

**Spicy Oriental Dressing:** Combine ¼ cup rice vinegar *or* white wine vinegar, 2 tablespoons vegetable oil, 2 tablespoons soy sauce, ½ teaspoon grated fresh ginger root, ¼ teaspoon red pepper flakes, ¼ teaspoon sesame oil and 1 clove garlic; mix well. Let stand at least 30 minutes; remove garlic before serving. *Makes ½ cup*

**Prep time:** About 45 minutes
*Broccoli flowerets may be substituted.

*Favorite recipe from **California Table Grape Commission***

## Southwest Ruffle Salad

**7 ounces MUELLER'S® Pasta Ruffles,
cooked and drained**
**⅔ cup HELLMANN'S® or BEST
FOODS® Real Mayonnaise**
**⅓ cup sour cream**
**¼ cup chopped cilantro**
**2 tablespoons milk**
**2 tablespoons lime juice**
**1 fresh jalapeño pepper, seeded and
minced**
**1 teaspoon salt**
**2 large tomatoes, seeded and chopped**
**1 yellow pepper, chopped**
**1 zucchini, quartered lengthwise and
thinly sliced**
**3 green onions with tops, sliced**

In large bowl, combine mayonnaise,
sour cream, cilantro, milk, lime juice,
jalapeño pepper and salt; mix well. Add
pasta, tomatoes, yellow pepper, zucchini
and green onions; toss lightly to coat.
Cover; refrigerate.

*Makes 6 to 8 servings*

## ABC Soup

**1 tablespoon vegetable oil**
**⅓ cup chopped onion**
**1 clove garlic, minced**
**1 can (14½ ounces) reduced-salt
chicken broth**
**1 can (14½ ounces) ready-cut
tomatoes, undrained**
**⅓ cup alphabet pasta, uncooked**
**¼ cup chopped fresh parsley**
**¾ cup diced DOLE® Carrots**
**¾ cup diced DOLE® Cauliflower**
**Salt and pepper**
**Grated Parmesan cheese**

• Heat oil in 3-quart saucepan over
medium-high heat. Add onion and
garlic; cook and stir until tender.

• Add broth, tomatoes, pasta and
parsley. Bring to a boil. Reduce heat to
medium; simmer 5 minutes.

• Add carrots and cauliflower; simmer
5 minutes or until vegetables are tender,
stirring occasionally. Season with salt
and pepper to taste. Sprinkle individual
servings with Parmesan cheese.

*Makes 4 servings*

**Prep time:** 10 minutes
**Cook time:** 15 minutes

## Marinated Shrimp & Pasta Salad

**1 package (7 ounces) *or* 2 cups
CREAMETTE® Salad Macaroni
Shells, cooked and drained**
**1 can (4¼ ounces) ORLEANS®
Shrimp, drained and soaked as
label directs**
**½ cup REALEMON® Lemon Juice from
Concentrate**
**½ cup vegetable oil**
**1 package (0.6 ounce) Italian salad
dressing mix**
**1 teaspoon prepared horseradish**
**1½ cups small broccoli flowerets**
**1½ cups sliced zucchini**
**1 cup coarsely shredded carrots**
**¼ cup chopped green onions with tops**

In large bowl, combine REALEMON®
brand, oil, salad dressing mix and
horseradish; mix until well blended.
Add pasta, shrimp, broccoli, zucchini,
carrots and onions; toss lightly to coat.
Cover; chill several hours, stirring
occasionally. Serve on lettuce, if desired.
Refrigerate leftovers.

*Makes 8 to 10 servings*

*Shaker Chicken and Noodle Soup*

Bring remaining 12 cups broth to a boil over medium-high heat in Dutch oven. Add noodles and celery. Reduce heat to low; simmer until noodles are just tender. Gradually add water to flour in medium bowl, stirring until smooth. Gradually stir into broth mixture. Simmer 2 minutes, stirring constantly; stir in cream mixture. Add chicken. Season with salt and pepper to taste. Heat just to serving temperature. (*Do not boil.*) Sprinkle with parsley. Garnish as desired.                    *Makes 15 servings*

**Note:** This soup freezes well.

*Favorite recipe from* **North Dakota Wheat Commission**

## Shaker Chicken and Noodle Soup

13 cups chicken broth, divided
¼ cup dry vermouth
¼ cup butter *or* margarine
1 cup heavy cream
1 package (12 ounces) frozen *or* dry
    egg noodles
1 cup thinly sliced celery
1½ cups water
¾ cup all-purpose flour
2 cups chopped cooked chicken
    Salt and pepper
¼ cup finely chopped fresh parsley,
    optional

Combine 1 cup broth, vermouth and butter in small saucepan. Bring to a boil over medium-high heat. Reduce heat to low; simmer until liquid is reduced to ¼ cup and has a syrupy consistency. Remove from heat. Stir in cream; set aside.

## Hot Pasta Salad

6 cups water
1 tablespoon vegetable oil
1½ cups uncooked rotini
1 cup sliced carrots
1 tablespoon olive oil
½ cup green pepper strips
½ cup chopped onion
1 can (14½ ounces) CONTADINA®
    Whole Peeled Tomatoes, cut up,
    undrained
1 can (8 ounces) garbanzo beans,
    drained
1 teaspoon Italian seasoning
1 teaspoon garlic salt
⅛ teaspoon ground black pepper
¼ cup (1 ounce) grated Parmesan
    cheese

Combine water and vegetable oil in medium saucepan. Bring to a boil over medium-high heat. Add rotini and carrots; return to a boil. Simmer 10 minutes; drain. Heat olive oil in same saucepan over medium-high heat. Add pepper strips and onion; cook and stir until crisp-tender. Add rotini mixture, tomatoes, beans, seasoning, garlic salt and black pepper. Reduce heat to low; simmer 5 minutes, stirring occasionally. Stir in Parmesan cheese. Serve immediately.                    *Makes about 5 cups*

## Antipasto Salad

1 cup MIRACLE WHIP® Salad
    Dressing
½ cup milk
2 packages (0.6 ounce *each*) GOOD
    SEASONS® Zesty Italian Salad
    Dressing Mix
5⅓ cups (1 pound) mostaccioli, cooked
    and drained
1 package (8 ounces) cotto salami
    slices, cut into strips
1 package (8 ounces) CASINO®
    Natural Low-Moisture Part-Skim
    Mozzarella Cheese, cubed
¾ cup thin red pepper strips
¾ cup thin zucchini strips
½ cup pitted ripe olives, drained,
    halved

• Mix together salad dressing, milk,
dressing mix and pasta in large shallow
bowl.

• Arrange remaining ingredients over
pasta mixture; cover and chill.
*Makes 18 servings, about 14 cups*

*Pasta Primavera Salad*

## Pasta Primavera Salad

12 ounces corkscrew pasta, cooked and
    drained
3 tablespoons olive *or* vegetable oil
2 medium zucchini, cut into ¼-inch
    slices
1 cup broccoli flowerets, cooked until
    crisp-tender
1 large red *or* green pepper, cut into
    small chunks
½ cup cherry tomato halves
⅓ cup sliced radishes
3 green onions with tops, chopped
2 tablespoons drained capers, optional
1 cup prepared HIDDEN VALLEY
    RANCH® Original Ranch® Salad
    Dressing

In large bowl, combine hot pasta with
oil; toss lightly to coat. Cool. Add
remaining ingredients; mix lightly.
Cover; refrigerate at least 2 hours. Add
additional salad dressing just before
serving, if desired.   *Makes 4 servings*

*Antipasto Salad*

*Spiral Pasta Salad*

In large bowl, combine pasta, tuna, pea pods, squash, asparagus, onion and olives; mix lightly. For dressing, combine all remaining ingredients in shaker jar. Cover and shake until well blended. Pour over salad; toss to coat. Serve on lettuce-covered plates, if desired.          *Makes 5 servings*

**Prep time:** 15 minutes

## Easy Macaroni Salad

1 cup HELLMANN'S® or BEST
   FOODS® Real, Light *or*
   Cholesterol Free Reduced Calorie
   Mayonnaise
2 tablespoons vinegar
1 tablespoon prepared yellow mustard
1 teaspoon sugar
1 teaspoon salt
¼ teaspoon freshly ground black
   pepper
8 ounces elbow macaroni, cooked and
   drained
1 cup sliced celery
1 cup chopped green *or* red pepper
¼ cup chopped onion

In large bowl, combine mayonnaise, vinegar, mustard, sugar, salt and black pepper; mix well. Add remaining ingredients; mix lightly. Cover; refrigerate. Garnish as desired.
*Makes about 8 servings*

**Note:** If desired, add small amount of milk to dressing mixture for a creamier consistency.

## Spiral Pasta Salad

*Pasta bow ties or shells are ideal for this salad too!*

8 ounces tri-color spiral pasta, cooked
   and drained
1 can (12½ ounces) STARKIST® Tuna,
   drained and broken into chunks
1 cup slivered pea pods
1 cup chopped yellow squash *or*
   zucchini
1 cup asparagus, cut into 2-inch pieces
½ cup slivered red onion
½ cup sliced pitted ripe olives

Dijon Vinaigrette:
⅓ cup white wine vinegar
¼ cup olive *or* vegetable oil
2 tablespoons water
2 teaspoons Dijon-style mustard
1 teaspoon dried basil leaves, crushed
¼ teaspoon pepper

## Zucchini-Tomato-Noodle Soup

10 cups cubed zucchini
¾ cup water
½ cup butter
4 cups chopped onion
8 cups quartered tomatoes
4 chicken bouillon cubes
3 cloves garlic, chopped
1 teaspoon Beau Monde seasoning
2 teaspoons salt
1 teaspoon pepper
4 cups 100% durum noodles, cooked
  and drained

Combine zucchini and water in Dutch oven. Bring to a boil over medium-high heat. Reduce heat to medium; simmer until zucchini is crisp-tender. In small skillet over medium heat, melt butter. Add onion; cook and stir until tender. Add to zucchini mixture with tomatoes, bouillon cubes, garlic and seasonings. Return to a boil. Reduce heat to low; simmer until zucchini is tender, stirring occasionally. Add cooked noodles; heat thoroughly.          *Makes 8 servings*

*Favorite recipe from* **North Dakota Wheat Commission**

## Artichokes with Smoked Salmon Pasta Salad

4 medium California artichokes,
  prepared and cooked as directed*
½ cup unflavored yogurt
½ cup reduced-calorie mayonnaise
¼ cup chopped fresh dill
4 teaspoons Dijon-style mustard
8 ounces orzo, cooked and drained
4 ounces smoked salmon, flaked
  Salt and pepper

Cut cooked artichokes in half lengthwise. Remove center petals and fuzzy centers of artichokes. Combine yogurt, mayonnaise, dill and mustard in medium bowl. Add orzo and smoked salmon; mix lightly. Season with salt and pepper to taste. Fill centers of artichokes with pasta mixture. Garnish with additional fresh dill, if desired.
*Makes 4 servings*

**\*To cook artichokes:** Trim stems so artichokes stand upright. Cut ¼ to ⅓ off tops of artichokes. Stand artichokes in deep saucepan or pot with 3 inches boiling salted water. If desired, add oil, lemon juice and seasonings to cooking water. Cover and simmer 25 to 40 minutes, depending on size of artichokes, until petal near center of artichoke pulls out easily. Remove artichokes from saucepan; stand upside down to drain.

*Favorite recipe from* **California Artichoke Advisory Board**

*Zucchini-Tomato-Noodle Soup*

# Italian Chicken Salad

¼ (1-pound) package CREAMETTE®
    Linguine, cooked and drained
¾ cup *plus* 1 tablespoon vegetable oil,
    divided
½ cup REALEMON® Lemon Juice from
    Concentrate
2 tablespoons grated Parmesan cheese
3 teaspoons WYLER'S® or STEERO®
    Chicken-Flavor Instant Bouillon,
    divided
1 teaspoon sugar
½ teaspoon dried oregano leaves,
    crushed
1 clove garlic, minced
⅛ teaspoon black pepper
1 pound boneless skinless chicken
    breasts, cut into strips
1 package (9 ounces) frozen artichoke
    hearts, cooked and drained
1 cup sliced fresh mushrooms
½ cup chopped red pepper
¼ cup sliced pitted ripe olives

In large bowl, combine ¾ cup oil,
REALEMON® brand, Parmesan cheese,
2 teaspoons bouillon, sugar, oregano,
garlic and black pepper; mix well. In
large skillet, heat remaining 1 tablespoon
oil over medium-high heat. Add chicken
and 1 teaspoon bouillon; cook and stir
until chicken is browned and tender.
Add chicken, pasta and all remaining
ingredients to oil mixture; mix lightly to
coat. Cover; chill. Serve on lettuce, if
desired. Garnish as desired. Refrigerate
leftovers.                    *Makes 4 servings*

# Mexicali Minestrone

*A Mexican interpretation of the classic
Italian soup. Substitute pinto beans for chick
peas, if you wish, and serve with crusty
toasted garlic bread.*

1 can (28 ounces) whole tomatoes, cut
    up, undrained
7 cups beef broth *or* beef stock
1 clove garlic, minced
1 can (16 ounces) chick peas, rinsed
    and drained
1 can (16 ounces) kidney beans, rinsed
    and drained
2 stalks celery, sliced
1 package (10½ ounces) frozen cut
    green beans
⅔ cup PACE® Picante Sauce
½ teaspoon dried thyme leaves,
    crushed
2 cups medium shell macaroni,
    uncooked
1 to 1½ cups chopped yellow squash

Combine tomatoes and all remaining
ingredients *except* macaroni and squash
in large saucepan or Dutch oven. Bring
to a boil over medium-high heat. Reduce
heat to low; cover. Simmer 30 minutes,
stirring occasionally. Stir in macaroni;
simmer 10 minutes or until macaroni
and vegetables are tender, adding
squash during last 5 minutes of cooking.
Serve with additional picante sauce, if
desired.

*Makes 10 servings, about 3 quarts*

*Italian Chicken Salad*

## Chicken Noodle Tortilla Soup

2 tablespoons vegetable oil
¾ pound boneless skinless chicken breasts, cut into bite-size pieces
½ cup sliced green onions with tops
1½ teaspoons chili powder
½ teaspoon dried oregano leaves, crushed
5 cups water
1 can (14½ ounces) whole peeled tomatoes, cut up, undrained
1 package LIPTON® Noodles & Sauce—Chicken Flavor
1 can (4 ounces) chopped green chilies, undrained
1 teaspoon garlic powder
1 can (7 ounces) whole kernel corn, drained
  Tortilla chips, coarsely broken
1 cup (4 ounces) shredded Cheddar or Monterey Jack cheese

In 3-quart saucepan, heat oil over medium-high heat. Add chicken, onions, chili powder and oregano. Cook, stirring frequently, until chicken is no longer pink in center; remove and set aside. Into saucepan, add water and tomatoes; bring to a boil. Reduce heat to medium. Stir in noodles & chicken flavor sauce, chilies and garlic powder. Simmer, stirring occasionally, 10 minutes or until noodles are tender. Just before serving, stir in corn and chicken mixture; heat thoroughly, stirring occasionally. Top individual servings with tortilla chips and cheese.      *Makes about 6 servings*

*Chicken Noodle Tortilla Soup*

## Pesto Rotini Salad with Prosciutto

1 pound Rotini, Spirals, Twists or other medium pasta shape, cooked and drained
7 ounces pesto (about ½ cup)
½ cup unflavored lowfat yogurt
1 tablespoon red wine vinegar
3 ounces thinly sliced prosciutto or other prepared ham, cut into julienne strips
2 cups fresh green beans, blanched and cut into 1-inch pieces
2 small yellow squash, cut into ¼-inch slices
1 cup cherry tomatoes, halved or quartered, if large
  Salt and freshly ground black pepper
½ cup toasted walnuts

Combine pesto, yogurt and vinegar in large bowl; mix well. Add rotini, prosciutto and vegetables; mix lightly. Season with salt and pepper to taste; cover. Chill 30 minutes. Sprinkle with walnuts just before serving.
      *Makes 6 to 8 servings*

*Favorite recipe from **National Pasta Association***

## Southwestern Pasta and Vegetable Salad

1 package (1 pound) bow tie pasta, cooked and drained
6 tablespoons vegetable oil
1 clove garlic, minced
1 jalapeño pepper, seeded, ribs removed and minced
1 can (15 ounces) black beans, rinsed and drained
3 DOLE® Bell Peppers (red, green *or* yellow), cut into ½-inch chunks
2 cups sliced DOLE® Celery
4 DOLE® Carrots, sliced
3 ripe medium tomatoes, seeded and chopped
2 cups (8 ounces) shredded Monterey Jack cheese
3 tablespoons grated Parmesan cheese
Freshly ground black pepper and salt to taste
3 tablespoons red wine vinegar
1 ripe avocado
½ head DOLE® Iceberg Lettuce, torn

• Heat oil in small saucepan over medium heat. Remove from heat; stir in garlic and jalapeño. Cook and stir until tender, about 1 minute. Set aside.

• In large bowl, combine pasta, beans, bell peppers, celery, carrots, tomatoes and Monterey Jack cheese; mix lightly.

• In small mixing bowl, combine oil mixture, Parmesan cheese, black pepper and salt. Whisk in vinegar. Pour over pasta mixture; toss to coat. Cover and refrigerate.

• Just before serving, peel avocado; cut into ½-inch chunks. Add to salad; toss lightly. Serve on bed of lettuce.
*Makes 10 to 12 servings*

**Prep time:** 15 minutes
**Cook time:** 10 minutes
**Chill time:** 30 minutes

*Smoked Turkey & Pepper Pasta Salad*

## Smoked Turkey & Pepper Pasta Salad

¾ cup MIRACLE WHIP® Salad Dressing
1 tablespoon Dijon-style mustard
½ teaspoon dried thyme leaves, crushed
8 ounces fettuccine, cooked and drained
1 cup (8 ounces) chopped LOUIS RICH® Smoked Boneless Turkey Breast
¾ cup zucchini slices, halved
½ cup red pepper strips
½ cup yellow pepper strips
Salt and black pepper

• Mix salad dressing, mustard and thyme until well blended.

• Add pasta, turkey and vegetables; mix lightly. Season with salt and black pepper to taste. Chill. Add additional salad dressing just before serving, if desired. *Makes 6 servings*

**Prep time:** 15 minutes plus chilling

*Greek-Style Pasta Salad*

## Greek-Style Pasta Salad

**4 ounces wagonwheel, shell *or* tubular
    shaped pasta, cooked and drained
1 cup pitted California ripe olives, cut
    into wedges
1 cup halved cherry tomatoes
½ cucumber, sliced, quartered
4 ounces feta cheese, crumbled
¼ cup sliced green onions with tops
2 tablespoons finely chopped fresh
    parsley
Greek Dressing (recipe follows)**

Combine all ingredients *except* Greek
Dressing in medium bowl. Add
dressing; toss to coat.

*Makes 4 to 6 servings*

**Greek Dressing:** In jar, combine 3
tablespoons lemon juice, 1 tablespoon
chopped fresh mint (*or* 1 teaspoon dried
mint leaves), 1 teaspoon finely chopped
fresh oregano leaves (*or* ½ teaspoon
dried oregano leaves, crushed), 1
teaspoon finely chopped fresh rosemary
leaves (*or* ½ teaspoon dried rosemary
leaves, crushed), ½ teaspoon sugar, ¼
teaspoon salt, ¼ teaspoon pepper and
½ cup olive oil. Shake well to blend.

*Favorite recipe from **California Olive Industry***

## Turkey Meatball Soup

**1 pound ground turkey
⅔ cup matzo meal
¼ cup EGG BEATERS® 99% Real Egg
    Product
2 tablespoons FLEISCHMANN'S®
    Sweet Unsalted Margarine
2 cloves garlic, minced
6 cups water
4 cups low-sodium tomato juice
1½ cups tri-color rotini, uncooked
2 large carrots, peeled and thinly
    sliced
2 large tomatoes, chopped
1 large onion, chopped
1 tablespoon Italian seasoning
½ teaspoon pepper
1 package (10 ounces) frozen chopped
    spinach, thawed**

In small bowl, thoroughly mix turkey,
matzo meal and egg product. Shape into
24 (1-inch) balls. In large saucepan over
medium-high heat, brown meatballs, in
batches, in margarine. Remove meatballs;
drain. In same saucepan, cook and stir
garlic in meat drippings 3 minutes or
until browned. Add water, tomato juice,
meatballs, rotini, carrots, tomatoes,
onion, Italian seasoning and pepper.
Bring to a boil. Cover; reduce heat to
low. Simmer 15 minutes, stirring
occasionally. Add spinach; simmer an
additional 5 minutes or until rotini is
tender. *Makes 10 servings*

## Rotini Salad

2 or 3 stalks broccoli
10 ounces rotini, cooked and drained
1 can (6 ounces) small pitted ripe olives, drained
10 to 12 cherry tomatoes, cut into halves
½ medium red onion, thinly sliced
½ cup Italian dressing
1 to 2 tablespoons grated Parmesan cheese, optional
Freshly ground black pepper

Cut flowerets from broccoli. Peel stalks; cut into chunks. Cook broccoli in boiling salted water in medium saucepan over medium-high heat just until broccoli is bright green and tender-crisp. Drain; rinse under cold water and drain thoroughly. Combine broccoli, rotini, olives, tomatoes, onion and dressing in large bowl. Stir in cheese. Season with pepper to taste; toss gently. Cover; refrigerate at least 2 hours. Garnish as desired.          *Makes 8 to 10 servings*

*Favorite recipe from* **North Dakota Wheat Commission**

## Neptune Salad

½ cup MIRACLE WHIP® Salad Dressing
½ cup sour cream
1 teaspoon dill weed
3 cups cooked orzo *or* white rice
2 packages (8 ounces *each*) LOUIS KEMP® CRAB DELIGHTS® Flakes
1 package (10 ounces) frozen peas, cooked and drained
2 stalks celery, sliced
2 tablespoons chopped onion

• Mix salad dressing, sour cream and dill in large bowl. Add remaining ingredients; mix lightly.
          *Makes 8 main-dish servings*

## Turkey Pasta Salad

½ pound LOUIS RICH®, fully cooked, Oven Roasted Breast of Turkey
5 ounces bow tie pasta *or* shell macaroni, cooked and drained
1 pound fresh spinach, torn into bite-size pieces
½ cup creamy Italian dressing
Leaf lettuce
2 tablespoons grated Parmesan cheese
Coarsely ground pepper
2 medium tomatoes, chopped
5 pitted ripe olives, sliced

• Cut turkey into ½-inch cubes; set aside.

• Mix pasta, spinach and dressing; place in large lettuce-lined bowl. Sprinkle with Parmesan cheese and pepper to taste.

• Arrange tomatoes around outside edge of bowl to form ring. Form second ring with turkey; place olives in center.
          *Makes 4 main-dish servings*

*Rotini Salad*

## Quick Country Minestrone

2 tablespoons olive *or* vegetable oil
1 cup chopped onion
1 tablespoon minced fresh garlic
5 cups water
1 package LIPTON® Pasta & Sauce—
    Herb Tomato
1 package (10 ounces) frozen cut green
    beans, thawed
½ teaspoon salt
⅛ teaspoon pepper
1 cup red kidney beans, rinsed and
    drained
    Grated Parmesan cheese, optional

In 3-quart saucepan, heat oil over
medium-high heat. Add onion and
garlic; cook, stirring occasionally, until
tender. Add water; bring to a boil. Stir in
pasta & herb tomato sauce, green beans,
salt and pepper. Reduce heat to medium;
simmer, stirring occasionally, 7 minutes
or until pasta is tender. Stir in kidney
beans; heat thoroughly. Serve with
grated Parmesan cheese. Garnish with
fresh basil leaves, if desired.

*Makes about 4 servings*

**Microwave:** Decrease water to 4½ cups.
In 3-quart microwave-safe round
casserole, combine oil, onion and garlic.
Microwave, uncovered, on HIGH (Full
Power) 2 minutes or until onion is
tender. Add water. Microwave 6 minutes
or until mixture comes to a boil. Stir in
pasta & herb tomato sauce, green beans,
salt and pepper. Microwave 13 minutes
or until pasta is tender, stirring after 7
minutes. Stir in kidney beans; let stand,
covered, 5 minutes. Serve as directed.

## Spicy Pasta Shrimp Salad

1 pound medium Shells *or* your
    favorite medium pasta shape,
    cooked and drained
2 tablespoons margarine
1 small onion, finely chopped
1½ pounds small fresh shrimp (35 to
    50 count), peeled and deveined
1 tablespoon ground seafood
    seasoning
½ teaspoon salt
¼ teaspoon freshly ground black
    pepper
2 tablespoons dry white wine
¼ cup reduced-calorie herb dressing
¼ cup unflavored yogurt
3 teaspoons fresh dill, finely chopped,
    divided
2 tablespoons horseradish sauce

Melt margarine over medium heat in
large nonstick skillet. Add onion; cook
and stir until tender, about 5 minutes.
Add shrimp; cook and stir until shrimp
are no longer gray and are fairly firm to
the touch. Reduce heat to low. Stir in
seafood seasoning, salt, pepper and
wine; simmer 2 to 3 minutes, or until
shrimp turn pink but are not overdone.
Set aside. (For the best flavor, make this
shrimp mixture ahead of time, cover and
refrigerate until time to cook the pasta
and assemble the salad.)

In large bowl, combine dressing, yogurt,
2 teaspoons dill and horseradish sauce.
Add pasta; toss gently. Discard shrimp
liquid. Add shrimp to pasta; mix lightly.
Serve in "cups" of lettuce leaves
garnished with red bell pepper strips, if
desired. Sprinkle with remaining 1
teaspoon dill.     *Makes 6 to 8 servings*

*Favorite recipe from* **National Pasta Association**

*Quick Country Minestrone*

## "Crab" & Cucumber Noodle Salad

8 ounces vermicelli
3 green onions with tops
4 ounces imitation crabmeat, flaked
1 cucumber, halved, seeded and cut into julienne strips
2 tablespoons chopped fresh cilantro
2 tablespoons vegetable oil
2 tablespoons minced fresh ginger root
2 large cloves garlic, minced
3 tablespoons KIKKOMAN® Lite Soy Sauce
3 tablespoons distilled white vinegar
2 teaspoons sugar
4 teaspoons dark sesame *or* Oriental oil

Cook vermicelli according to package directions, omitting salt; drain. Rinse with cold water; drain thoroughly. Separate white parts of green onions from tops; chop whites. Cut tops into thin strips. Combine vermicelli, crabmeat, cucumber, cilantro and green onion tops in large bowl. Heat vegetable oil in small skillet over medium heat. Add whites of green onions, ginger and garlic; stir-fry 1 minute. Remove pan from heat; stir in lite soy sauce, vinegar, sugar and sesame oil until sugar dissolves. Pour over vermicelli mixture; toss to coat. Cover and refrigerate 1 hour, stirring occasionally.

*Makes 6 servings*

*Rainbow Pasta Salad*

## Rainbow Pasta Salad

¼ cup mayonnaise
¼ cup French dressing
1 teaspoon finely chopped onion
8 ounces tri-color corkscrew pasta, cooked and drained
2 cans (4½ ounces *each*) medium shrimp, drained, *or* ½ pound cooked fresh shrimp, peeled and deveined
½ cup chopped walnuts, optional
2 tablespoons sliced pimiento-stuffed green olives

Combine mayonnaise, French dressing and onion in large bowl; mix well. Add remaining ingredients; mix lightly to coat. Garnish as desired.

*Makes 4 servings*

*Favorite recipe from **North Dakota Wheat Commission***

## Picnic Perfect Pasta Salad

2 cups cooked spiral pasta
1 can (8 ounces) DOLE® Pineapple
    Chunks in Juice, undrained
2 tablespoons sesame oil
1 tablespoon honey
1 tablespoon soy sauce
1 tablespoon minced crystallized
    ginger
1 large clove garlic, minced
1 cup chopped cooked chicken*
2 tablespoons sliced DOLE® Green
    Onion with top
2 cups cooked DOLE® Broccoli
    florettes
⅓ cup DOLE® Red Bell Pepper strips
1 tablespoon sesame seeds, toasted

• Drain pineapple, reserving ⅓ cup juice for dressing.

• For dressing, in screw-top jar, combine ⅓ cup reserved juice, sesame oil, honey, soy sauce, ginger and garlic. Shake well.

• In large bowl, combine pineapple, pasta, chicken and onion. Add dressing; toss to coat. Cover; refrigerate at least 2 hours.

• Just before serving, add broccoli and red pepper; toss lightly. Sprinkle with sesame seeds. *Makes 4 servings*

**Prep time:** 20 minutes
**Cook time:** 10 minutes
**Chill time:** 2 hours

*Use deli chicken, if desired.

## Pasta Chicken Salad with Snow Peas

8 ounces Rotini, Spirals, Twists *or*
    your favorite medium pasta shape,
    cooked and drained
4 ounces pea pods
2 cups chopped cooked chicken *or*
    smoked turkey breast
⅓ cup reduced-calorie mayonnaise *or*
    salad dressing
1 tablespoon horseradish sauce,
    optional
2 teaspoons fresh lemon juice
3 green onions with tops, chopped
½ teaspoon dried tarragon leaves,
    crushed
    Salt and freshly ground black
    pepper

Remove ends and strings from pea pods. Using kitchen shears, cut snow peas in half on the diagonal. Add to boiling water; let stand 2 minutes. Rinse in cold water; drain. Place pea pods, chicken, mayonnaise, horseradish sauce, lemon juice, onions and tarragon in large bowl; mix lightly. Add pasta; toss gently. Season with salt and pepper to taste. Cover and chill until serving time.
*Makes 4 to 6 servings*

*Favorite recipe from* **National Pasta Association**

*Picnic Perfect Pasta Salad*

*JONES® Ham Stir-Fry Pasta Salad*

Heat 2 tablespoons oil in large skillet over medium heat. Add cabbage, red pepper and pea pods. Stir-fry 3 minutes; remove from skillet. Add remaining 2 tablespoons oil to skillet. Add garlic and ginger. Stir-fry 30 seconds. Add ham; stir-fry 3 minutes. Stir in soy sauce, sherry, vinegar and hot pepper sauce. Bring to a boil, stirring frequently. Reduce heat to low; simmer 1 minute. Remove from heat. Add pasta and vegetables; toss to coat. Chill.

*Makes 6 servings*

# JONES® Ham Stir-Fry Pasta Salad

¾ pound JONES® Ham, cut into ½-inch cubes
6 ounces macaroni, cooked and drained
4 tablespoons vegetable oil, divided
4 cups shredded cabbage
1 red pepper, cut into thin strips
6 ounces pea pods, cut crosswise in half
2 cloves garlic, minced
½ teaspoon ground ginger
3 tablespoons soy sauce
3 tablespoons dry sherry
1 tablespoon cider vinegar
½ teaspoon hot pepper sauce

## Taco Pasta Salad

1 pound Elbow Macaroni *or* your favorite medium pasta shape, cooked, drained and cooled
1 pound ground beef
1 package (1.5 ounces) taco seasoning mix
¾ cup water
1 avocado
2 tomatoes, chopped
1 medium onion, chopped
2 cups (8 ounces) shredded Cheddar cheese
1 cup pitted ripe olives, sliced, optional
1½ cups taco sauce *or* salsa
4 cups shredded lettuce
Crushed corn chips for topping

Brown meat in large skillet over medium-high heat; drain. Stir in taco seasoning mix and ¾ cup water. Bring to a boil. Reduce heat to low; simmer, uncovered, 10 minutes, stirring occasionally.

Peel and chop avocado. In large bowl, combine pasta, meat mixture, tomatoes, onion, cheese and olives. Add taco sauce; toss gently. Serve on bed of lettuce. Top with avocado and corn chips. Tastes great served hot, too!

*Makes 6 servings*

*Favorite recipe from **National Pasta Association***

## Beef & Pasta Salad

    3 cups CREAMETTE® Rotini, cooked
      and drained
    2 tablespoons vegetable *or* olive oil
    1 pound boneless stir-fry beef strips
    2 teaspoons WYLER'S® or STEERO®
      Beef-Flavor Instant Bouillon,
      divided
    1 cup Italian dressing
    6 ounces Provolone cheese, cut into
      cubes
    1 large green pepper, cut into strips
    1 cup cherry tomato halves
    ½ cup sliced pitted ripe olives
      Grated Parmesan cheese, optional

In large skillet, heat oil over medium-
high heat. Add beef and 1 teaspoon
bouillon; cook and stir until beef is
browned. In large bowl, combine beef,
rotini, dressing and remaining 1
teaspoon bouillon; let stand 15 minutes.
Add Provolone, green pepper, tomatoes
and olives; mix well. Cover; chill.
Sprinkle with Parmesan cheese just
before serving, if desired. Refrigerate
leftovers.          *Makes 4 servings*


## Mustardy VEG-ALL® Pasta Salad

    8 ounces rotini, cooked and drained
    1 can (16 ounces) VEG-ALL® Mixed
      Vegetables, drained
    ½ cup sliced pitted ripe olives
    ½ cup chopped red onion
    ¼ cup (1 ounce) grated Parmesan
      cheese
    ½ cup prepared Dijon-style oil and
      vinegar dressing

Combine first 5 ingredients in large
bowl. Add dressing; toss to coat.
Refrigerate several hours before serving.
(Leftover chopped cooked ham, chicken
or turkey can also be added for a main-
dish salad.)      *Makes 6 to 8 servings*


## Couscous Salad

*Add variety to your menu with this North
African staple.*

    ½ cup reduced-calorie mayonnaise
    ½ cup plain *or* lemon nonfat yogurt
    1½ tablespoons Dijon-style mustard
    1½ cups water
    1 cup couscous
    1 cup finely chopped roasted turkey
      breast, optional
    3 tablespoons finely chopped red
      onion
    ½ cup chopped red pepper
    3 tablespoons chopped fresh parsley
    1 teaspoon LAWRY'S® Garlic Salt
    ⅓ cup pine nuts *or* slivered almonds

In small bowl, combine mayonnaise,
yogurt and mustard; chill. In medium
saucepan, bring 1½ cups water to a boil.
Add couscous; remove from heat. Cover
and let stand 10 minutes or until water
is absorbed. Combine all ingredients;
mix well. Refrigerate until ready to
serve.          *Makes 8 servings*

**Presentation:** Serve in halved, hollowed
bell peppers or on lettuce-lined plates.

*Beef & Pasta Salad*

# PASTA TOPPERS

## Chunky Pasta Sauce with Meat

6 ounces ground beef
6 ounces mild *or* hot Italian sausage,
   sliced
½ medium onion, coarsley chopped
1 clove garlic, minced
2 cans (14½ ounces *each*)
   DEL MONTE® Chunky Pasta
   Style Tomatoes
1 can (8 ounces) DEL MONTE®
   Tomato Sauce
¼ cup red wine, optional
   Hot cooked pasta
   Grated Parmesan cheese

In large saucepan, brown beef and
sausage over medium-high heat; drain
all but 1 tablespoon drippings. Add
onion and garlic; cook and stir until
tender. Add tomatoes, tomato sauce and
wine. Reduce heat to low; simmer,
uncovered, 15 minutes, stirring
frequently. Serve over hot pasta; sprinkle
with Parmesan cheese.
*Makes 4 cups sauce*

**Variation:** Serve sauce over vegetables,
omelets or frittatas.

## Bell Pepper and Mushroom Pasta Sauce

1 tablespoon WESSON® Vegetable Oil
2 cups julienne-cut green peppers
1 cup chopped onion
1 teaspoon minced fresh garlic
1 can (15 ounces) HUNT'S® Tomato
   Sauce
1 can (14½ ounces) HUNT'S® Whole
   Tomatoes, cut up, undrained
1 can (4 ounces) sliced mushrooms,
   drained
1 teaspoon dried basil leaves, crushed
½ teaspoon dried oregano leaves,
   crushed
¼ teaspoon black pepper
2 tablespoons grated Parmesan cheese
4 cups mostaccioli, cooked and
   drained

In medium saucepan, heat oil over
medium-high heat. Add green peppers,
onion and garlic; cook and stir until
crisp-tender. Add all remaining
ingredients *except* Parmesan cheese and
mostaccioli. Reduce heat to medium.
Simmer, uncovered, 20 minutes. Stir in
Parmesan cheese; serve over hot
mostaccioli.      *Makes 4 to 6 servings*

*Chunky Pasta Sauce with Meat*

*Tomato Caper Sauce*

## Tomato Caper Sauce

3 tablespoons olive oil
2 cloves garlic, crushed
1 can (28 ounces) CONTADINA®
    Whole Peeled Tomatoes, cut up,
    undrained
½ cup rinsed capers
¼ cup chopped fresh cilantro
1 tablespoon chopped fresh basil
    leaves
1 tablespoon chopped fresh thyme
    leaves
    Dash pepper
1 pound rigatoni, cooked and drained

Heat oil in medium saucepan over
medium-high heat. Add garlic; cook and
stir 1 to 2 minutes or until lightly
browned. Add tomatoes and capers.
Reduce heat to low; simmer, uncovered,
15 to 20 minutes. Stir in cilantro, basil,
thyme and pepper; simmer an
additional 5 minutes. Serve over hot
pasta.          *Makes 8 servings*

**Microwave:** Combine oil and garlic in
2-quart microwave-safe dish. Microwave
on HIGH 3 minutes. Add tomatoes and
capers. Microwave 8 minutes, stirring
after 4 minutes. Stir in cilantro, basil,
thyme and pepper. Microwave 1 minute.
Serve as directed.

## Classic No-Cook Tomato Sauce

*Enough for one pound of your favorite
pasta shape.*

8 fresh ripe tomatoes, chopped,
    undrained
1¼ cups coarsely chopped fresh basil
    leaves
4 cloves garlic, minced
¼ cup vegetable oil
    Salt and freshly ground black
    pepper

Combine tomatoes and basil in medium
bowl. Add combined garlic and oil; mix
lightly. Season with salt and pepper to
taste. Serve immediately over hot
cooked pasta. Sprinkle with grated
Parmesan cheese, if desired.

*Makes 4 to 6 servings*

*Favorite recipe from **National Pasta Association***

## White Clam Sauce

¼ cup olive oil
2 cloves garlic, minced
2 cans (6½ ounces *each*) DOXSEE® or
    SNOW'S® Minced *or* Chopped
    Clams, drained, reserving liquid
1 bottle (8 ounces) DOXSEE® or
    SNOW'S® Clam Juice
1 tablespoon chopped fresh parsley
¼ teaspoon dried basil leaves, crushed
    Dash pepper

In medium saucepan, heat oil over
medium-high heat. Add garlic; cook and
stir until lightly browned. Stir in reserved
clam liquid, clam juice, parsley, basil
and pepper. Bring to a boil. Reduce heat
to low; simmer 5 minutes. Add clams;
heat thoroughly. Serve over hot cooked
CREAMETTE® Linguine with grated
Parmesan cheese. Refrigerate leftovers.

*Makes about 2½ cups sauce*

## Turkey Eggplant Sauce for Pasta

*Eggplant adds both flavor and texture to this unique sauce.*

2 teaspoons olive *or* vegetable oil
1½ cups cubed eggplant
½ cup chopped onion
¾ teaspoon LAWRY'S® Garlic Powder
    with Parsley
1 pound ground turkey
1 can (28 ounces) whole tomatoes, cut
    up, undrained
1 package (1.5 ounces) LAWRY'S®
    Original Style Spaghetti Sauce
    Spices & Seasonings
¾ teaspoon dried rosemary leaves,
    crushed

In large skillet, heat oil over medium-high heat. Add eggplant, onion and Garlic Powder with Parsley; cook 10 to 12 minutes or until eggplant and onion are tender, stirring frequently. Add turkey; cook 2 to 3 minutes or until no longer pink, stirring occasionally. Add remaining ingredients. Bring to a boil; reduce heat to low. Simmer, uncovered, 10 to 15 minutes.          *Makes 4 cups*

**Presentation:** Serve over hot cooked egg noodles.

**Hint:** Crumbled sausage can be substituted for turkey.

## POLLY-O® Tomato Sauce with Mushrooms

¼ cup olive oil
1 small onion, chopped
1 clove garlic, minced
2 cups sliced fresh mushrooms
1 cup water
1 can (7 ounces) tomato paste
½ can (14 ounces) crushed tomatoes
1 teaspoon dried basil leaves, crushed
    Salt and pepper

1. In medium saucepan, heat oil over medium-high heat. Add onion and garlic; cook and stir until tender. Add mushrooms; cook and stir 2 minutes.

2. Gradually add water to tomato paste in small bowl, stirring until well blended. Add to mushroom mixture with tomatoes and basil. Reduce heat to low. Simmer 1 hour, stirring occasionally. Season with salt and pepper to taste.
*Makes 3 cups*

*Favorite recipe from **Pollio Dairy Products Corporation***

## Garden Vegetable Sauce for Pasta

2 tablespoons vegetable oil
1 clove garlic, minced
2 medium zucchini, cut into bite-size
    chunks (about 3½ cups)
1½ cups sliced fresh mushrooms
2 medium tomatoes, coarsely chopped
1 cup HEINZ® Chili Sauce
2 tablespoons chopped fresh parsley
½ teaspoon dried oregano leaves,
    crushed
¼ teaspoon dried basil leaves, crushed
¼ teaspoon salt
    Dash pepper
    Hot cooked linguine *or* spaghetti
    Grated Parmesan cheese

In large skillet, heat oil over medium-high heat. Add garlic; cook and stir 1 to 2 minutes or until lightly browned. Add zucchini and mushrooms; cook and stir 4 to 5 minutes or until tender. Stir in tomatoes, chili sauce, parsley, oregano, basil, salt and pepper. Reduce heat to low. Simmer, uncovered, 10 to 15 minutes or until sauce is desired consistency, stirring occasionally. Serve over hot pasta; sprinkle with Parmesan cheese.
*Makes about 4 cups sauce*

# Bolognese Sauce

1 slice prosciutto (about 1 ounce)
1 parsley sprig
1 medium onion
1 celery stalk
1 medium carrot
2 tablespoons sweet butter
3 tablespoons olive oil
1 pound mixture of chopped beef, veal
     and pork
¼ teaspoon sage
¼ cup dry white wine
3 tablespoons tomato paste
2 cups chicken *or* beef broth
½ cup cream
     Salt and pepper

1. Chop prosciutto, parsley and all vegetables together. Mixture should be very fine. (This is done best in a food processor.)

2. Melt butter with oil in medium saucepan over medium-high heat. Add chopped vegetable mixture; cook and stir until tender, about 2 minutes.

3. Add meat mixture; cook until meat is no longer pink in center. Stir in sage and wine. Reduce heat to low; simmer, uncovered, until wine evaporates, stirring occasionally.

4. Stir in tomato paste and broth; cover. Bring to a boil over medium-high heat. Reduce heat to low; simmer 1 hour, stirring occasionally.

5. Remove sauce from heat. Stir in cream. Season with salt and pepper to taste.          *Makes 2½ cups*

**Note:** This sauce can be prepared in advance and gently reheated. It can also be frozen. In either case, do not add the cream until ready to serve.

*Favorite recipe from **Pollio Dairy Products***

# Sweety Meaty Sauce for Ziti

2 tablespoons CHEF PAUL
     PRUDHOMME'S Poultry Magic®,
     divided
1 pound ground turkey
2 tablespoons olive oil
2 tablespoons margarine
1 cup chopped onion
1 cup chopped green pepper
2 cups canned crushed tomatoes
1 cup tomato puree
¾ cup finely chopped carrots
1½ cups chicken stock *or* water, divided
1 tablespoon granulated sugar
½ teaspoon salt
1 tablespoon dark brown sugar,
     optional
12 ounces ziti pasta, cooked and
     drained

Mix 1 tablespoon plus 2 teaspoons Poultry Magic® with turkey, working it in well with your hands; set aside.

Heat oil and margarine in 3½-quart saucepan over medium-high heat 1 minute or until margarine has melted and mixture begins to sizzle. Add turkey; cook, stirring occasionally to separate chunks, until turkey is no longer pink, about 6 minutes. Add onion and green pepper; cook and stir 3 to 4 minutes or until tender. Add the remaining 1 teaspoon Poultry Magic®, tomatoes, tomato puree, carrots, ½ cup stock, granulated sugar and salt; mix well. (If you like a sweeter sauce, add the brown sugar.) Cook, stirring occasionally, 3 to 4 minutes or until mixture comes to a boil. Reduce heat to low; cover. Simmer 30 minutes, stirring occasionally. Stir in remaining 1 cup stock; cover. Simmer an additional 20 minutes or until sauce has thickened and has changed from bright red to dark red in color, stirring occasionally. Remove from heat. Serve over hot pasta.
     *Makes 4 servings*

*Zesty Artichoke Basil Sauce*

## Zesty Artichoke Basil Sauce

1 jar (6 ounces) marinated artichoke
    hearts, drained, reserving
    marinade
1 cup chopped onion
1 large clove garlic, minced
1 can (14½ ounces) CONTADINA®
    Whole Peeled Tomatoes, cut up,
    undrained
1 can (6 ounces) CONTADINA®
    Tomato Paste
1 cup water
2 tablespoons chopped fresh basil
    leaves
½ teaspoon salt

In medium saucepan, cook and stir onion and garlic in reserved marinade over medium heat 2 to 3 minutes or until tender. Chop artichoke hearts; add to saucepan with tomatoes, tomato paste, water, basil and salt. Bring to a boil; reduce heat to low. Simmer, uncovered, 20 minutes, stirring occasionally. *Makes 4 cups*

**Savory Caper and Olive Sauce:** Omit artichoke hearts and basil. In medium saucepan, cook and stir onion and garlic in 2 tablespoons olive oil over medium heat 2 to 3 minutes. Add ¾ cup sliced and quartered zucchini, tomatoes, tomato paste, water, salt, 1 can (2¼ ounces) drained sliced pitted ripe olives and 2 tablespoons drained capers. Continue as directed.

# Microwave Marinara Sauce

½ cup chopped onion
2 cloves garlic, minced
2 tablespoons olive oil
1 can (14½ ounces) CONTADINA®
    Whole Peeled Tomatoes, cut up,
    undrained
1 can (8 ounces) CONTADINA®
    Tomato Sauce
½ teaspoon salt
½ teaspoon dried basil leaves, crushed
½ teaspoon dried oregano leaves,
    crushed
    Hot cooked pasta (tortellini, ravioli,
    spaghetti, fusilli, linguine, twists,
    fettuccine, gnochi or small shells)

In 2-quart microwave-safe dish, combine onion, garlic and oil. Microwave on HIGH (100%) power 3 minutes or until onion is tender. Stir in tomatoes, tomato sauce, salt, basil and oregano. Microwave on HIGH power 7 to 8 minutes, stirring occasionally. Serve over hot pasta.

*Makes about 2 cups sauce*

**Conventional:** In medium saucepan, heat oil over medium-high heat. Add onion and garlic; cook and stir until onion is tender. Stir in tomatoes, tomato sauce, salt, basil and oregano. Bring to a boil; reduce heat to low. Simmer 15 minutes, stirring occasionally. Serve as directed.

# Seafood Sauce for Pasta

1 tablespoon vegetable oil
1 small green pepper, coarsely
    chopped
1 small onion, coarsely chopped
1 clove garlic, minced
2 medium tomatoes, peeled, coarsely
    chopped
1 cup HEINZ® Seafood Cocktail Sauce
½ cup bottled clam juice
½ teaspoon dried basil leaves, crushed
¼ teaspoon dried thyme leaves,
    crushed
¼ teaspoon black pepper
1 pound scallops, peeled and deveined
    shrimp or cubed fish
    Hot cooked linguine or fettuccine

Heat oil in medium saucepan over medium-high heat. Add green pepper, onion and garlic; cook and stir until crisp-tender. Add all remaining ingredients *except* scallops and pasta. Reduce heat to low; simmer, uncovered, 15 minutes, stirring occasionally. Add scallops; cook 3 to 4 minutes or until scallops are tender. Serve over hot pasta.

*Makes about 4½ cups sauce*

*Microwave Marinara Sauce*

## First-Class Pasta Sauce

1 pound lean ground beef
1 cup chopped onion
1 large clove garlic, minced
1 can (28 ounces) CONTADINA®
    Whole Peeled Tomatoes, cut up,
    undrained
2 cans (6 ounces *each*) CONTADINA®
    Tomato Paste
1 cup water
1 cup sliced fresh mushrooms
1 bay leaf
1 teaspoon dried oregano leaves,
    crushed
½ teaspoon dried basil leaves, crushed
1 teaspoon salt
⅛ teaspoon pepper
1 pound pasta, cooked and drained
½ cup (2 ounces) grated Parmesan
    cheese

Brown ground beef with onion and garlic over medium-high heat in large saucepan; drain. Add tomatoes, tomato paste, water, mushrooms, bay leaf, oregano, basil, salt and pepper. Bring to a boil. Reduce heat to low. Simmer, uncovered, 30 minutes, stirring occasionally. Remove bay leaf. Serve over hot cooked pasta. Sprinkle with Parmesan cheese.     *Makes 8 servings*

**Microwave:** Crumble meat into 3-quart microwave-safe dish. Add onion and garlic. Microwave on HIGH 4 to 6 minutes or until meat is no longer pink, stirring occasionally; drain. Add tomatoes, tomato paste, water, mushrooms, bay leaf, oregano, basil, salt and pepper. Microwave on HIGH 8 minutes, stirring after 4 minutes. Remove bay leaf. Serve as directed.

*Southwestern Pasta Sauce*

## Southwestern Pasta Sauce

¼ cup olive oil
2 medium onions, sliced
1 clove garlic, minced
1 can (28 ounces) tomatoes, coarsely
    chopped, undrained
2 to 3 tablespoons chopped fresh
    cilantro
¾ teaspoon TABASCO® pepper sauce
¼ teaspoon sugar
¼ teaspoon salt
12 ounces angel hair pasta, cooked and
    drained
    Grated Parmesan cheese, optional

Heat oil over medium-high heat in large, heavy non-aluminum saucepan. Add onions and garlic; cook and stir 10 to 12 minutes or until onions are tender. Add tomatoes, cilantro, TABASCO® sauce, sugar and salt; bring to a boil. Reduce heat to low; simmer, uncovered, 30 minutes or until slightly thickened, stirring occasionally. Place hot pasta on heated serving platter; top with sauce. Sprinkle with Parmesan cheese.

*Makes 4 servings*

## Italian Spaghetti Sauce

1 package (12 ounces) JONES® Hot
   Roll Sausage
1 medium onion, finely chopped
2 cloves garlic, minced
1 can (6 ounces) tomato paste
1 cup water
1 can (16 ounces) pear-shaped
   tomatoes, cut up, undrained
1 can (8 ounces) tomato sauce
2 bay leaves
½ teaspoon sugar

Brown sausage in large skillet over
medium-high heat, stirring occasionally
to separate sausage; drain. Add onion
and garlic; cook and stir until tender.
Add tomato paste; mix well. Stir in
water. Reduce heat to low; simmer 10
minutes, stirring occasionally.

In medium or large saucepan, heat
tomatoes over medium heat. Stir in
sausage mixture, tomato sauce, bay
leaves and sugar. Reduce heat to low;
simmer 1 to 2 hours or to desired
consistency. Remove bay leaves just
before serving.　　*Makes 4 servings*

## Homemade Tomato Sauce with Pasta

½ cup WISH-BONE® Robusto Italian
   Dressing*
½ cup chopped onion
1 can (28 ounces) whole plum
   tomatoes, cut up, undrained
3 tablespoons chopped fresh basil
   leaves
8 ounces pasta, cooked and drained
   Grated Parmesan cheese

In large skillet, heat robusto Italian
dressing over medium heat. Add onion;
cook and stir 3 minutes or until tender.
Add tomatoes. Reduce heat to low;
simmer 10 minutes or until sauce is
thickened, stirring occasionally. Stir in
basil. Serve over hot pasta; sprinkle with
cheese.

*Makes 4 side-dish or 2 main-dish servings*

*Also terrific with WISH-BONE® Italian,
Blended Italian *or* Lite Italian Dressing.

**Variation:** Substitute 2 teaspoons dried
basil leaves, crushed, for 3 tablespoons
fresh basil leaves.

**Microwave:** In 2-quart microwave-safe
casserole, combine robusto Italian
dressing and onion. Microwave,
uncovered, on HIGH (Full Power)
3 minutes or until onion is tender. Add
tomatoes; microwave on HIGH 20
minutes or until thickened, stirring
occasionally; stir in basil. Serve as
directed.

## Clam Spaghetti Sauce

3 tablespoons CRISCO® Shortening
¼ cup chopped celery
¼ cup chopped onion
1 jar (48 ounces) spaghetti sauce
2 cans (6½ ounces *each*) minced clams,
   drained

1. Melt CRISCO® in large saucepan over
medium-high heat. Add celery and
onion; cook and stir until tender, about
4 minutes.

2. Stir in spaghetti sauce and clams; heat
thoroughly, stirring occasionally. Serve
over hot cooked spaghetti.

*Makes 1½ quarts sauce*

*HUNT'S® Homemade Spaghetti Sauce Made Easy*

## White Cheese Sauce

*This simple light sauce goes well with tortellini and ravioli.*

2 cups part-skim POLLY-O® Ricotta Cheese
¼ cup plain unflavored yogurt
¼ cup (1 ounce) grated Parmesan cheese
Dash white pepper
6 fresh basil *or* tarragon leaves, chopped
1 clove garlic, minced, optional

Combine all ingredients in medium saucepan; beat until smooth and creamy. Stir over medium heat until thoroughly heated. Serve over hot cooked pasta. *Makes 2½ cups sauce*

## HUNT'S® Homemade Spaghetti Sauce Made Easy

½ pound ground beef
¼ cup chopped onion
1½ cups water
1 can (6 ounces) HUNT'S® Tomato Paste
1 teaspoon sugar
¾ teaspoon salt
¾ teaspoon dried basil leaves, crushed
½ teaspoon dried oregano leaves, crushed
½ teaspoon garlic powder
¼ teaspoon pepper

In medium saucepan, brown meat with onion over medium-high heat; drain. Stir in all remaining ingredients. Reduce heat to low; cover. Simmer 20 minutes, stirring occasionally. *Makes 2 cups*

## Peppery Pasta Toss

1 cup FLEISCHMANN'S® Extra Light Margarine
1 tablespoon dry sherry
2 cloves garlic, minced
½ teaspoon dried oregano leaves, crushed
½ teaspoon dried basil leaves, crushed
¼ teaspoon black pepper
¼ teaspoon crushed red pepper
Hot cooked pasta

In small saucepan, melt margarine over medium heat. Stir in sherry, garlic, oregano, basil, black pepper and red pepper. Bring mixture to a boil. Reduce heat to low; simmer 10 minutes, stirring occasionally. Serve over hot pasta.
*Makes ¾ cup sauce*

# LUSCIOUS LASAGNAS

## Easy Family Lasagna

½ **pound bulk Italian sausage** *or*
   **ground turkey**
½ **cup chopped onion**
 1 **can (28 ounces) PROGRESSO®**
   **Peeled Tomatoes Italian Style, cut**
   **up, undrained**
 1 **jar (14 ounces) PROGRESSO®**
   **Spaghetti Sauce**
 2 **teaspoons Italian seasoning**
 9 **lasagna noodles, uncooked**
 1 **container (15 ounces) ricotta cheese**
 3 **cups (12 ounces) shredded**
   **mozzarella cheese**
¼ **cup (1 ounce) PROGRESSO® Grated**
   **Parmesan Cheese**

1. In medium skillet, brown sausage and onion; drain.

2. Stir in tomatoes, spaghetti sauce and Italian seasoning.

3. In lightly greased 12×8-inch baking dish, layer ⅓ *each* of the *uncooked* lasagna noodles, ricotta cheese, meat mixture, mozzarella cheese and Parmesan cheese; repeat layers twice. Cover.

4. Refrigerate at least 8 hours or up to 24 hours.

5. When ready to bake, remove cover; place in cold oven. Turn oven on to 350°F. Bake 45 to 50 minutes or until bubbly. Let stand 15 minutes before cutting to serve.          *Makes 8 servings*

**Prep time:** 20 minutes
**Chilling/cooling time:** 8 hours
**Baking time:** 50 minutes
**Variations:**
Stir 1 package (10 ounces) frozen chopped spinach, thawed and well drained, into the ricotta cheese.

To prepare and bake lasagna immediately, cook lasagna noodles according to package directions. Prepare recipe as directed, *except* drain tomatoes before chopping, discarding liquid. Bake in preheated 350°F oven 35 minutes.

**Microwave:** Crumble sausage into a medium microwave-safe bowl; cover. Microwave on HIGH (100% power) 4 minutes, stirring and breaking sausage into small pieces after 2 minutes. Stir in onion. Microwave on HIGH 2 minutes; drain. Break up any remaining large pieces of sausage. Continue as directed in Steps 2 through 4, *except* drain tomatoes and use 12×8-inch microwave-safe baking dish; cover with plastic wrap. When ready to microwave, cut a few slits in center of plastic wrap to vent. Microwave on HIGH 10 minutes, rotating dish after 5 minutes. Microwave on MEDIUM (50% power) 25 minutes, rotating dish every 5 minutes. Let stand 5 minutes before cutting to serve.

*Easy Family Lasagna*

# Lasagna Deliciousa

½ (1-pound) package CREAMETTE®
    Lasagna
1 pound bulk Italian sausage
½ pound ground beef
1 cup chopped onion
2 cloves garlic, minced
1 can (28 ounces) tomatoes, cut up,
    undrained
2 cans (6 ounces *each*) tomato paste
2 teaspoons sugar
1½ teaspoons salt, divided
1½ teaspoons dried basil leaves, crushed
¼ teaspoon fennel seeds
¼ teaspoon pepper
1 egg, slightly beaten
1 container (15 ounces) ricotta cheese
1 tablespoon dried parsley flakes
1 cup sliced pitted ripe olives
4 cups (1 pound) shredded mozzarella
    cheese
¾ cup (3 ounces) grated Parmesan
    cheese

Prepare Creamette® lasagna according to package directions; drain. Brown sausage and ground beef with onion and garlic in large skillet over medium-high heat; drain. Stir in tomatoes, tomato paste, sugar, 1 teaspoon salt, basil, fennel seeds and pepper. Bring to a boil over high heat. Reduce heat to low. Simmer, uncovered, 20 minutes, stirring occasionally.

In small bowl, blend egg, ricotta, parsley and remaining ½ teaspoon salt. Spoon 1½ cups meat sauce into 13×9-inch baking dish. Cover with layers of ⅓ *each* of the noodles, remaining meat sauce, ricotta mixture, olives, mozzarella cheese and Parmesan cheese; repeat layers twice. Cover with foil. Bake at 375°F, 25 minutes. Uncover. Continue baking 20 minutes or until heated through. Let stand 10 minutes before cutting to serve. Refrigerate leftovers.

*Makes 8 to 10 servings*

# Tuna Lasagna

2 tablespoons vegetable oil
1 cup chopped zucchini
1 cup sliced fresh mushrooms
½ cup sliced green onions with tops
1 clove garlic, minced
1 can (12½ ounces) STARKIST® Tuna,
    drained and broken into chunks
1½ cups spaghetti sauce
½ teaspoon dried thyme *or* basil
    leaves, crushed
½ teaspoon dried oregano leaves,
    crushed
1 large egg, slightly beaten
1½ cups lowfat cottage cheese
6 lasagna noodles, cooked and drained
3 slices low-fat mozzarella cheese, cut
    into ½-inch strips
2 tablespoons grated Parmesan *or*
    Romano cheese
2 tablespoons chopped fresh parsley

In large skillet, heat oil over medium-high heat. Add zucchini, mushrooms, onions and garlic; cook and stir 3 minutes or until crisp-tender. Stir in tuna, spaghetti sauce and herbs; bring to a boil. Remove from heat.

Preheat oven to 375°F. In small bowl, combine egg and cottage cheese. Spray 12×8-inch baking dish with aerosol shortening. Spread ½ cup tuna mixture onto bottom of dish. Place 3 lasagna noodles over tuna mixture; cover with layers of ½ *each* of the cottage cheese mixture, remaining tuna mixture and mozzarella cheese. Repeat layers of noodles, cottage cheese mixture, tuna mixture and mozzarella cheese. Sprinkle with Parmesan cheese; cover with foil. Bake 30 minutes; uncover. Continue baking 10 minutes or until sauce is bubbly and lasagna is heated through. Sprinkle with parsley. Let stand 10 minutes before cutting to serve.

*Makes 4 to 6 servings*

**Prep time:** 40 minutes

## Lasagna Verde
### (Green Lasagna)

**Sauce:**

¼ cup olive oil
2 cloves garlic, minced
2 cans (28 ounces *each*) Italian peeled
    tomatoes, cut up, drained
1 teaspoon salt
¼ teaspoon pepper
¼ cup chopped fresh basil leaves

**Filling:**

1 pound spinach lasagna noodles,
    cooked and drained
2 eggs, slightly beaten
3 cups POLLY-O® Ricotta Cheese
1 package (16 ounces) POLLY-O®
    Mozzarella Cheese, shredded
½ cup freshly grated Parmesan cheese

In medium saucepan, heat oil over
medium heat. Add garlic; cook and stir
until lightly browned. Stir in tomatoes,
salt and pepper. Bring to a boil. Reduce
heat to low; simmer, uncovered, 1 hour
or until thickened, stirring occasionally.
Stir in basil; cool to room temperature.

In medium bowl, combine eggs and
ricotta cheese. Into 13×9-inch baking
dish, pour a thin layer of sauce; cover
with a layer of ¼ of the noodles. Top
with layers of ¼ of the remaining sauce,
1 cup ricotta mixture and 1 cup
mozzarella; sprinkle with 2 tablespoons
Parmesan cheese. Repeat layers of
noodles, sauce, ricotta mixture,
mozzarella and Parmesan cheeses twice.
Top with remaining noodles, sauce,
mozzarella and Parmesan cheeses.
(Recipe can be made ahead to this point.
Cover with plastic wrap and refrigerate
several hours or overnight.)

Preheat oven to 375°F. Bake lasagna 45
to 60 minutes or until hot and bubbly.
Let stand 10 minutes before cutting to
serve.                    *Makes 8 servings*

**Variation:** Substitute 2 teaspoons dried
basil leaves, crushed, *and* 2 tablespoons
chopped fresh parsley for fresh basil.

*Lasagna Italiano*

## Lasagna Italiano

1½ pounds ground beef
½ cup chopped onion
1 can (14 ounces) tomatoes, cut up,
    undrained
1 can (6 ounces) tomato paste
⅓ cup cold water
1 clove garlic, minced
1 teaspoon dried oregano leaves,
    crushed
¼ teaspoon pepper
6 ounces lasagna noodles, cooked and
    drained
2 packages (6 ounces *each*) 100%
    Natural KRAFT® Low Moisture
    Part-Skim Mozzarella Cheese
    Slices
½ pound VELVEETA® Pasteurized
    Process Cheese Spread, thinly
    sliced
½ cup (2 ounces) KRAFT® 100% Grated
    Parmesan Cheese

Heat oven to 350°F. Brown meat with
onions in large skillet; drain. Stir in
tomatoes, tomato paste, water, garlic and
seasonings. Cover; simmer 30 minutes,
stirring occasionally. In 12×8-inch
baking dish, layer ½ *each* of the noodles,
meat sauce, mozzarella, process cheese
spread and parmesan; repeat layers.
Bake 30 minutes. Let stand 10 minutes.
                    *Makes 6 to 8 servings*

**Prep time:** 40 minutes
**Baking time:** 30 minutes plus standing

**LUSCIOUS LASAGNAS    59**

## Luscious Vegetarian Lasagna

8 ounces lasagna noodles, cooked and drained
1 can (14½ ounces) tomatoes, cut up, undrained
1 can (12 ounces) tomato sauce
1 teaspoon dried oregano leaves, crushed
1 teaspoon dried basil leaves, crushed
Dash black pepper
2 tablespoons olive oil
1 large onion, chopped
1½ teaspoons minced fresh garlic
2 small zucchini, chopped
8 ounces mushrooms, sliced
1 large carrot, chopped
1 green pepper, chopped
1 cup (4 ounces) shredded mozzarella cheese
2 cups cottage cheese
1 cup (4 ounces) grated Parmesan or Romano cheese

Preheat oven to 350°F. Combine tomatoes, tomato sauce, oregano, basil and black pepper in medium saucepan. Bring to a boil over medium-high heat. Reduce heat to low; simmer 10 to 15 minutes, until slightly thickened, stirring occasionally. Set aside. Heat oil in large skillet over medium-high heat. Add onion and garlic; cook and stir until crisp-tender. Add zucchini, mushrooms, carrot and green pepper. Cook and stir until vegetables are tender, 5 to 10 minutes. Add vegetables to tomato mixture; simmer 15 minutes, stirring occasionally. Combine mozzarella, cottage and Parmesan cheeses in large bowl; mix well.

Spoon about 1 cup sauce into 12×8-inch baking dish. Cover with layers of ½ *each* of the noodles, cheese mixture and remaining sauce; repeat layers of noodles, cheese mixture and sauce. Bake 30 to 45 minutes or until hot and bubbly. Let stand 10 minutes before cutting to serve. Garnish with fresh parsley sprigs, if desired.

*Makes 6 to 8 servings*

**Variation:** Substitute your favorite vegetables for the ones listed.

*Favorite recipe from* **North Dakota Dairy Promotion Commission**

## Turkey Lasagna

1½ cups (½ to ¾ pound) chopped cooked BUTTERBALL® Turkey
1 egg, slightly beaten
1¼ cups ricotta cheese
⅔ cup (about 3 ounces) grated Parmesan cheese, divided
2 tablespoons dried parsley flakes
½ teaspoon pepper
1 jar (15½ ounces) spaghetti sauce
2 teaspoons dried oregano leaves, crushed
6 lasagna noodles, cooked and drained
1½ cups (6 ounces) shredded mozzarella cheese, divided

Preheat oven to 350°F. Combine egg, ricotta cheese, turkey, ¼ cup Parmesan cheese, parsley and pepper in medium bowl. Combine spaghetti sauce and oregano in separate bowl. Trim lasagna noodles to 9-inch lengths.

Place 3 lasagna noodles on bottom of 9-inch square baking dish; cover with layers of ½ of the turkey mixture, 2 tablespoons Parmesan cheese and ½ cup mozzarella cheese. Top with 1 cup spaghetti sauce (sauce will not cover cheese completely). Repeat layers of noodles, turkey mixture, Parmesan cheese, mozzarella cheese and sauce. Sprinkle with remaining Parmesan and mozzarella cheeses. Bake, uncovered, 35 to 40 minutes or until hot and bubbly. Let stand 10 to 15 minutes before cutting to serve. *Makes 6 servings*

## Lasagna Florentine

2 tablespoons olive oil
¾ cup chopped onion
2 cloves garlic, minced
2 jars (26 ounces *each*) CLASSICO®
  Pasta Sauce, any flavor
2 eggs, slightly beaten
1 container (15 or 16 ounces) ricotta
  cheese
1 package (10 ounces) frozen chopped
  spinach, thawed and well drained
1 pound mozzarella cheese, shredded,
  divided
½ cup (2 ounces) grated Parmesan
  cheese
1 package (1 pound) CREAMETTE®
  Lasagna, cooked as package
  directs, drained
Chopped fresh parsley

Preheat oven to 350°F. In large saucepan, heat oil over medium-high heat. Add onion and garlic; cook and stir until tender. Stir in pasta sauce. Reduce heat to low; simmer, uncovered, 15 minutes, stirring occasionally. Meanwhile, in medium bowl, combine eggs, ricotta, spinach, ½ cup mozzarella cheese and Parmesan cheese; mix well.

*Lasagna Florentine*

Into 13×9-inch baking dish, pour 2 cups sauce; cover with layers of ½ *each* of the noodles and remaining sauce; cover with spinach mixture and ½ of the remaining mozzarella. Top with remaining noodles and sauce; cover. Bake 45 minutes or until hot and bubbly. Uncover; sprinkle with remaining mozzarella and parsley. Continue baking 15 minutes. Let stand 15 minutes before cutting to serve. Refrigerate leftovers.

*Makes 12 to 15 servings*

## Double Cheese Lasagna

1 pound lasagna noodles, cooked and
  drained
3 eggs, slightly beaten
1 container (2 pounds) POLLY-O®
  Ricotta Cheese
1 teaspoon dried oregano leaves,
  crushed
1 teaspoon dried basil leaves, crushed
2 packages (16 ounces *each*) POLLY-O®
  Mozzarella Cheese, divided
3 cups marinara sauce
¼ cup (1 ounce) POLLY-O® Grated
  Parmesan Cheese

In medium bowl, combine eggs, ricotta cheese, oregano and basil. Reserve 4 ounces (¼ of one package) of mozzarella; shred for topping. Cut remaining mozzarella into ¼-inch slices.

Preheat oven to 350°F. Into 13×9-inch baking dish, pour a thin layer of marinara sauce; top with ⅓ of the noodles. Cover with layers of ½ *each* of the ricotta mixture and sliced mozzarella; top with ½ cup sauce. Repeat layers of noodles, ricotta mixture, sliced mozzarella and sauce; cover with remaining noodles and sauce. Sprinkle with Parmesan and shredded mozzarella. Bake 40 minutes or until hot and bubbly. Let stand 10 minutes before cutting to serve. *Makes 8 servings*

*Lasagna with White and Red Sauce*

## Lasagna with White and Red Sauce

Béchamel Sauce (recipe follows)
2 to 3 tablespoons vegetable oil
½ medium onion, sliced
1 clove garlic, minced
1 pound lean ground beef
1 can (28 ounces) crushed tomatoes *or*
    1 can (28 ounces) whole tomatoes,
    cut up, undrained
½ cup thinly sliced celery
½ cup thinly sliced carrot
1 teaspoon dried basil leaves, crushed
1 package (1 pound) lasagna noodles,
    cooked and drained
6 ounces BEL PAESE® cheese,* thinly
    sliced
6 hard-cooked eggs, sliced, optional
2 tablespoons butter *or* margarine, cut
    into small pieces
1 cup (about 2 ounces) freshly grated
    Parmigiano-Reggiano *or* Grana
    Padano cheese

Preheat oven to 350°F. Prepare Béchamel Sauce; set aside. Heat oil in Dutch oven over medium-high heat. Add onion and garlic; cook and stir until tender. Add ground beef; cook until no longer pink, stirring occasionally to separate meat. Add tomatoes, celery, carrot and basil. Reduce heat to low; cover. Simmer 45 minutes, stirring occasionally. Remove cover; simmer an additional 15 minutes.

Arrange ⅓ of the lasagna noodles on bottom of greased 13×9-inch baking dish. Cover with layers of ½ *each* of the BEL PAESE® and eggs; top with meat sauce. Repeat layers of noodles, remaining BEL PAESE® and eggs; cover with layers of Béchamel Sauce and remaining noodles. Dot with butter. Sprinkle with Parmigiano-Reggiano. Bake 30 to 40 minutes or until heated through. Let stand 10 minutes before cutting to serve. *Makes 6 servings*

*Remove wax coating and moist, white crust from cheese.

**Béchamel Sauce:** Melt 2 tablespoons butter *or* margarine in small saucepan over medium-low heat. Stir in 2 tablespoons all-purpose flour. Gradually blend in ¾ cup milk. Season with white pepper to taste. Cook until thick and bubbly, stirring constantly. *Makes ¾ cup sauce*

*Three-Cheese Vegetable Lasagna*

## Three-Cheese Vegetable Lasagna

---

  **9 lasagna noodles, cooked and drained**
  **1 can (16 ounces) VEG-ALL® Mixed**
     **Vegetables, undrained**
**¼ cup butter**
**¼ cup chopped onion**
**¼ cup all-purpose flour**
  **1 cup chicken broth**
  **2 eggs, divided**
  **8 ounces ricotta cheese**
**1¾ cups (7 ounces) grated Parmesan**
     **cheese, divided**
**⅛ teaspoon ground nutmeg**
  **1 package (10 ounces) frozen chopped**
     **spinach, cooked**
  **2 cups (8 ounces) shredded mozzarella**
     **cheese**

1. Drain VEG-ALL®, reserving ½ cup liquid. Melt butter in medium saucepan over medium heat. Add onion; cook and stir until tender. Blend in flour. Gradually add reserved vegetable liquid and chicken broth. Cook and stir until thickened; set aside.

2. Prepare ricotta filling by combining 1 egg, ricotta cheese, ¾ cup Parmesan cheese, nutmeg and VEG-ALL®.

3. Prepare spinach filling by combining remaining egg, ¼ cup sauce and spinach.

4. To assemble lasagna, spoon small amount of sauce into lightly greased 13×9-inch baking dish; cover with 3 noodles. Top with layers of spinach filling, ½ cup sauce and ⅓ cup Parmesan cheese.

5. Cover with layers of 3 more noodles, ricotta filling, 1 cup mozzarella cheese and ⅓ cup Parmesan cheese. Top with layers of the remaining noodles, sauce, mozzarella and Parmesan cheeses.

6. Bake at 400°F, 30 minutes.

*Makes 8 servings*

## Tomato Pesto Lasagna

---

  **8 ounces lasagna noodles, cooked and**
     **drained**
  **1 pound pork sausage *or* ground beef**
  **1 can (14½ ounces) DEL MONTE®**
     **Chunky Pasta Style Stewed**
     **Tomatoes**
  **1 can (6 ounces) DEL MONTE®**
     **Tomato Paste**
**¾ cup water**
  **8 ounces ricotta cheese**
  **1 package (4 ounces) frozen pesto,**
     **thawed**
  **2 cups (8 ounces) shredded mozzarella**
     **cheese**

Brown meat in 10-inch skillet, stirring occasionally to separate meat; drain. Stir in tomatoes, tomato paste and water. Spoon ⅓ of the meat sauce into 2-quart or 9-inch square baking dish; cover with layers of ½ *each* of the noodles, ricotta cheese, pesto and mozzarella cheese. Repeat layers of meat sauce, noodles, ricotta cheese, pesto and mozzarella cheese. Top with remaining meat sauce. Bake at 350°F, 30 minutes or until heated through. *Makes 6 servings*

**Prep time:** 20 minutes
**Bake time:** 30 minutes

# Chicken and Zucchini Lasagna

1 tablespoon butter *or* margarine
2 medium zucchini, sliced ¼-inch thick (about 3 cups)
1 jar (12 ounces) HEINZ® HomeStyle Chicken Gravy
⅔ cup half-and-half *or* milk
½ cup (2 ounces) grated Romano *or* Parmesan cheese, divided
½ teaspoon dried basil leaves, crushed
¼ teaspoon dried thyme leaves, crushed
1 egg, slightly beaten
1½ cups ricotta cheese
3 green onions with tops, sliced
2 tablespoons chopped fresh parsley
8 lasagna noodles, cooked and drained
2 cups chopped cooked chicken
1 cup (4 ounces) shredded mozzarella cheese
¼ cup dry bread crumbs
1 tablespoon butter *or* margarine, melted
Paprika

In large skillet, melt butter over medium-high heat. Add zucchini; cook and stir until crisp-tender. Set aside. In medium bowl, combine gravy, half-and-half, ¼ cup Romano cheese, basil and thyme; set aside. In separate medium bowl, combine egg, ricotta cheese, onions and parsley.

Pour ⅓ of gravy mixture into 3-quart oblong baking dish; top with 4 lasagna noodles. Cover with layers of ½ *each* of the ricotta mixture, zucchini, chicken and mozzarella cheese; top with ⅓ of the gravy mixture. Repeat layers of noodles, ricotta mixture, zucchini, chicken and mozzarella cheese; cover with remaining gravy mixture. In small bowl, combine remaining ¼ cup Romano cheese, bread crumbs and melted butter; mix well. Sprinkle over top of lasagna; dust with paprika. Bake at 350°F, 45 minutes; let stand 10 minutes before cutting to serve.
*Makes 6 to 8 servings*

# Tuna Lasagna Bundles

6 lasagna noodles, cooked in unsalted water and drained
1 can (10¾ ounces) condensed cream of chicken soup
½ cup milk
1 egg, slightly beaten
1 can (6½ ounces) tuna, drained and flaked
1 package (10 ounces) frozen chopped spinach *or* broccoli, thawed and well drained
¼ cup seasoned dry bread crumbs
¼ teaspoon DURKEE® Garlic Salt
1 cup (4 ounces) shredded Cheddar Cheese, divided
1 can (2.8 ounces) DURKEE® French Fried Onions, divided

Preheat oven to 350°F. Place hot noodles under cold running water until cool enough to handle; drain and set aside. In small bowl, blend soup and milk; set aside. In medium bowl, combine egg, tuna, spinach, bread crumbs, Garlic Salt, ½ cup cheese and ½ can onions; stir in ½ cup soup mixture. Cut noodles crosswise in half. Spoon equal amounts of tuna mixture onto center of each noodle; roll up, starting at short end. Place tuna rolls, seam-side down, in greased 12×8-inch baking dish. Top with remaining soup mixture; cover. Bake at 350°F, 35 minutes or until heated through. Uncover. Top with remaining cheese and onions. Continue baking 5 minutes or until onions are golden brown. *Makes 6 servings*

**Microwave:** Assemble tuna rolls as directed. Place rolls, seam-side down, in 12×8-inch microwave-safe dish; top with remaining soup mixture. Cover. Microwave on HIGH 10 to 12 minutes or until heated through, rotating dish after 6 minutes. Top with remaining cheese and onions. Microwave, uncovered, 1 minute or until cheese melts. Let stand 5 minutes.

# Spinach Lasagna

1 pound lean ground beef
2 jars (15½ ounces *each*) spaghetti
    sauce
1 can (6 ounces) tomato paste
1 can (4 ounces) mushroom stems and
    pieces, drained
¼ cup chopped onion
½ teaspoon dried parsley flakes
½ teaspoon dried oregano leaves,
    crushed
½ teaspoon dried basil leaves, crushed
¼ teaspoon garlic powder
    Seasoned salt and pepper to taste
1 egg, slightly beaten
1 pound dry curd cottage cheese
3 cups (12 ounces) shredded
    mozzarella cheese, divided
¾ cup (3 ounces) grated Romano
    cheese
1 package (10 ounces) frozen chopped
    spinach, thawed and squeezed dry
8 ounces lasagna noodles, cooked and
    drained
3 ounces sliced pepperoni, optional
½ cup (2 ounces) grated Parmesan
    cheese

Preheat oven to 350°F. Brown meat in large skillet over medium-high heat, stirring occasionally to separate meat; drain. Stir in spaghetti sauce, tomato paste, mushrooms, onion, herbs and seasonings. Bring to a boil, stirring frequently. Remove from heat; set aside. Combine egg, cottage cheese, 1 cup mozzarella cheese, Romano cheese and spinach in medium bowl.

Spoon 1½ cups meat sauce into 13×9-inch baking dish. Cover with layers of ½ *each* of the noodles and spinach mixture; top with layers of pepperoni, Parmesan cheese and remaining meat sauce. Repeat layers of noodles and spinach mixture; sprinkle with remaining 2 cups mozzarella cheese. Bake 30 to 45 minutes or until hot and bubbly. If a browner top is desired, place lasagna under broiler for a few minutes to brown cheese. Let stand 10 minutes before cutting to serve.
*Makes 8 to 10 servings*

*Favorite recipe from* **North Dakota Wheat Commission**

# Asparagus Ham Lasagna

6 lasagna noodles
2 tablespoons butter *or* margarine
2 cloves garlic, minced
½ teaspoon dried thyme leaves,
    crushed
2 tablespoons all-purpose flour
1⅓ cups milk
    Salt and pepper
1 cup (4 ounces) shredded mozzarella
    cheese
1 cup julienne ham
1 can (15 ounces) DEL MONTE®
    Tender Green Asparagus Spears,
    drained

**Microwave:** Cook noodles according to package directions; rinse and cut in half crosswise. Set aside. In medium saucepan, melt butter over medium-low heat. Add garlic and thyme; cook and stir until garlic is lightly browned. Blend in flour; cook, stirring constantly, 2 minutes. Stir in milk; cook, stirring constantly, until thickened. Season with salt and pepper to taste. In buttered 8-inch square microwave-safe dish, layer ⅓ *each* of the noodles, sauce, cheese, ham and asparagus. Repeat layers twice; cover. Microwave on HIGH 9 to 10 minutes or until heated through, turning twice. *Makes 4 servings*

**Prep time:** 20 minutes
**Cook time:** 10 minutes
**Helpful Hint:** Good use of leftover ham.

*Spinach Lasagna*

## Pasta Roll-Ups

*A great recipe you can prepare in a snap!*

1 package (1.5 ounces) LAWRY'S®
   Spaghetti Sauce Seasoning
   Blended with Imported
   Mushrooms
1 can (6 ounces) tomato paste
2¼ cups water
2 tablespoons butter *or* vegetable oil
2 cups cottage cheese *or* ricotta cheese
1 cup (4 ounces) shredded mozzarella
   cheese
¼ cup (1 ounce) grated Parmesan
   cheese
2 eggs, slightly beaten
½ to 1 teaspoon LAWRY'S® Garlic Salt
½ teaspoon dried basil leaves, crushed,
   optional
8 ounces lasagna noodles, cooked and
   drained

**Microwave:** In medium saucepan,
prepare Spaghetti Sauce Seasoning
Blend with Imported Mushrooms
according to package directions, using
tomato paste, water and butter; set
aside. In large bowl, combine all
remaining ingredients *except* noodles;
blend well. Spread ¼ cup cheese
mixture onto entire length of each
lasagna noodle; roll up, starting at short
end.

Place noodles, seam-side down, in
microwave-safe baking dish; cover with
vented plastic wrap. Microwave on
HIGH 6 to 7 minutes or until cheese
begins to melt. Pour sauce over rolls.
Microwave on HIGH 1 minute, if
necessary, to reheat sauce.

*Makes 6 servings*

**Presentation:** Sprinkle with additional
grated Parmesan cheese. Garnish with
fresh basil leaves.

**Hint:** For quick microwaveable meals,
wrap prepared rolls individually and
freeze. Sauce may be frozen in ¼ cup
servings. Reheat just before serving.

*Pasta Roll-Ups*

## SARGENTO® Classic Lasagna

1 pound lean ground beef
1 cup chopped onion
3 cloves garlic, minced
2 cans (14½ ounces *each*) whole
   peeled tomatoes, cut up,
   undrained
2 cups sliced mushrooms
1 can (6 ounces) tomato paste
1 tablespoon Worcestershire sauce
1 teaspoon dried oregano leaves,
   crushed
1 teaspoon dried parsley flakes
½ teaspoon salt
⅛ teaspoon pepper
8 ounces lasagna noodles
2 cups (15 ounces) SARGENTO®
   Ricotta Cheese*
1 cup (4 ounces) SARGENTO® Grated
   Cheese**
2 cups (8 ounces) SARGENTO®
   Classic Supreme Shredded *or*
   Fancy Supreme Shredded
   Mozzarella Cheese

In large saucepan, brown ground beef with onion and garlic over medium-high heat; drain. Add tomatoes, mushrooms, tomato paste, Worcestershire sauce, oregano, parsley, salt and pepper. Bring to a boil. Reduce heat to low; cover and simmer 30 minutes, stirring occasionally. Cook noodles according to package directions. In lightly greased 13×9-inch baking dish, layer ⅓ *each* of the noodles, Ricotta cheese, Grated cheese, Mozzarella cheese and meat sauce. Repeat layers twice. Sprinkle with additional Grated cheese, if desired; cover. Bake at 350°F, 45 minutes. Uncover; continue baking 15 minutes or until top begins to brown. Remove from oven; let stand 10 minutes before cutting to serve.            *Makes 8 servings*

*SARGENTO® Ricotta, Part-Skim Ricotta *or* Lite Ricotta can be used.

**SARGENTO® Parmesan, Parmesan and Romano *or* Italian-Style Grated Cheese can be used.

# Lentil Lasagna

*This all-vegetable lasagna has a creamy texture and the slightly "nut-like" flavor of lentils.*

1 tablespoon PROGRESSO® Olive Oil
½ cup chopped onion
2 cloves garlic, minced
1 can (19 ounces) PROGRESSO® Lentil Soup
1 can (8 ounces) PROGRESSO® Tomato Sauce
1 can (6 ounces) PROGRESSO® Tomato Paste
2 teaspoons Italian seasoning
9 lasagna noodles, cooked and drained
1 container (15 ounces) ricotta cheese
1 package (12 ounces) mozzarella cheese slices
¼ cup (1 ounce) PROGRESSO® Grated Parmesan Cheese

1. Preheat oven to 350°F.

2. In medium skillet, heat olive oil over medium-high heat. Add onion and garlic; cook and stir 2 to 3 minutes or until tender.

3. Stir in soup, tomato sauce, tomato paste and Italian seasoning. Reduce heat to low; simmer 10 minutes, stirring occasionally.

4. In greased 12×8-inch baking dish, layer ⅓ *each* of the noodles, ricotta cheese, mozzarella cheese, soup mixture and Parmesan cheese; repeat layers twice. Cover with foil.

5. Bake 35 to 40 minutes or until hot and bubbly. Let stand 15 minutes before cutting to serve.            *Makes 8 servings*

**Prep time:** 30 minutes
**Baking time:** 40 minutes

**Microwave:** In small microwave-safe container, combine olive oil, onion and garlic; cover. Microwave on HIGH (100% power) 1 to 2 minutes or until tender. Stir in soup, tomato sauce, tomato paste and Italian seasoning; cover. Microwave on HIGH 3 minutes or until hot and bubbly, stirring after 2 minutes. Continue as directed above in Step 4, *except* using 12×8-inch microwave-safe baking dish and covering with plastic wrap; cut a few slits in center of wrap to vent. Microwave on HIGH 5 minutes; rotate dish. Microwave on MEDIUM (50% power) 20 minutes or until hot and bubbly, rotating dish after 10 minutes. Let stand 5 minutes before cutting to serve.

## Spring Fresh Lasagna

**Ricotta Filling:**

2 eggs, slightly beaten
2 cups ricotta cheese *or* small-curd
    cottage cheese
½ cup chopped fresh parsley
2 teaspoons garlic salt
¼ teaspoon ground nutmeg

**Sauce:**

3 cups tomato puree
2 teaspoons ground cumin
2 teaspoons dried oregano leaves,
    crushed
2 teaspoons onion powder
2 teaspoons garlic salt
1½ teaspoons chili powder

**Spring Vegetable Filling:**

2 tablespoons vegetable oil
1 medium onion, minced
6 cloves garlic, minced
2 teaspoons salt
1 teaspoon ground cumin
1 teaspoon chili powder
1 teaspoon dried oregano leaves,
    crushed
2 cups coarsely shredded zucchini
2 cups shredded carrots
2 cups sliced mushrooms
1 green pepper, chopped
1 cup chopped fresh parsley
¼ cup chopped cilantro (*or* use
    additional ¼ cup parsley)

8 lasagna noodles, cooked and drained
4 cups shredded Classic Jarlsberg
    cheese
2 medium California avocados
2 tablespoons lemon juice
1 teaspoon garlic salt

Combine Ricotta Filling ingredients; set aside. Mix together Sauce ingredients; set aside. To prepare Spring Vegetable Filling, heat oil over medium-high heat in large skillet. Add onion and garlic; cook and stir until tender. Stir in seasonings. Add vegetables, parsley and cilantro; set aside.

To assemble lasagna, place 4 noodles on bottom of 13×9-inch baking dish; cover with layers of ½ *each* of the Ricotta Filling, Spring Vegetable Filling, Sauce and cheese. Repeat layers of noodles, fillings, Sauce and cheese. Bake at 350°F, 45 minutes. Let stand 10 minutes before cutting to serve. Meanwhile, mash avocado with lemon juice and garlic salt. Top each serving of lasagna with avocado mixture. *Makes 12 servings*

*Favorite recipe from* **Norseland Foods, Inc.**

## Lasagna Supreme

½ pound ground Oklahoma beef
½ pound mild Italian sausage
½ cup chopped onion
2 cloves garlic, minced
1 can (16 ounces) tomatoes, cut up,
    undrained
1 can (6 ounces) tomato paste
2 teaspoons dried basil leaves, crushed
1 teaspoon dried marjoram leaves,
    crushed
1 can (4 ounces) sliced mushrooms,
    drained
2 eggs, slightly beaten
1 pound cream-style cottage cheese
¾ cup (3 ounces) grated Parmesan
    cheese, divided
2 tablespoons dried parsley flakes
½ teaspoon salt
½ teaspoon pepper
8 ounces lasagna noodles, cooked and
    drained
2 cups (8 ounces) shredded Cheddar
    cheese
3 cups (12 ounces) shredded
    mozzarella cheese

Preheat oven to 375°F. Brown meats with onion and garlic in large skillet over medium-high heat, stirring occasionally to separate meat; drain. Stir in tomatoes, tomato paste, basil and marjoram. Reduce heat to low; cover. Simmer 15 minutes, stirring frequently. Stir in mushrooms; set aside.

Combine eggs, cottage cheese, ½ cup Parmesan cheese, parsley, salt and pepper in large bowl; mix well. In greased 13×9-inch baking dish, layer ½ *each* of the noodles, cottage cheese mixture, meat mixture, Cheddar cheese and mozzarella cheese; repeat layers. Sprinkle with remaining ¼ cup Parmesan cheese. Bake 40 to 45 minutes or until hot and bubbly. Let stand 10 minutes before cutting to serve.

*Makes 8 to 10 servings*

**Note:** Lasagna may be assembled ahead of time, covered and refrigerated. Bake in preheated 375°F oven, 1 hour or until hot and bubbly.

*Favorite recipe from **Oklahoma Agriculture Organizations***

**Lasagna Supreme**

# Spinach-Cheese Lasagna Rolls

1 tablespoon olive *or* vegetable oil
½ cup chopped onion
1 clove garlic, minced
1 can (15 ounces) whole leaf spinach, well drained, finely chopped
1 egg, slightly beaten
1 cup lowfat ricotta cheese
½ cup (2 ounces) grated Parmesan cheese
1 teaspoon sugar
⅛ teaspoon pepper
6 lasagna noodles, cooked and drained
2 cans (8 ounces *each*) no-salt-added tomato sauce
1 can (4 ounces) no-salt-added mushroom pieces and stems, drained
1 teaspoon dried basil leaves, crushed
1 teaspoon dried oregano leaves, crushed
2 thinly sliced green onions with tops *or* 1 tablespoon chopped fresh parsley

Preheat oven to 350°F. Heat oil in medium skillet over medium-high heat. Add chopped onion and garlic; cook and stir until tender. Reduce heat to medium. Add spinach; cook, stirring occasionally, until mixture is very dry. In medium bowl, combine egg, spinach mixture, cheeses, sugar and pepper. Spread scant ½ cup spinach mixture onto each lasagna noodle; roll up, starting at short end. Place lasagna rolls, seam-side down, in greased 13×9-inch baking dish; cover. Bake 20 minutes or until hot and bubbly.

Heat tomato sauce, mushrooms and herbs in small saucepan. Spoon sauce onto serving plates. Cut lasagna rolls into thirds; serve over sauce. Sprinkle with green onions. *Makes 6 servings*

*Favorite recipe from **Canned Food Information Council***

# Lazy Lasagna

1 pound ground beef
1 jar (32 ounces) spaghetti sauce
16 ounces cottage cheese
2 cups sour cream
8 uncooked lasagna noodles
3 packages (6 ounces *each*) sliced mozzarella cheese (12 slices)
½ cup (2 ounces) grated Parmesan cheese
1 cup water

Preheat oven to 350°F. Brown meat in large skillet over medium-high heat, stirring occasionally to separate meat; drain. Stir in spaghetti sauce. Reduce heat to low. Heat thoroughly, stirring occasionally; set aside. Combine cottage cheese and sour cream in medium bowl; blend well.

Spoon 1½ cups meat sauce into 13×9-inch baking dish. Cover with layers of ½ *each* of the *uncooked* noodles and cottage cheese mixture. Top with layers of 4 slices mozzarella, ½ of the remaining meat sauce and ¼ cup Parmesan cheese. Repeat layers of noodles, cottage cheese mixture, mozzarella, meat sauce and Parmesan cheese. Top with remaining 4 slices mozzarella. Carefully add water to baking dish, pouring around edges of dish; cover tightly with foil. Bake 1 hour. Uncover; continue baking 20 minutes or until hot and bubbly. Let stand 15 to 20 minutes before cutting to serve. Garnish as desired.      *Makes 8 to 10 servings*

*Favorite recipe from* **North Dakota Dairy Promotion Commission**

# Four-Cheese Lasagna

6 ounces lasagna noodles, cooked and drained
½ pound ground beef
½ cup chopped onion
⅓ cup chopped celery
1 clove garlic, minced
1½ teaspoons dried basil leaves, crushed
¼ teaspoon dried oregano leaves, crushed
¼ teaspoon salt
⅛ teaspoon pepper
1 package (3 ounces) cream cheese, cubed
⅓ cup light cream *or* milk
½ cup dry white wine
½ cup (2 ounces) shredded Wisconsin Cheddar *or* Gouda cheese
1 egg, slightly beaten
1 cup cream-style cottage cheese
6 ounces sliced Wisconsin Mozzarella cheese

In large skillet, brown meat with onion, celery and garlic; drain. Stir in basil, oregano, salt and pepper. Reduce heat to low. Add cream cheese and cream. Cook, stirring frequently, until cream cheese is melted. Stir in wine. Gradually add Cheddar cheese, stirring until Cheddar cheese is almost melted. Remove from heat. In small bowl, combine egg and cottage cheese.

Into greased 10×6-inch baking dish, layer ½ *each* of the noodles, meat sauce, cottage cheese mixture and Mozzarella cheese; repeat layers. Bake, uncovered, at 375°F, 30 to 35 minutes or until hot and bubbly. Let stand 10 minutes before cutting to serve.      *Makes 6 servings*

**Prep time:** 1½ hours

*Favorite recipe from* **Wisconsin Milk Marketing Board** © *1992*

*Lazy Lasagna*

# Seafood Lasagna

2 tablespoons butter *or* margarine
1 large onion, chopped
1½ cups cream-style cottage cheese
1 package (8 ounces) cream cheese, cubed and softened
2 teaspoons dried basil leaves, crushed
½ teaspoon salt
⅛ teaspoon pepper
1 egg, slightly beaten
2 cans (10¾ ounces *each*) cream of mushroom soup
⅓ cup milk
1 clove garlic, minced
½ cup dry white wine
½ pound bay scallops
½ pound flounder fillets, cubed
½ pound medium shrimp, peeled and deveined
1 package (1 pound) lasagna noodles, cooked and drained
1 cup (4 ounces) shredded mozzarella cheese
2 tablespoons grated Parmesan cheese

Preheat oven to 350°F. Melt butter in medium skillet over medium heat. Add onion; cook and stir until tender. Stir in cottage cheese, cream cheese, basil, salt and pepper. Remove from heat. Blend in egg; set aside.

Combine soup, milk and garlic in large bowl; mix until well blended. Stir in wine, scallops, flounder and shrimp.

Place ⅓ of the noodles on bottom of greased 13×9-inch baking dish. Cover with layers of ½ *each* of the cottage cheese mixture, remaining noodles and seafood mixture; repeat layers of cottage cheese mixture, noodles and seafood mixture. Sprinkle with mozzarella cheese and Parmesan cheese. Bake 45 minutes or until hot and bubbly. Let stand 10 minutes before cutting to serve.

*Makes 8 to 10 servings*
*Favorite recipe from* **New Jersey Department of Agriculture**

*Seafood Lasagna*

# Green Market Lasagna with Three Cheeses

8 ounces lasagna noodles, cooked and drained
2 eggs, slightly beaten
2 cups Wisconsin Ricotta cheese
8 ounces asparagus, trimmed and cut into ½-inch pieces
1 cup peas
⅔ cup sliced green onions with tops
¾ cup chopped fresh parsley, divided
  Salt and black pepper
2 tablespoons butter
1½ tablespoons all-purpose flour
1 cup milk
¼ teaspoon ground nutmeg
  Dash cayenne pepper
3 cups (12 ounces) Wisconsin Medium Cheddar cheese, thinly sliced
2 tablespoons grated Wisconsin Parmesan cheese

In large bowl, combine eggs and Ricotta cheese. Stir in vegetables and all but 1 tablespoon parsley. Season with salt and black pepper to taste; set aside.

Melt butter in 1-quart saucepan over medium-low heat. Whisk in flour; cook 1 minute. Gradually whisk in milk. Cook 4 to 5 minutes until thickened, stirring occasionally. Stir in nutmeg and cayenne.

Line bottom of lightly oiled 12×8-inch baking dish with ⅓ of the noodles; cover with layers of ½ of the Ricotta mixture and ⅓ of the Cheddar. Repeat layers of noodles, Ricotta mixture and Cheddar. Cover with remaining noodles and Cheddar; top with sauce and Parmesan. Bake, covered, at 375°F, 40 minutes. Uncover. Continue baking 10 minutes. Sprinkle with remaining 1 tablespoon parsley. Let stand 10 minutes.

*Makes 6 to 8 servings*

*Favorite recipe from* **Wisconsin Milk Marketing Board**
**© 1992**

## Lasagna with a Difference

1 pound ground turkey
1 medium onion, chopped
3 cloves garlic, minced
4 ounces mushrooms, sliced
2 tablespoons vegetable oil
4 cups tomato juice
1 can (6 ounces) tomato paste
2 teaspoons dried oregano leaves, crushed
1 teaspoon dried basil leaves, crushed
1 teaspoon salt, divided
½ teaspoon pepper, divided
2 eggs, slightly beaten
1 pound ricotta cheese
1 cup (4 ounces) grated Parmesan cheese
1 tablespoon dried parsley flakes
1 package (8 ounces) lasagna noodles, uncooked
2 cups (8 ounces) shredded mozzarella cheese

*Lasagna with a Difference*

In large saucepan over medium-high heat, brown turkey with onion, garlic and mushrooms in oil. Add tomato juice, tomato paste, oregano, basil, ½ teaspoon salt and ¼ teaspoon pepper. Bring to a boil. Reduce heat to low; simmer 30 minutes, stirring occasionally.

Meanwhile, in medium bowl, combine eggs, ricotta cheese, Parmesan cheese, parsley flakes, remaining ½ teaspoon salt and remaining ¼ teaspoon pepper.

Spoon 1 cup meat sauce into lightly greased 13×9-inch baking dish; cover with ½ of the *uncooked* noodles. Top with layers of ½ *each* of the ricotta cheese mixture, remaining meat sauce and mozzarella cheese. Repeat layers of noodles, ricotta cheese mixture, meat sauce and mozzarella cheese; cover with foil. Bake at 375°F, 30 minutes. Remove foil; continue baking 15 minutes. Let stand 10 minutes before cutting to serve.

*Makes 8 to 10 servings*

**Note:** To prepare ahead, assemble lasagna to point of baking; cover with foil. Refrigerate. Bake, covered, 45 minutes. Uncover; continue baking 15 minutes or until hot and bubbly.

*Favorite recipe from* **California Poultry Industry Federation**

# Apple Lasagna

1 egg, slightly beaten
2 cups (8 ounces) shredded Cheddar
    cheese
1 cup ricotta cheese
¼ cup granulated sugar
1 teaspoon almond extract
2 cans (20 ounces *each*) apple pie
    filling
8 lasagna noodles, cooked and drained
6 tablespoons all-purpose flour
⅔ cup packed brown sugar, divided
¼ cup quick-cooking oats
½ teaspoon ground cinnamon
    Dash ground nutmeg
3 tablespoons cold margarine
1 cup sour cream

Preheat oven to 350°F. Combine egg, Cheddar cheese, ricotta cheese, granulated sugar and almond extract in medium bowl; blend well. Spoon 1 can pie filling into greased 13×9-inch baking dish. Cover with ½ of the noodles; top with cheese mixture. Cover with remaining noodles and pie filling.

Combine flour, ⅓ cup brown sugar, oats, cinnamon and nutmeg in small bowl. Cut in margarine until mixture is crumbly; sprinkle over pie filling. Bake 45 minutes. Cool 15 minutes.

Meanwhile, prepare garnish by blending sour cream and remaining ⅓ cup brown sugar in small bowl. Cover; refrigerate.

When ready to serve, cut lasagna into squares; garnish with sour cream mixture. *Makes 12 to 15 servings*

*Favorite recipe from **North Dakota Wheat Commission***

# Lasagna Olé

6 Lasagna Noodles
1 pound ground turkey
1 envelope (1.25 ounces) taco
    seasoning mix
½ cup water
1 can (4 ounces) chopped green chiles,
    undrained
2 cups (8 ounces) shredded Monterey
    Jack cheese with or without
    jalapeño peppers
1 container (16 ounces) sour cream
1 cup sliced pitted ripe olives, optional
1 can (15 ounces) creamy textured
    refried beans

Prepare pasta according to package directions; drain. While pasta is cooking, brown ground turkey in large nonstick skillet over medium-high heat, stirring occasionally to separate turkey; drain. Stir in taco seasoning and ½ cup water. Reduce heat to low; simmer 8 to 10 minutes, until turkey is cooked and most of liquid has evaporated, stirring occasionally. Stir in chiles. Cool slightly.

Spray 13×9-inch baking dish with vegetable spray. In medium bowl, gently mix cheese, sour cream and olives. Spread ½ of the turkey mixture onto bottom of dish; cover with 3 noodles and layers of ½ *each* of the refried beans and cheese mixture. Top with 3 noodles and layers of the remaining turkey mixture, beans and cheese mixture; sprinkle with Parmesan cheese, if desired. Bake at 350°F, 30 to 40 minutes or until hot and bubbly. Let stand 10 minutes before cutting to serve. *Makes 8 to 10 servings*

*Favorite recipe from **National Pasta Association***

*Apple Lasagna*

# Spetzque

2 pounds ground beef
1 can (4½ ounces) chopped pitted ripe olives, drained
1 can (4 ounces) mushroom stems and pieces, drained
1 small onion, chopped
1 jar (16 ounces) spaghetti sauce
Dash pepper
Dash dried oregano leaves, crushed
Dash Italian seasoning
9 lasagna noodles, cooked and drained
1¼ cups frozen corn
1¼ cups frozen peas
2 cups (8 ounces) shredded mozzarella cheese

*Spetzque*

Preheat oven to 350°F. Brown beef in large skillet over medium-high heat, stirring occasionally to separate beef; drain. Add olives, mushrooms and onion. Cook, stirring occasionally, until vegetables are tender. Add spaghetti sauce, pepper, oregano and Italian seasoning. Heat thoroughly, stirring occasionally; set aside.

Place ⅓ of the noodles on bottom of greased 13×9-inch baking dish; cover with layers of ½ *each* of the beef mixture, corn and peas. Repeat layers of noodles, beef mixture, corn and peas. Top with remaining noodles; sprinkle with mozzarella cheese. Bake 25 minutes or until hot and bubbly. (If desired, lasagna may be covered with foil during last few minutes of baking time to prevent over-browning of cheese.) Let stand 10 minutes before cutting to serve. Garnish as desired.          *Makes 6 servings*

*Favorite recipe from* **North Dakota Beef Commission**

# 7 Spice Lasagna

10 PASTA DeFINO No Boil® Lasagna noodles

**Meat Sauce:**

1 pound ground turkey
1 large clove garlic, minced
1 jar (16 ounces) Original *or* Spicy TABASCO® 7 Spice Chili Recipe
2 cups tomato juice
1 can (6 ounces) tomato paste
1 teaspoon dried oregano leaves, crushed

**Cheese Sauce:**

1 egg, slightly beaten
1 container (16 ounces) lowfat cottage cheese
½ package (8 ounces) reduced-calorie cream cheese, softened
¼ cup finely chopped fresh parsley

½ cup (2 ounces) grated Parmesan cheese
2 cups (8 ounces) shredded Monterey Jack cheese

• **Microwave:** In large skillet, brown turkey over medium heat, stirring occasionally to separate turkey. Add garlic; cook 1 minute. Stir in 7 Spice Chili Recipe, tomato juice, tomato paste and oregano. Bring to a boil. Reduce heat to low; simmer 10 minutes, stirring occasionally.

• In medium bowl, combine egg, cottage cheese, cream cheese and parsley; mix until well blended.

• Spoon 1½ cups meat sauce into 13×9-inch microwave-safe baking dish. Cover with layers of ½ *each* of the noodles, remaining meat sauce, cottage cheese mixture, Parmesan cheese and Monterey Jack cheese; repeat layers ending with Monterey Jack cheese.

• Cover with vented plastic wrap. Microwave on HIGH 17 to 20 minutes or until hot and bubbly, turning dish after 10 minutes. Let stand 10 minutes before cutting to serve.     *Makes 6 to 8 servings*

## Artichoke Lasagna

3 medium California artichokes
¾ to 1 pound ground turkey *or* turkey sausage
1 cup chopped onion
1 to 2 cloves garlic, minced
2 tablespoons olive oil
1 can (14½ ounces) ready-cut peeled tomatoes, undrained
1 teaspoon dried rosemary leaves, crushed
1 teaspoon dried basil leaves, crushed
    Salt and pepper to taste
12 lasagna noodles, cooked and drained
1 cup ricotta cheese *or* small curd cottage cheese
½ cup (2 ounces) grated Parmesan cheese
1 cup (4 ounces) shredded mozzarella cheese

Trim stems so artichokes stand upright. Cut ¼ to ⅓ off top of artichokes. Bend back outer petals of artichokes until they snap off easily near base. (Edible portion of petals should remain on artichoke hearts.) Continue to snap off and discard petals until central cores of pale green petals are reached. Trim dark outer green layers from artichokes. Slice artichokes lengthwise into ½-inch strips.

In large skillet over medium heat, brown turkey with onion and garlic in oil, stirring occasionally to separate turkey. Add artichokes; cook until crisp-tender, stirring occasionally. Stir in tomatoes, rosemary, basil, salt and pepper. Reduce heat to low; simmer 5 minutes, stirring occasionally.

Trim noodles to 9-inch lengths. Place 4 noodles on bottom of 9-inch square baking dish. Cover with layers of ½ cup ricotta cheese, ½ of the artichoke mixture and ¼ cup Parmesan cheese. Repeat layers of noodles, ricotta cheese, artichoke mixture and Parmesan cheese. Top with remaining noodles. Sprinkle with mozzarella cheese. Bake at 375°F, 30 minutes or until thoroughly heated.
*Makes 9 servings*

**Prep time:** About 1 hour
**Tip:** Individual portions can be packaged and frozen for later use.
**Microwave:** Prepare recipe as directed, using microwave-safe baking dish. Microwave at MEDIUM-HIGH (70%) 10 to 15 minutes or until thoroughly heated, turning dish after 5 minutes.

*Favorite recipe from **California Artichoke Advisory Board***

# IN-A-MINUTE ENTRÉES

## 15-Minute Pasta Combo

**8 ounces spaghetti, broken in half**
**½ cup KRAFT® House Italian Dressing**
**2 large tomatoes, seeded and chopped**
**2 cups LOUIS RICH® Hickory Smoked
Breast of Turkey cubes**
**1 cup (4 ounces) KRAFT® 100% Grated
Parmesan Cheese**

• Cook spaghetti according to package
directions; drain. Keep warm.

• In same pan used to cook pasta, heat
dressing over medium heat. Add hot
spaghetti; toss until well coated.

• Add tomatoes, turkey and Parmesan
cheese; toss lightly. Garnish as desired.
*Makes 6 servings*

**Prep time:** 5 minutes
**Cook time:** 10 minutes

## Quick Spaghetti

**1 pound ground beef**
**1 jar (16 ounces) prepared spaghetti
sauce**
**½ (1-pound) package CREAMETTE®
Spaghetti**
**Grated Parmesan cheese**

In medium skillet, brown ground beef;
drain. Stir in spaghetti sauce; heat
thoroughly, stirring occasionally.
Meanwhile, prepare Creamette®
Spaghetti according to package
directions; drain. Top with spaghetti
sauce and Parmesan cheese. Refrigerate
leftovers.          *Makes 4 to 6 servings*

## Fettuccine Primavera

**1 package (12 ounces) fettuccine
noodles,\* cooked and drained**
**¾ cup BLUE BONNET® Margarine**
**1 cup broccoli flowerets**
**1 cup sliced zucchini**
**½ cup finely chopped red *or* green
pepper**
**½ cup chopped onion**
**½ teaspoon dried basil leaves, crushed**
**2 medium tomatoes, cut into wedges**
**½ cup sliced mushrooms**

Melt margarine in large skillet over
medium-high heat. Add broccoli,
zucchini, peppers, onion and basil; cook
and stir until vegetables are tender. Stir
in tomatoes and mushrooms.

Combine vegetable mixture with hot
fettuccine; toss lightly. Serve with grated
Parmesan cheese, if desired.
*Makes 5 servings*

\*Other pasta may be substituted.

*Mostaccioli and Sausage*

## Mostaccioli and Sausage

1 (1-pound) package CREAMETTE®
    Mostaccioli, cooked and drained
1½ pounds link Italian sausage, sliced
1 cup chopped onion
¾ cup chopped green pepper
2 jars (26 ounces *each*) CLASSICO®
    Pasta Sauce, any flavor
½ cup (2 ounces) grated Parmesan
    cheese
2 tablespoons olive oil

In large saucepan over medium heat,
brown sausage; drain. Add onion and
peppers; cook and stir until tender. Add
pasta sauce and Parmesan cheese. Bring
to a boil; reduce heat to low. Cover and
simmer 15 minutes, stirring occasionally.
Combine hot cooked mostaccioli with
oil; toss lightly to coat. Serve with sauce.
Garnish as desired. Refrigerate leftovers.
*Makes 6 to 8 servings*

## Garlic Parmesan Pasta

*A dish with robust flavor that's also quick
and convenient to prepare.*

8 ounces fettuccine, cooked and
    drained
½ cup butter *or* margarine
2 teaspoons dried basil leaves, crushed
2 teaspoons lemon juice
1¼ teaspoons LAWRY'S® Garlic Powder
    with Parsley
¾ teaspoon LAWRY'S® Seasoned Salt
1½ cups broccoli flowerettes, cooked
    until crisp-tender
3 tablespoons chopped walnuts
½ cup (2 ounces) grated Parmesan *or*
    Romano cheese

In large skillet, melt butter over medium
heat. Add basil, lemon juice, Garlic
Powder with Parsley and Seasoned Salt;
mix well. Add hot fettuccine, broccoli,
walnuts and Parmesan cheese; toss
lightly to coat. *Makes 4 servings*

**Presentation:** Serve with a fresh spinach
salad.

## Creamy Chicken Fettuccine

2 cups hot cooked and drained
    spinach fettuccine (about 8 ounces
    uncooked)
1 jar (12 ounces) HEINZ® HomeStyle
    Chicken Gravy
1 package (4 ounces) garlic and spice
    *or* herb and garlic flavored soft
    spreadable cheese
2 cups chopped cooked chicken
    Snipped fresh chives, basil, thyme *or*
    tarragon leaves

Combine gravy and cheese in 2-quart
saucepan. Cook and stir over medium
heat until cheese melts and sauce is
smooth. Stir in chicken; heat thoroughly,
stirring occasionally. Serve over hot
fettuccine. Sprinkle with chives.
*Makes 4 servings*

# Singapore Spicy Noodles

*A pasta dish with a taste of the Orient.*

**8 ounces linguine, cooked and drained**
**1¼ cups water**
**2 tablespoons ketchup**
**2½ teaspoons packed brown sugar**
**1½ teaspoons chopped cilantro**
**1 teaspoon cornstarch**
**¾ teaspoon LAWRY'S® Seasoned Salt**
**¾ teaspoon LAWRY'S® Garlic Powder**
**    with Parsley**
**¼ teaspoon crushed red pepper**
**2½ tablespoons chunky peanut butter**
**1 cup shredded red cabbage**
**¼ cup sliced green onions with tops**

*Singapore Spicy Noodles*

In medium saucepan, combine water, ketchup, sugar, cilantro, cornstarch and seasonings. Bring to a boil over medium-high heat. Reduce heat to low; simmer, uncovered, 5 minutes. Cool 10 minutes; blend in peanut butter. Add to hot linguine with cabbage and onions; toss lightly.                    *Makes 4 servings*

**Presentation:** Garnish with green onion curls. Serve with a marinated cucumber salad.

**Hint:** For a heartier entrée, add shredded cooked chicken or pork.

# Savory Bacon 'n Cheese Pasta

**1 package (12 ounces) VELVEETA®**
**    Shells & Cheese Dinner**
**8 OSCAR MAYER® Bacon Slices,**
**    crisply cooked, crumbled**
**1 package (9 ounces) BIRDS EYE®**
**    Italian Green Beans, thawed,**
**    drained**
**2 tablespoons chopped fresh chives**

• Prepare Dinner as directed on package.

• Stir in remaining ingredients; continue cooking until thoroughly heated.
                    *Makes 4 to 6 servings*

**Prep time:** 20 minutes

**Microwave:** • Prepare Dinner as directed on package. Stir in remaining ingredients. • Microwave on HIGH 3 to 5 minutes or until thoroughly heated, stirring every 2 minutes.

## Flavorful Tortellini à la VEG-ALL®

14 ounces tortellini, cooked and
    drained
¼ cup butter
1 medium onion, chopped
⅓ cup chopped red pepper
3 cloves garlic, minced
1 can (16 ounces) VEG-ALL® Mixed
    Vegetables, drained
½ cup (2 ounces) grated Parmesan
    cheese

Melt butter in medium skillet over
medium heat. Add onion, red pepper
and garlic; cook and stir until tender,
about 2 minutes. Add VEG-ALL®; heat
thoroughly, stirring occasionally. Spoon
mixture into large bowl. Add hot tortellini
and Parmesan cheese; toss to coat.
Garnish with fresh herbs, if desired.

*Makes 8 servings*

## Chicken and Pasta in Cream Sauce

5 ounces thin spaghetti, cooked and
    drained
6 tablespoons unsalted butter
1 tablespoon CHEF PAUL
    PRUDHOMME'S® Poultry Magic®
½ pound finely chopped skinless
    boneless chicken breast
¼ cup finely chopped green onions
    with tops
2 cups heavy cream *or* half-and-half

*Flavorful Tortellini à la VEG-ALL®*

In large skillet, melt butter over medium
heat. Add Poultry Magic® and chicken;
cook 1 minute. Add onions; cook and
stir 1 to 2 minutes. Gradually add cream,
stirring until well blended. Bring to a
boil. Reduce heat to low; simmer 2 to 3
minutes, until sauce starts to thicken,
stirring frequently. Add hot spaghetti;
toss to coat. Heat thoroughly, stirring
occasionally. Serve immediately.

*Makes 2 main-dish servings*

**Variation:** Substitute shelled, deveined
medium shrimp for chicken. Substitute 2
teaspoons CHEF PAUL PRUDHOMME'S®
Seafood Magic® for Poultry Magic®.
Remove shrimp from skillet after cooking
about 1 minute; return to skillet with
cooked spaghetti.

## Turkey Pasta Primavera

1 pound LOUIS RICH®, fully cooked, Hickory Smoked Breast of Turkey
2 tablespoons vegetable oil
2 green onions with tops, sliced
1 clove garlic, minced
2 tablespoons water
4 cups broccoli flowerets
4 ounces spaghetti *or* fettuccine, cooked and drained
8 cherry tomatoes, halved
1 container (8 ounces) plain lowfat yogurt
1 teaspoon dried basil leaves, crushed
¼ cup (1 ounce) grated Parmesan cheese

• Cut turkey into ½-inch cubes; set aside.

• Heat oil in large skillet over medium heat. Add onions and garlic; cook and stir 3 minutes. Add water, broccoli and turkey; bring to a boil. Reduce heat to low; cover and simmer 5 to 10 minutes or until broccoli is crisp-tender, stirring occasionally.

• Combine spaghetti with turkey mixture; toss lightly. Place on serving platter; top with tomatoes.

• Blend together yogurt and basil in small bowl; spoon over spaghetti mixture. Sprinkle with Parmesan cheese.
*Makes 4 servings*

## Linguine with Oil and Garlic

½ cup FILIPPO BERIO® Extra-Virgin Flavorful Olive Oil, divided
10 cloves garlic, minced
12 ounces linguine
¼ teaspoon pepper
¼ teaspoon salt, optional

1. Heat 2 tablespoons olive oil in small saucepan over medium heat. Add garlic; cook and stir until lightly browned. Remove from heat; set aside.

2. Cook linguine according to package directions until tender. *(Do not overcook.)*

3. Drain linguine; return to pan. Add garlic mixture, remaining 6 tablespoons olive oil, pepper and salt; toss lightly to coat.          *Makes 4 servings*

**Prep time:** 5 minutes
**Cook time:** 20 minutes

## Easy Beef Stroganoff

2 tablespoons vegetable oil
2 teaspoons minced fresh garlic
½ pound boneless sirloin steak, cut into thin strips
¼ cup dry red wine
2 teaspoons Worcestershire sauce
1¼ cups water
½ cup milk
2 tablespoons butter *or* margarine
1 package LIPTON® Noodles & Sauce—Stroganoff*
½ cup pearl onions

In large skillet, heat oil over medium-high heat. Add garlic; cook and stir 30 seconds or until lightly browned. Add steak; cook and stir 1 minute or until almost done. Add wine and Worcestershire sauce. Cook 30 seconds; remove steak from skillet. Into same skillet, stir water, milk, butter and noodles & stroganoff sauce. Bring to a boil. Reduce heat to medium; simmer 7 minutes, stirring occasionally. Stir in onions and steak; simmer an additional 2 minutes or until noodles are tender. Garnish, if desired, with chopped parsley and paprika.
*Makes about 2 servings*

*Also terrific with LIPTON® Noodles & Sauce—Beef Flavor.

## Salmon Tortellini

*This creamy tortellini can be served as a main dish with a variety of colorful fresh vegetables or as an accompaniment for poultry or seafood.*

1 package (7 ounces) cheese-filled
  tortellini, cooked and drained
1 container (8 ounces)
  PHILADELPHIA BRAND® Soft
  Cream Cheese with Smoked
  Salmon
½ cup finely chopped cucumber
1 teaspoon dried dill weed *or*
  2 teaspoons fresh dill

• Lightly toss hot tortellini with remaining ingredients. Serve immediately.          *Makes 6 to 8 servings*

**Prep time:** 25 minutes

## Spaghetti with Quick Clam Sauce

½ (1-pound) package CREAMETTE®
  Spaghetti, cooked and drained
2 cans (6½ ounces *each*) SNOW'S® *or*
  DOXSEE® Chopped Clams,
  drained, reserving ⅓ cup liquid
1 jar (26 ounces) CLASSICO® Pasta
  Sauce, any flavor
  Grated Parmesan cheese

In large saucepan over medium heat, combine reserved clam liquid and pasta sauce; simmer, uncovered, 10 minutes, stirring occasionally. Add clams; heat thoroughly. Serve over hot spaghetti. Sprinkle with Parmesan cheese. Refrigerate leftovers.
          *Makes 3 to 4 servings*

## Ham Carrot Fettuccine

4 ounces fettuccine noodles, cooked
  and drained
1 tablespoon margarine
1 tablespoon olive oil
1 cup sliced DOLE® Carrots
1 cup sliced DOLE® Celery
1 cup DOLE® Asparagus tips *or* green
  beans
½ cup julienne smoked ham
1 large clove garlic, minced
1 teaspoon Italian seasoning
2 tablespoons grated Parmesan cheese

• Heat margarine and oil in large skillet over medium-high heat. Add vegetables, ham, garlic and seasoning; cook and stir 3 to 4 minutes or until vegetables are crisp-tender.

• Add hot noodles; mix lightly. Add cheese; toss lightly. Serve immediately.
          *Makes 2 servings*

**Prep time:** 15 minutes
**Cook time:** 7 minutes

## Springtime Pasta Italiano

2 cups broccoli florets
¾ cup thinly sliced pepperoni
½ cup WISH-BONE® Robusto Italian
  Dressing
8 ounces spaghetti, cooked and
  drained
2 tablespoons grated Parmesan cheese

In medium saucepan, steam or boil broccoli florets until tender; drain. Add pepperoni, robusto Italian dressing and hot spaghetti; heat thoroughly, stirring occasionally. Sprinkle with cheese.
          *Makes 4 main-dish servings*

*Also terrific with WISH-BONE® Italian, Lite Italian *or* Blended Italian Dressing.

*Salmon Tortellini*

# Chili Mac 'n Cheddar

1 package (7 ounces) CREAMETTES®
    Elbow Macaroni, cooked and
    drained
2 cans (15 ounces *each*) chili with
    beans
1 can (16 ounces) whole tomatoes, cut
    up, undrained
1 can (4 ounces) diced green chilies *or*
    jalapeño peppers, drained
1 cup (4 ounces) shredded Cheddar
    cheese
    Sour cream
    Corn chips

In large skillet over low heat, combine
chili, tomatoes and green chilies; mix
well. Simmer 10 minutes, stirring
occasionally. Stir in hot macaroni;
sprinkle cheese over top. Cover; simmer
an additional 5 minutes or until cheese
melts. Serve with sour cream and corn
chips. Refrigerate leftovers.

*Makes 6 to 8 servings*

# Italian Sausage with Kraut and Fettuccine

7 ounces fettuccine, cooked and
    drained
4 bacon slices
1 large onion, chopped
1 small red pepper, sliced into strips
1 cup thinly sliced mushrooms
1 tablespoon packed brown sugar
¼ cup red wine
1 can (14 ounces) FRANK'S® or
    SNOWFLOSS® Kraut, drained
1 package (12 ounces) precooked link
    Italian sausage, thickly sliced
2 tablespoon dried parsley flakes
¼ cup butter

In large skillet over medium heat, cook
bacon until crisp; remove bacon from
skillet, reserving drippings in skillet.
Drain bacon on paper towels; crumble
and set aside. Add onion, peppers and
mushrooms to reserved drippings in
skillet; cook and stir until tender. Stir in
brown sugar, wine and kraut. Add
sausage and parsley; cover. Reduce heat
to low; simmer 8 minutes or until
thoroughly heated, stirring occasionally.
Add butter to hot pasta; toss to coat.
Add bacon and kraut mixture; mix
lightly. *Makes 4 to 6 servings*

# San Francisco Stir-Fry

6 ounces linguine, cooked and drained
1 cup carrot slices
4 ounces pea pods
½ teaspoon dried tarragon leaves,
    crushed
2 tablespoons PARKAY® Margarine
¾ pound VELVEETA® Pasteurized
    Process Cheese Spread, cubed
¼ cup milk

• Stir-fry vegetables and tarragon in
margarine in large skillet over medium-
high heat until crisp-tender. Reduce
heat to low.

• Add process cheese spread and milk;
stir until process cheese spread is
melted. Add hot linguine; toss lightly.

*Makes 4 to 6 servings*

**Prep time:** 10 minutes
**Cooking time:** 15 minutes

**Microwave:** • In 1½-quart microwave-
safe bowl, microwave vegetables,
tarragon and margarine on HIGH 3 to 5
minutes or until crisp-tender, stirring
every 2 minutes. • Stir in process cheese
spread and milk; microwave on HIGH 2
to 4 minutes or until process cheese
spread is melted, stirring after 2
minutes. Add hot linguine; toss lightly.

*Creamy Fettuccine Toss*

# Speedy Stroganoff

1 pound beef sirloin, cut into thin
  strips
1 tablespoon CRISCO® Shortening
1 medium onion, sliced
1 clove garlic, minced
1 can (10½ ounces) condensed cream
  of mushroom soup
1 cup sour cream
1 can (3 ounces) sliced mushrooms,
  undrained
2 tablespoons ketchup
2 teaspoons Worcestershire sauce
  Poppy Seed Noodles (recipe follows)

In large skillet, brown beef strips in hot
CRISCO® over medium-high heat. Add
onion and garlic; cook and stir until
tender. Combine soup, sour cream,
mushrooms, ketchup and
Worcestershire; pour over beef mixture.
Reduce heat to low. Heat thoroughly,
stirring occasionally. Serve over Poppy
Seed Noodles.          *Makes 4 servings*

**Poppy Seed Noodles:** Combine 4 cups
hot cooked noodles with 1 tablespoon
butter and 1 teaspoon poppy seed; mix
lightly.

# Creamy Fettuccine Toss

¼ cup margarine *or* butter
1 tablespoon all-purpose flour
2 teaspoons WYLER'S® or STEERO®
  Chicken-Flavor Instant Bouillon
¾ teaspoon dried basil leaves, crushed
¼ teaspoon garlic powder
⅛ teaspoon pepper
1 cup (½ pint) BORDEN® or
  MEADOW GOLD® Coffee Cream
  *or* Half-and-Half
1 cup BORDEN® or MEADOW
  GOLD® Milk
½ (1-pound) package CREAMETTE®
  Fettuccini
¼ cup (1 ounce) grated Parmesan
  cheese
  Chopped fresh parsley, walnuts and
  cooked crumbled bacon

In medium saucepan over medium heat,
melt margarine. Stir in flour, bouillon,
basil, garlic powder and pepper.
Gradually add cream and milk. Cook,
stirring occasionally, until bouillon
dissolves and sauce thickens slightly,
about 15 minutes. Meanwhile, cook
fettuccine according to package
directions; drain. Place in large bowl.
Remove sauce from heat; stir in cheese.
Add to hot fettuccine; toss to coat.
Sprinkle with parsley, walnuts and
bacon. Serve immediately. Refrigerate
leftovers.          *Makes 6 to 8 servings*

*Fettuccine Alfredo*

## Chicken Pesto

3 cups hot cooked pasta
1½ tablespoons olive oil
4 skinless boneless chicken breast
    halves (about 1 pound)
1 jar (12 ounces) HEINZ® HomeStyle
    Chicken Gravy
¼ cup water
2 tablespoons prepared pesto sauce
2 teaspoons lemon juice
2 tablespoons grated Parmesan cheese

Heat oil in large skillet over medium heat. Add chicken; cook until browned on both sides. Cover; continue cooking 6 to 8 minutes or until chicken is tender. Remove chicken from skillet; keep warm. Combine gravy, water, pesto and lemon juice in same skillet; heat until bubbly, stirring occasionally. To serve, place chicken on hot pasta; spoon sauce over chicken and sprinkle with cheese.

*Makes 4 servings*

## Fettuccine Alfredo

4 ounces spinach fettuccine noodles,
    cooked and drained
4 ounces egg fettuccine noodles,
    cooked and drained
¼ cup PARKAY® Margarine
1 cup whipping cream
¼ teaspoon salt
⅛ teaspoon pepper
1 package (3 ounces) KRAFT® 100%
    Shredded Parmesan Cheese,
    divided

• Melt margarine in 3-quart saucepan over low heat. Stir in cream, salt and pepper. Heat thoroughly, stirring occasionally.

• Add fettuccine and ½ cup Parmesan cheese, stirring until thoroughly heated. Serve with remaining cheese.

*Makes 4 to 6 servings*

**Prep time:** 5 minutes
**Cooking time:** 15 minutes

**Pasta Carbonara:** Prepare recipe as directed. Stir in 2 tablespoons chopped fresh parsley and 4 strips OSCAR MAYER® Bacon cooked, crumbled.

**Pasta Primavera:** In 10-inch skillet over medium-high heat, cook and stir 2 cups freshly cut vegetables in 2 tablespoons margarine 4 to 5 minutes. Stir into hot fettuccine. Continue as directed above.

**Lighter Fettuccine:** Substitute ½ cup 2% milk for ½ cup of the whipping cream. Prepare as above.

# Pasta Vegetable Medley

1½ cups (6 ounces) tri-color corkscrew
    noodles, cooked and drained
**2 cups broccoli flowerets**
**2 cups mushroom slices**
**1 medium red** *or* **green pepper, cut**
    **into strips**
**2 tablespoons PARKAY® Margarine**
½ pound VELVEETA® Mexican
    Pasteurized Process Cheese
    Spread with Jalapeño Pepper,
    cubed
**1 tablespoon milk**

• Stir-fry vegetables in margarine in
large skillet over medium-high heat
until crisp-tender. Reduce heat to low.

• Add process cheese spread and milk;
stir until process cheese spread is
melted. Add hot noodles; toss lightly.

*Makes 4 to 6 servings*

**Prep time:** 15 minutes
**Cooking time:** 15 minutes

**Microwave:** • Microwave broccoli,
peppers and margarine in 1½-quart
microwave-safe casserole on HIGH 2 to
3 minutes or until vegetables are crisp-
tender. • Add mushrooms. Microwave
on HIGH 2 minutes; drain. Add process
cheese spread and milk. • Microwave on
HIGH 2 to 3 minutes or until process
cheese spread is melted, stirring after 2
minutes. Add hot noodles; toss lightly.

# Easy Linguine Tutto Mare

*A very easy seafood pasta prepared from
on-hand ingredients.*

**8 ounces linguine, cooked and drained**
**1 jar (12 ounces) PROGRESSO® White**
    **Clam Sauce**
**1 can (6 ounces) lump crabmeat,**
    **rinsed and drained**
**1 can (4½ ounces) deveined medium**
    **shrimp, rinsed and drained**

1. In small saucepan over medium heat,
combine white clam sauce, crabmeat
and shrimp. Bring just to a boil. Remove
from heat.

2. Add to hot linguine; toss gently to
coat. (If necessary, add 2 tablespoons
water for desired consistency.) Serve
immediately. *Makes 4 servings*

**Prep time:** 15 minutes

**Microwave:** In 1-quart microwave-safe
casserole, combine clam sauce, crabmeat
and shrimp. Microwave on HIGH (100%
power) 4½ to 5 minutes or until hot,
stirring every 2 minutes. Continue as
directed above in Step 2.

# Ziti & Tuna Bake

*Here's a quick supper dish you can pull right
from your pantry.*

**6 ounces ziti pasta, cooked and**
    **drained**
**1 jar (15 ounces) spaghetti sauce with**
    **mushrooms**
**1 can (9¼ ounces) STARKIST® Tuna,**
    **drained and broken into chunks**
½ cup sliced pitted ripe olives
**1 cup (4 ounces) shredded low-fat**
    **mozzarella cheese, divided**
**Chopped fresh parsley**

**Microwave:** In large bowl, combine hot
pasta, spaghetti sauce, tuna, olives and
½ cup mozzarella cheese; mix lightly.
Transfer mixture to 10×6-inch
microwave-safe baking dish; cover with
waxed paper. Microwave on HIGH
power 9 minutes, rotating dish ¼ turn
every 3 minutes. Sprinkle with remaining
½ cup cheese. Let stand, covered, 2
minutes to melt cheese. Sprinkle with
parsley. *Makes 4 servings*

**Prep time:** 20 minutes

## Pasta Alfredo

8 ounces thin vegetable-flavored
    noodles, cooked and drained
1/2 cup (2 ounces) grated Parmesan
    cheese
1/2 cup prepared HIDDEN VALLEY
    RANCH® Original Ranch® Salad
    Dressing
2 tablespoons chopped fresh parsley
    Additional Parmesan cheese and
    freshly ground black pepper

In large saucepan over medium heat,
combine hot noodles, cheese, salad
dressing and parsley; toss to coat. Heat
until cheese melts, stirring occasionally.
Sprinkle individual servings with
additional cheese and pepper to taste.
*Makes 4 servings*

## Fettuccine with Herbed Cheese Sauce

3 tablespoons butter *or* margarine
1/3 cup sliced green onions with tops
1 clove garlic, minced
1 tablespoon all-purpose flour
1/2 teaspoon salt
1/2 teaspoon dried basil leaves, crushed
1/2 teaspoon dried oregano leaves,
    crushed
1/4 teaspoon pepper
1 3/4 cups milk
1 cup (4 ounces) SARGENTO® Classic
    Supreme Shredded *or* Fancy
    Supreme Shredded Mozzarella
    Cheese
1 cup (8 ounces) SARGENTO® Ricotta
    Cheese*
3 tablespoons chopped fresh parsley
10 ounces fettuccine *or* spaghetti

In medium saucepan over medium heat,
melt butter. Add onions and garlic; cook
and stir until tender, about 5 minutes.
Stir in flour, salt, basil, oregano and
pepper. Gradually stir in milk. Heat until
thick and bubbly, stirring occasionally.
Remove from heat. Add cheeses; stir
until melted. Stir in parsley; keep warm.
Meanwhile, cook fettuccine according to
package directions. Add cheese sauce;
toss lightly to coat. *Makes 6 servings*
*SARGENTO® Old Fashioned Ricotta,
Part Skim Ricotta *or* Light Ricotta can be
used.

## Pasta Cintoro

*Lightly sautéed fresh vegetables make this
recipe quick and easy.*

8 ounces angel hair pasta, cooked and
    drained
2 tablespoons IMPERIAL® Margarine
2 tablespoons olive *or* vegetable oil
1 teaspoon dried basil leaves, crushed
3/4 teaspoon LAWRY'S® Garlic Powder
    with Parsley
1/2 teaspoon LAWRY'S® Lemon Pepper
    Seasoning
1/2 cup chopped green pepper
1 medium zucchini, julienne-cut into
    1-inch pieces
1 cup thinly sliced mushrooms
2 medium tomatoes, chopped
1/4 to 1/2 cup chicken broth

In large skillet, melt margarine over
medium-high heat. Add oil, basil, Garlic
Powder with Parsley and Lemon Pepper
Seasoning; blend well. Add vegetables;
cook and stir until zucchini is crisp-
tender. Stir in chicken broth; heat 1
minute. Add hot pasta; toss until well
coated. *Makes 4 servings*

**Presentation:** Serve with a light
sprinkling of grated Parmesan cheese.

*Pasta Alfredo*

*New Orleans Sausage and Noodles*

## New Orleans Sausage and Noodles

1 package (4½ or 5¼ ounces) Alfredo
   noodles and sauce mix
¼ teaspoon ground red pepper
1 package (9 ounces) frozen artichoke
   hearts, thawed
1 tablespoon olive oil
1 package (1 pound) LOUIS RICH®
   fully cooked Turkey Smoked
   Sausage, cut diagonally into
   ¼-inch slices
1 clove garlic, minced
1 tomato, chopped

• Prepare Alfredo noodle mix according
to package directions, stirring in red
pepper and artichoke hearts during last
3 minutes of cooking time.

• Meanwhile, heat oil in large skillet
over medium heat. Add sausage and
garlic; cook and stir 5 minutes or until
sausage is lightly browned.

• Stir tomato into sausage mixture; cook
an additional 2 minutes. Serve over hot
noodle mixture.      *Makes 4 to 6 servings*

## Nokkelost Macaroni & Cheese

4 ounces elbow macaroni, cooked and
   drained
1 cup evaporated skim milk
1½ tablespoons all-purpose flour
½ cup (2 ounces) shredded Nokkelost
   *or* Classic Jarlsberg cheese
2 green onions with tops, sliced
2 tablespoons chopped pimiento
1 tablespoon chopped fresh parsley
1 cup blanched cauliflowerets
   Salt

In small saucepan over medium heat,
gradually add milk to flour, stirring until
well blended. Cook until thickened,
stirring constantly. Add cheese; stir until
melted. Stir in onions, pimiento and
parsley. Add to hot macaroni with
cauliflowerets; mix lightly. Season with
salt to taste.      *Makes 4 servings*

*Favorite recipe from* **Norseland Foods, Inc.**

## Easy Cheesy Tomato Macaroni

2 packages (7 ounces *each*) macaroni
   and cheese dinner
1 tablespoon olive *or* vegetable oil
1 cup finely chopped onion
1 cup thinly sliced celery
1 can (28 ounces) CONTADINA®
   Crushed Tomatoes
   Grated Parmesan cheese, optional
   Sliced green onions *or* celery leaves,
   optional

Cook macaroni (from macaroni and cheese dinner) according to package directions; drain. Heat oil in large skillet over medium-high heat. Add chopped onion and celery; cook and stir 3 minutes or until tender. Combine tomatoes and cheese mix from dinner; mix well. Add to vegetable mixture in skillet. Reduce heat to low; simmer, stirring constantly, until mixture is thickened. Simmer an additional 2 minutes to heat through. Add hot macaroni; toss lightly. Sprinkle with Parmesan cheese and garnish with green onions, if desired.

*Makes 6 to 8 servings*

## Savory Cheese Tortellini

**1 package (7 ounces) cheese-filled tortellini, cooked and drained**
**2 pounds VELVEETA® Pasteurized Process Cheese Spread, cubed**
**¼ cup milk**
**¼ teaspoon ground nutmeg**

Combine process cheese spread, milk and nutmeg in medium saucepan. Stir over low heat until process cheese spread is melted. Add hot tortellini; mix lightly. Garnish as desired.

*Makes 4 servings*

**Prep time:** 10 minutes
**Cooking time:** 10 minutes

**Microwave:** • Combine process cheese spread, milk and nutmeg in 1-quart microwave-safe bowl. Microwave on HIGH 2½ to 4½ minutes or until process cheese spread is melted, stirring after 2 minutes. • Add hot tortellini; mix lightly. Garnish as desired.

# Fettuccine with Creamy Tuna Sauce

*A quick and easy recipe that uses canned tuna in a new way.*

**8 ounces fettuccine, cooked and drained**
**1 tablespoon vegetable oil**
**1½ cups sliced fresh mushrooms**
**⅓ cup sour cream**
**2 tablespoons water**
**¾ teaspoon LAWRY'S® Garlic Powder with Parsley**
**¾ teaspoon LAWRY'S® Seasoned Salt**
**1 can (6½ ounces) water-packed tuna, drained and broken into chunks**
**3 tablespoons chopped pimientos**
**2 tablespoons grated Parmesan cheese**

In medium skillet, heat oil over medium-high heat. Add mushrooms; cook and stir until tender. Stir in sour cream, water, Garlic Powder with Parsley and Seasoned Salt. Combine with hot noodles, tuna and pimientos; mix lightly. Heat 1 minute. Sprinkle with Parmesan cheese. Serve immediately.

*Makes 4 servings*

**Presentation:** Garnish with chopped fresh parsley. Serve with broiled tomato slices.

# FAMILY FIXIN'S

## Layered Pasta Ricotta Pie

¼ (1-pound) package CREAMETTE®
    Vermicelli, uncooked
1 tablespoon olive *or* vegetable oil
⅓ cup finely chopped onion
4 cloves garlic, minced
1 cup grated fresh Romano cheese,
    divided
3 eggs, divided
1 container (15 or 16 ounces) ricotta
    cheese
1 package (10 ounces) frozen chopped
    spinach, thawed and *well drained*
½ teaspoon salt
1 jar (26 ounces) CLASSICO® Di
    Sicilia (Ripe Olives &
    Mushrooms) Pasta Sauce, divided

Preheat oven to 350°F. Break vermicelli
into thirds; cook according to package
directions. Drain. Meanwhile, in large
skillet, heat oil over medium-high heat.
Add onion and garlic; cook and stir until
tender. Remove from heat. Add
vermicelli, ½ cup Romano cheese and
one egg; mix well. Press onto bottom of
well-greased 9-inch springform pan.
Combine 2 egg *yolks*, ricotta cheese,
spinach, salt and remaining ½ cup
Romano cheese. Spread over pasta layer.
In small mixer bowl, beat 2 egg *whites*
until stiff but not dry; fold into 1½ cups
pasta sauce. Pour over spinach mixture.
Bake 50 to 60 minutes or until set; let
stand 10 minutes before cutting to serve.
Meanwhile, heat remaining pasta sauce;
serve with pie. Garnish as desired.
Refrigerate leftovers.

*Makes 6 to 8 servings*

## Five Wisconsin Cheese Pasta Bake

12 to 14 ounces macaroni *or* desired
    pasta shape, cooked and drained
1 cup (4 ounces) shredded Wisconsin
    Swiss cheese
1 cup (4 ounces) shredded Wisconsin
    Mozzarella cheese
2 tablespoons grated Wisconsin
    Parmesan cheese
1 cup (4 ounces) shredded Wisconsin
    Provolone cheese
½ cup Wisconsin Ricotta cheese
½ cup sour cream
½ cup heavy cream
1 tablespoon chopped fresh parsley
¾ teaspoon garlic powder
½ teaspoon pepper

In large bowl, combine Swiss,
Mozzarella and Parmesan cheeses.
Reserve ¾ cup cheese mixture; add pasta
to remaining cheese mixture in bowl.
Combine remaining ingredients. Add to
pasta mixture; mix lightly. Pour into
greased 13×9-inch baking dish. Sprinkle
with reserved cheese mixture. Broil on
middle oven rack 10 minutes or until
thoroughly heated.

*Makes 10 to 12 servings*

*Favorite recipe from* **Wisconsin Milk Marketing Board**
*© 1992*

*Layered Pasta Ricotta Pie*

*Vegetable 'n Chicken Alfredo*

## Pepper-Chicken Fettuccine Toss

1 package (1 pound) CREAMETTE®
    Fettuccini, cooked and drained
¼ cup olive *or* vegetable oil
3 whole boneless skinless chicken
    breasts, cut into strips (about
    1½ pounds)
2 large red peppers, cut into strips
2 large yellow peppers, cut into strips
1 medium green pepper, cut into strips
1 medium onion, cut into chunks
2 cups sliced fresh mushrooms
1 teaspoon any herb seasoning
2 tablespoons grated Parmesan cheese

In large skillet, heat oil over medium
heat. Add chicken, peppers, onion,
mushrooms and seasoning; cook and
stir until chicken is no longer pink in
center, 8 to 10 minutes. Add hot
fettuccine and Parmesan cheese; toss to
coat. Serve immediately. Refrigerate
leftovers.     *Makes 10 to 12 servings*

## Vegetable 'n Chicken Alfredo

8 ounces pasta, cooked and drained
4 tablespoons butter *or* margarine,
    divided
3 tablespoons all-purpose flour
3 cups milk
¾ cup (3 ounces) SARGENTO® Grated
    Cheese*
½ teaspoon dried basil leaves, crushed
¼ teaspoon salt
¼ teaspoon black pepper
1 tablespoon vegetable oil
3 chicken breast halves, skinned,
    boned and cut into thin strips
¼ cup thinly sliced green onions with
    tops
4 cups sliced fresh vegetables
    (broccoli, mushrooms, green or
    red bell peppers, celery, green
    beans, carrots or zucchini)

In medium saucepan, melt 2
tablespoons butter over low heat. Add
flour; cook 2 minutes, stirring
occasionally. Gradually whisk in milk.
Bring to a boil over medium heat;
simmer until thickened, stirring
constantly. Stir in grated cheese, basil,
salt and black pepper. Set aside; keep
warm.

Heat remaining 2 tablespoons butter
and oil in large skillet. Add chicken;
cook over medium heat, stirring
constantly, until no longer pink in
center. Remove chicken from skillet; set
aside.

In same skillet, cook and stir onions
with other vegetables until crisp-tender,
about 5 minutes. Combine vegetables
with hot pasta and chicken in large
bowl; toss lightly. Serve with sauce.
Sprinkle with additional grated cheese,
if desired.     *Makes 4 servings*

*SARGENTO® Parmesan, Parmesan and
Romano or Italian-Style Grated Cheese
may be used.

## Old-Fashioned Tuna Noodle Casserole

**3 tablespoons butter** *or* **margarine, divided**
**¼ cup plain dry bread crumbs**
**1 tablespoon finely chopped fresh parsley**
**½ cup chopped onion**
**½ cup chopped celery**
**1 cup water**
**1 cup milk**
**1 package LIPTON® Noodles & Sauce—Butter**
**2 cans (6½ ounces** *each***) tuna, drained and flaked**

Melt 1 tablespoon butter. Combine with bread crumbs and parsley in small bowl; set aside.

Melt remaining 2 tablespoons butter in medium saucepan over medium heat. Add onion and celery; cook and stir 2 minutes or until tender. Add water and milk; bring to a boil. Stir in noodles & butter sauce. Simmer 8 minutes or until noodles are tender, stirring occasionally. Stir in tuna. Spoon into greased 1-quart casserole; top with bread crumb mixture. Broil until crumbs are golden brown.     *Makes about 4 servings*

**Microwave:** Prepare bread crumb mixture as directed. In 1½-quart microwave-safe casserole, combine remaining 2 tablespoons butter, onion and celery. Microwave on HIGH (Full Power) 2 minutes or until vegetables are tender. Stir in water, milk and noodles & butter sauce. Microwave 11 minutes or until noodles are tender, stirring after 6 minutes. Stir in tuna. Top with bread crumb mixture. Microwave 1 minute.

## Rotelle with Pork & Pepper Pasta Sauce

**3 tablespoons olive oil, divided**
**½** *each* **green and red pepper, cut into strips**
**1 medium onion, cut into wedges**
**1 (¾- to 1-pound) pork tenderloin, cut into ½-inch cubes**
**2 cloves garlic, minced**
**1 jar (26 ounces) CLASSICO® Di Roma Arrabbiata (Spicy Red Pepper) Pasta Sauce**
**¼ teaspoon dried thyme leaves, crushed**
**½ (1-pound) package CREAMETTE® Rotelle**

In large skillet, heat 2 tablespoons oil over medium-high heat. Add vegetables; cook and stir until tender. Remove from skillet. In same skillet, cook and stir pork and garlic until pork is no longer pink in center. Stir in pasta sauce and thyme. Reduce heat to low; simmer, uncovered, 20 minutes or until pork is tender, stirring occasionally. Meanwhile, cook pasta according to package directions; drain. Combine hot pasta with remaining 1 tablespoon oil; toss lightly. Stir vegetables into sauce. Serve over pasta. Refrigerate leftovers.
     *Makes 4 to 6 servings*

*Rotelle with Pork & Pepper Pasta Sauce*

## Mexican Mac 'n Cheese Dinner

1 package (7 ounces) elbow macaroni, cooked and drained
¾ pound VELVEETA® Mexican Pasteurized Process Cheese Spread with Jalapeño Pepper, cubed
¼ cup milk
1 tablespoon chopped cilantro
1 pound ground beef
1 can (8 ounces) tomato sauce
½ cup chopped tomato
¼ cup green onion slices with tops
¼ cup pitted ripe olive slices

• Mix together hot macaroni, process cheese spread, milk and cilantro in medium saucepan; stir until process cheese spread is melted.

• Crumble meat into 1-quart microwave-safe bowl. Microwave on HIGH 5 to 6 minutes or until meat loses pink color when stirred; drain. Stir in tomato sauce.

• Spoon ½ of macaroni mixture into 2-quart microwave-safe casserole; top with meat mixture and remaining macaroni mixture. Cover with lid.

• Microwave 5 to 7 minutes or until thoroughly heated, turning dish after 3 minutes. Top with remaining ingredients.          *Makes 4 to 6 servings*

**Prep time:** 15 minutes
**Microwave cooking time:** 13 minutes
**Conventional:** • Preheat oven to 350°F.
• Prepare macaroni mixture as directed.
• Brown meat; drain. Stir in tomato sauce. • Assemble recipe as directed.
• Bake, uncovered, 15 minutes or until thoroughly heated. Top with remaining ingredients.

## Fettuccine with Ham & Mushroom Sauce

8 ounces fettuccine noodles, cooked and drained
¼ cup butter *or* margarine
8 ounces fresh mushrooms, sliced, *or* 1 can (8 ounces) sliced mushrooms, drained
1 medium onion, chopped
1 pound cooked ham, chopped
1 recipe White Sauce Base (recipe follows)
¼ cup (1 ounce) grated Parmesan cheese

In large skillet, melt butter over medium heat. Add mushrooms and onion; cook and stir 5 minutes or until tender. Add ham; mix well. Prepare White Sauce Base. Stir in Parmesan cheese; pour over ham mixture. Heat until bubbly, stirring frequently. Serve over hot noodles. Garnish with chopped fresh parsley and additional grated Parmesan cheese, if desired.          *Makes 4 servings*

### White Sauce Base

2 tablespoons butter *or* margarine
2 tablespoons all-purpose flour
¼ teaspoon salt
½ teaspoon TABASCO® pepper sauce
1¼ cups milk

In small saucepan, melt butter over low heat. Blend in flour, salt and TABASCO® sauce. Gradually stir in milk. Bring to a boil over medium heat, stirring constantly. Simmer 1 minute.
          *Makes about 1 cup*

**Microwave:** In 1-quart microwave-safe bowl, melt butter on HIGH 30 to 45 seconds. Stir in flour. Microwave, uncovered, on HIGH 30 seconds or until bubbly. Gradually stir in milk, salt and TABASCO® sauce. Microwave, uncovered, on HIGH 2½ to 3½ minutes, until thickened, stirring every minute.

## Chili Mostaccioli

1 pound ground beef
1 cup soft bread crumbs
½ cup milk
1 teaspoon salt
  Dash pepper
2 tablespoons CRISCO® Shortening
¼ cup chopped onion
1 clove garlic, minced
2 cans (11¼ ounces *each*) condensed
    chili-beef soup
1 soup can water
7 ounces mostaccioli *or* tubular
    macaroni (about 3 cups)
  Grated Parmesan cheese

Combine meat, crumbs, milk, salt and
pepper; shape into five oblong patties.
In skillet, brown patties in hot CRISCO®.
Remove patties; set aside. Add onion
and garlic to skillet; cook and stir until
tender. Blend in soup and water. Return
patties to skillet. Bring mixture to a boil;
simmer, covered, 15 minutes.
Meanwhile, cook mostaccioli according
to package directions; drain. Place on
large heated platter. Arrange patties on
mostaccioli; top with sauce. Sprinkle
with Parmesan cheese.

*Makes 5 servings*

## Polish Reuben Casserole

2 cans (10¾ ounces *each*) condensed
    cream of mushroom soup
1⅓ cups milk
½ cup chopped onion
1 tablespoon prepared mustard
2 cans (16 ounces *each*) sauerkraut,
    rinsed and drained
1 package (8 ounces) uncooked
    medium noodles
1½ pounds Polish sausage, cut into
    ½-inch pieces
2 cups (8 ounces) shredded Swiss
    cheese
¾ cup whole-wheat bread crumbs
2 tablespoons butter, melted

*Polish Reuben Casserole*

Preheat oven to 350°F. Combine soup,
milk, onion and mustard in medium
bowl; blend well. Spread sauerkraut
onto bottom of greased 13×9-inch
baking dish. Cover with *uncooked*
noodles; spoon soup mixture evenly
over top. Top with sausage and cheese.
Combine bread crumbs and butter in
small bowl; sprinkle over cheese. Cover
pan tightly with foil. Bake 1 hour or
until noodles are tender. Garnish as
desired. *Makes 8 to 10 servings*

*Favorite recipe from **North Dakota Wheat Commission***

# Beef Oriental

3 cups corkscrew pasta, cooked and
    drained
1 pound ground beef
7 green onions with tops, diagonally
    sliced into 2-inch pieces
3 tablespoons soy sauce
¼ teaspoon ground ginger
2 to 3 ribs celery, diagonally sliced
    into 1-inch pieces
8 mushrooms, sliced
1 package (20 ounces) frozen pea pods,
    rinsed under hot water
1 can (8 ounces) tomato sauce
3 fresh tomatoes, cut into wedges
1 cup (4 ounces) shredded Cheddar
    cheese, divided
1 green pepper, cut into thin slices

Brown beef with onions, soy sauce and
ginger in wok or large skillet over
medium-high heat, stirring occasionally
to separate meat. Push mixture up onto
side of wok. Add celery and mushrooms;
stir-fry 2 minutes. Push up onto side.
Add pea pods and tomato sauce; cook 4
to 5 minutes, stirring every minute. Add
pasta, tomatoes and ¾ cup cheese. Stir
gently to combine all ingredients. Cook
1 minute. Add green pepper; sprinkle
remaining cheese over top. Reduce heat
to low; heat thoroughly, stirring
occasionally.            *Makes 4 servings*

*Favorite recipe from* **North Dakota Beef Commission**

# Spinach-Noodle Casserole

*Serve a shredded carrot salad and fresh fruit
for dessert along with this easy-to-make
main course.*

4 ounces wide egg noodles *or* fusilli,
    cooked and drained
1 package (10 ounces) frozen chopped
    spinach
2 cups lowfat ricotta cheese
¼ cup reduced-calorie mayonnaise *or*
    salad dressing
1 egg
2 teaspoons dried chives
1 teaspoon dried basil leaves, crushed
½ teaspoon dill weed
¼ teaspoon salt
⅛ teaspoon pepper
1 can (9¼ ounces) STARKIST® Tuna,
    drained and broken into chunks
½ cup (2 ounces) shredded lowfat
    mozzarella cheese

**Microwave:** Place opened spinach
package in shallow microwave-safe
bowl. Microwave, uncovered, on HIGH
power 4 to 6 minutes or until thawed,
turning every 2 minutes. Let stand 2
minutes; drain well and squeeze out
excess moisture. In blender container or
food processor bowl, combine spinach,
ricotta cheese, mayonnaise, egg, chives
and seasonings; cover. Blend until
smooth.

Onto bottom of 9-inch square
microwave-safe casserole or 4 individual
microwave-safe ramekins, place noodles.
Top with layers of tuna and ricotta
cheese mixture, spreading to edge of
dish; cover loosely. Microwave on HIGH
power 8 to 11 minutes or until mixture
is hot in center, turning dish after 5
minutes. Sprinkle with mozzarella
cheese. Let stand, covered, 5 minutes or
until cheese is melted.

*Makes 4 servings*

**Prep time:** 15 minutes

*Beef Oriental*

## Fiesta Chicken Breasts

12 ounces spinach fettuccine *or*
    linguine, cooked and drained
3 tablespoons butter *or* margarine
3 whole chicken breasts, split, skinned
    and boned
1 jar (7 ounces) roasted red peppers,
    drained and sliced into ½-inch
    strips (about 1 cup)
¼ cup sliced green onions with tops
¼ cup all-purpose flour
1 cup chicken broth
1 cup milk
¼ cup dry white wine
1½ cups (6 ounces) SARGENTO®
    Classic Supreme Shredded
    Monterey Jack Cheese *or* Mild
    Cheddar Cheese
¼ cup coarsely chopped fresh cilantro

Melt butter in large skillet over medium heat. Add chicken; cook until golden brown and no longer pink in center, about 5 minutes per side. Remove chicken from skillet, reserving drippings in skillet; place chicken over fettuccine. Top with red pepper strips; keep warm. Add green onions to drippings in skillet; cook and stir 1 minute. Add flour; cook 1 minute, stirring constantly. Stir in broth, milk and wine. Bring to a boil; cook until thickened, stirring constantly. Add Monterey Jack cheese; stir until melted. Pour evenly over peppers, chicken and hot fettuccine; sprinkle with cilantro.

*Makes 6 servings*

*Fiesta Chicken Breasts*

## Speedy Chili-Mac

2 cups elbow macaroni, cooked in
    unsalted water and drained
1 can (15 ounces) chili without beans
1 can (10¾ ounces) condensed cream
    of mushroom soup
1 cup (4 ounces) shredded Cheddar
    cheese, divided
1 can (2.8 ounces) DURKEE® French
    Fried Onions, divided

Preheat oven to 350°F. Combine hot macaroni with chili, soup, ½ cup cheese and ½ can French Fried Onions; mix lightly. Spoon into greased 2-quart casserole; cover. Bake, 25 minutes or until thoroughly heated. Top with remaining cheese and onions. Bake, uncovered, 5 minutes or until onions are golden brown. *Makes 4 to 6 servings*

**Microwave:** Assemble macaroni mixture as directed; spoon into 2-quart microwave-safe casserole. Microwave, covered, on HIGH 8 to 10 minutes or until thoroughly heated, stirring after 5 minutes. Stir. Top with remaining cheese and onions. Microwave, uncovered, 1 minute or until cheese melts. Let stand 5 minutes.

## Sausage & Peppers with Pasta

1 tablespoon olive *or* vegetable oil
1 teaspoon minced fresh garlic
1 pound sweet Italian sausage, sliced
    diagonally into 1-inch pieces
1 cup sliced onion
2 medium red *or* green peppers, cut
    into thin strips
2½ cups water
1 package LIPTON® Pasta & Sauce—
    Herb Tomato
Black pepper

In large skillet, heat oil over medium
heat. Add garlic; cook and stir 30
seconds. Add sausage; cook over
medium-high heat 5 minutes or until
browned, stirring occasionally. Drain.
Add onion and red peppers; cook,
stirring frequently, 7 minutes or until
vegetables are tender. Drain. Add water.
Bring to a boil. Reduce heat to medium.
Stir in pasta & herb tomato sauce;
simmer 12 minutes or until pasta is
tender, stirring occasionally. Season
with black pepper to taste.
*Makes about 4 servings*

*Sausage & Peppers with Pasta*

## Mandarin Pork Noodles

8 ounces vermicelli noodles, cooked
    and drained
1 DOLE® Fresh Pineapple
¼ pound pork butt *or* shoulder
2 large cloves garlic, minced
2 tablespoons minced fresh ginger
    root
5 tablespoons soy sauce
¼ teaspoon crushed red pepper flakes
2 DOLE® Carrots, slivered
1 DOLE® Green Bell Pepper, slivered
4 DOLE® Green Onions with tops, cut
    into 2-inch pieces
1 tablespoon sesame oil

• Twist crown from pineapple. Cut
pineapple in half lengthwise. Reserve ½
for another stir-fry or salad. Cut
remaining pineapple into quarters. Cut
fruit from shells; core and chunk.

• Cut fat from pork; cut meat into thin
strips. Cook fat in wok or large skillet
until translucent. Remove fat from wok,
reserving meat drippings in wok. Add
pork strips to hot drippings; cook and
stir until pork is no longer pink in
center. Add garlic and ginger; cook and
stir until tender. Stir in soy sauce and
pepper flakes. Add carrots and bell
pepper. Reduce heat to low; cover.
Steam until vegetables are crisp-tender,
2 to 3 minutes. Add hot noodles; stir
until coated with sauce. Add pineapple,
onion and sesame oil. Cover; heat
thoroughly, stirring occasionally.
*Makes 4 servings*

**Prep time:** 15 minutes
**Cook time:** 10 minutes

# Meatballs and Pasta Picante con Queso

1 egg, slightly beaten
1 pound ground beef
1 cup fresh bread crumbs (about
    2 slices bread)
¾ cup PACE® Picante Sauce, divided
¼ cup chopped onion
2 tablespoons chopped fresh parsley
1 teaspoon salt
2 teaspoons ground cumin, divided
1 can (15 ounces) tomato sauce
½ pound pasteurized process cheese
    spread, cubed
1½ teaspoons chili powder
1 teaspoon ground coriander
1 pound thin linguine *or* other pasta
⅓ cup chopped fresh cilantro, optional

Combine egg, meat, bread crumbs, ¼
cup picante sauce, onion, parsley, salt
and ½ teaspoon cumin; mix well. Shape
into 1-inch balls. Place meatballs in
15×10-inch baking pan. Bake at 350°F, 15
minutes; drain. (*Or*, arrange about ⅓ of
the meatballs in circle in 9-inch glass pie
plate; cover with waxed paper.
Microwave on HIGH (100% power) 3
minutes, rotating dish after 2 minutes;
drain. Repeat with remaining meatballs.)

Combine remaining ½ cup picante
sauce, tomato sauce, process cheese
spread, chili powder, coriander and
remaining 1½ teaspoons cumin in large
saucepan. Cook over low heat, stirring
frequently, until process cheese spread
is melted. Add meatballs; simmer until
heated through. Meanwhile, cook pasta
according to package directions; drain.
Spoon sauce mixture over hot pasta;
sprinkle with cilantro, if desired. Serve
with additional picante sauce, if desired.
*Makes 6 servings*

*Meatballs and Pasta Picante con Queso*

# Hearty Manicotti

1¼ cups water, divided
1 pound sweet (mild) Italian sausage
    links
1 pound ground beef
1 medium onion, chopped
1 can (15 ounces) tomato puree
1 can (6 ounces) tomato paste
1 teaspoon sugar
½ teaspoon black pepper
1¾ teaspoons dried basil leaves,
    crushed, divided
1½ teaspoons salt, divided
1 package (12 ounces) manicotti shells
2 cups (15 ounces) SARGENTO®
    Ricotta Cheese*
2 cups (8 ounces) SARGENTO®
    Classic Supreme Shredded Low
    Moisture Part-Skim Mozzarella
    Cheese, divided
2 tablespoons chopped fresh parsley
    SARGENTO® Grated Cheese**

In 5-quart covered Dutch oven, place ¼ cup water and sausage; cook over medium heat 5 minutes. Uncover. Continue cooking until sausage is browned and no longer pink in center. Remove sausage from pan; drain on paper towels.

Add beef and onion to Dutch oven; cook over medium heat, stirring occasionally to separate meat; drain. Stir in tomato puree, tomato paste, sugar, pepper, 1 teaspoon basil, 1 teaspoon salt and remaining 1 cup water; cover. Simmer 45 minutes, stirring occasionally.

Cut sausage into bite-size pieces. Add to beef mixture; simmer 15 minutes, stirring occasionally.

Meanwhile, cook manicotti shells according to package directions; rinse and drain well.

In large bowl, combine Ricotta cheese, 1 cup Mozzarella cheese, parsley, remaining ¾ teaspoon basil and remaining ½ teaspoon salt. Spoon into shells; set aside.

Spoon ½ of meat sauce into large shallow baking dish. Arrange cheese-stuffed shells over sauce. Spoon remaining sauce over shells. Sprinkle with remaining 1 cup Mozzarella cheese. Bake at 375°F, 30 minutes. Serve with grated cheese.          *Makes 6 servings*

*SARGENTO® Old Fashioned Ricotta, Part Skim Ricotta or Light Ricotta can be used.

**SARGENTO® Parmesan, Parmesan and Romano or Italian-Style Grated Cheese can be used.

# Cacciatore-Style Chicken Fillets

4 cups rotini pasta, cooked and drained
¼ cup all-purpose flour
½ teaspoon garlic salt
¼ teaspoon pepper
4 boneless skinless chicken breasts, pounded to ¼-inch thickness
3 tablespoons WESSON® Vegetable Oil
1 cup *each* chopped onion and green pepper strips
1 teaspoon minced fresh garlic
2 cups sliced fresh mushrooms
1 cup sliced zucchini
1 can (15 ounces) HUNT'S® Tomato Sauce
1 can (14½ ounces) HUNT'S® Whole Tomatoes, cut up, undrained
⅓ cup dry white wine
2 teaspoons dried basil leaves, crushed
1 teaspoon *each* sugar and chicken bouillon granules
½ teaspoon dried oregano leaves, crushed

In large plastic bag, combine flour, garlic salt and pepper. Add chicken; shake to coat thoroughly. Heat oil in large skillet over medium heat. Add chicken; cook 4 to 5 minutes on each side or until no longer pink in center. Remove chicken from skillet; set aside. Add onion, green pepper and garlic to skillet. Cook and stir until crisp-tender. Add mushrooms and zucchini; cook and stir 1 to 2 minutes. Stir in all remaining ingredients *except* chicken and pasta. Bring to a boil. Add chicken; spoon sauce over chicken. Simmer, covered, 5 minutes. Serve over hot pasta.
*Makes 4 servings*

# Stuffed Pasta Shells

**4 ounces (about 18) large pasta shells,
cooked and drained**
**2 cups finely chopped cooked ham** *or*
**turkey**
**1 cup ricotta cheese**
**½ cup MIRACLE WHIP® Salad
Dressing**
**¼ cup chopped red onion**
**2 tablespoons cold water**
**¼ cup (1 ounce) KRAFT® 100% Grated
Parmesan Cheese**
**¼ cup dry bread crumbs**
**1 to 2 tablespoons chopped fresh
parsley**
**1 tablespoon PARKAY® Margarine,
melted**

• Heat oven to 350°F.

• Combine ham, ricotta cheese, salad
dressing and onions; mix lightly.

• Fill shells with ham mixture; place,
filled-side up, in shallow baking dish.

• Add 2 tablespoons cold water to dish;
cover with foil. Bake 30 minutes or until
thoroughly heated.

• Combine parmesan cheese, crumbs,
parsley and margarine; sprinkle over
shells. Continue baking, uncovered, 5
minutes. Serve with your favorite
accompaniments.     *Makes 6 servings*

**Prep time:** 15 minutes
**Cook time:** 35 minutes

**Microwave:** • Omit cold water.
• Microwave margarine in 9-inch
microwave-safe pie plate on HIGH 30
seconds or until melted. • Stir in
parmesan cheese and crumbs.
Microwave on HIGH 2 minutes, stirring
every 1 minute. Stir in parsley; set aside.

• Assemble shells as directed; place in
shallow microwave-safe baking dish.
Cover with plastic wrap; vent.
• Microwave on HIGH 7 to 8 minutes or
until thoroughly heated, turning dish
after 4 minutes. • Sprinkle with
parmesan cheese mixture. Let stand 5
minutes. Serve as directed.

# Italian Rice and Vegetables

**5 tablespoons BUTTER FLAVOR
CRISCO®, divided**
**1 cup uncooked long-grain rice**
**½ cup uncooked spaghetti pieces
(about 1-inch long)**
**½ teaspoon salt**
**½ teaspoon Italian seasoning**
**⅛ teaspoon pepper**
**2 cups water**
**1 package (10 ounces) frozen chopped
broccoli, thawed**
**1 cup sliced fresh mushrooms**
**¾ cup quartered cherry tomatoes**

In 2-quart saucepan, melt 3 tablespoons
BUTTER FLAVOR CRISCO®. Add
*uncooked* rice and spaghetti. Cook and
stir over medium heat until rice and
noodles are golden brown. Stir in salt,
Italian seasoning, pepper and water.
Bring to a boil. Reduce heat to low;
cover and simmer 15 minutes or until
water is absorbed. Set aside.

In large skillet, melt remaining 2
tablespoons BUTTER FLAVOR CRISCO®
over medium heat. Add broccoli,
mushrooms and tomatoes. Cook and stir
until mushrooms are tender. Add rice
mixture. Cook and stir until thoroughly
heated.     *Makes 6 servings*

*Stuffed Pasta Shells*

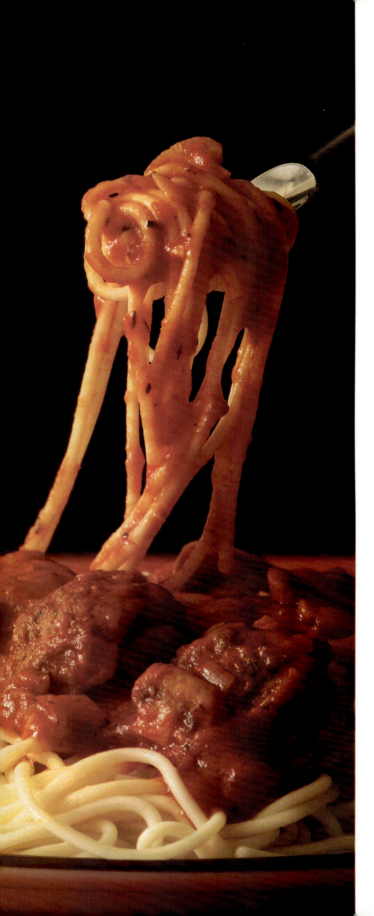

## Spaghetti & Meatballs

1 package (1 pound) CREAMETTE®
   Spaghetti, cooked and drained
1 egg, slightly beaten
1 pound lean ground beef
¾ cup (3 ounces) grated Parmesan
   cheese
½ cup finely chopped onion
½ cup fresh bread crumbs (about
   1 slice bread)
1 jar (26 ounces) CLASSICO® Pasta
   Sauce, any flavor, divided
2 teaspoons WYLER'S® or STEERO®
   Beef-Flavor Instant Bouillon
1 teaspoon Italian seasoning
8 ounces fresh mushrooms, sliced
   (about 2 cups)

In large bowl, combine egg, meat,
Parmesan cheese, onion, crumbs, ½ cup
pasta sauce, bouillon and Italian
seasoning; mix well. Shape into balls. In
large kettle or Dutch oven, brown
meatballs; drain. Stir in remaining pasta
sauce and mushrooms; simmer,
uncovered, 10 minutes or until
thoroughly heated, stirring occasionally.
Serve over hot spaghetti. Refrigerate
leftovers.          *Makes 6 to 8 servings*

## Favorite Mac 'n Cheese

2 cups (7 ounces) elbow macaroni,
   cooked and drained
¼ cup chopped green pepper
¼ cup chopped red pepper
¼ cup chopped onion
2 tablespoons PARKAY® Margarine
1 pound VELVEETA® Pasteurized
   Process Cheese Spread, cubed
½ cup milk

*Spaghetti & Meatballs*

- Preheat oven to 350°F.

- Cook and stir vegetables in margarine until vegetables are crisp-tender. Reduce heat to low.

- Add process cheese spread and milk; stir until process cheese spread is melted. Stir in macaroni; spoon into 2-quart casserole.

- Bake 15 minutes. Sprinkle with KRAFT® 100% Grated Parmesan Cheese, if desired.          *Makes 6 servings*

**Prep time:** 15 minutes
**Cook time:** 15 minutes

**Microwave:** • Microwave vegetables and margarine in 2-quart casserole on HIGH 2 to 2½ minutes or until vegetables are crisp-tender. • Add process cheese spread and milk; microwave 3 to 4 minutes or until process cheese spread is melted, stirring after 2 minutes. • Stir in macaroni. Microwave 4 to 6 minutes or until thoroughly heated, stirring after 3 minutes. Sprinkle with KRAFT® 100% Grated Parmesan Cheese, if desired.

*Sweet & Sour Tortellini*

# Sweet & Sour Tortellini

**1 package (7 to 12 ounces) cheese-filled tortellini**
**½ pound boneless tender beef steak (sirloin, rib eye *or* top loin)**
**2 teaspoons cornstarch**
**2 teaspoons KIKKOMAN® Soy Sauce**
**1 small clove garlic, minced**
**½ cup KIKKOMAN® Sweet & Sour Sauce**
**⅓ cup chicken broth**
**1 tablespoon sugar**
**2 tablespoons dry sherry**
**2 tablespoons vegetable oil, divided**
**1 medium onion, chunked**
**1 small red pepper, chunked**
**1 small green pepper, chunked**

Cook tortellini according to package directions, omitting salt; drain. Cut meat into thin bite-size pieces. Combine cornstarch, soy sauce and garlic in small bowl; stir in meat. Let stand 15 minutes. Meanwhile, combine sweet & sour sauce, chicken broth, sugar and sherry; set aside. Heat 1 tablespoon oil in hot wok or large skillet over high heat. Add meat mixture; stir-fry 1 minute. Remove from wok. Heat remaining 1 tablespoon oil in wok. Add onion and peppers; stir-fry 3 minutes. Add meat mixture, sweet & sour sauce mixture and tortellini. Heat thoroughly, stirring occasionally.
          *Makes 4 servings*

## Quick Chili Bake

7 ounces MUELLER'S® Pasta Swirls®,
   cooked 5 minutes and drained
1 can (15 to 16 ounces) chili
1 jar (12 ounces) mild *or* medium
   chunky salsa
1 can (12 ounces) corn, drained
½ cup (2 ounces) shredded Cheddar
   cheese

In large bowl, combine chili, salsa and
corn. Add pasta; toss to coat. Spoon into
2-quart casserole; top with cheese. Bake
at 400°F, 30 minutes or until thoroughly
heated. Serve with corn chips, if desired.

*Makes 6 servings*

**Microwave:** Prepare pasta mixture as
directed; spoon into 2-quart microwave-
safe casserole. Microwave on HIGH
(100% power) 15 minutes or until
thoroughly heated, turning dish after 8
minutes. Top with cheese. Microwave on
HIGH 1 minute or until cheese is
melted.

*Spaghetti Pizza Deluxe*

## Spaghetti Pizza Deluxe

1 package (7 ounces) CREAMETTE®
   Spaghetti, cooked and drained
1 egg, slightly beaten
½ cup skim milk
   Vegetable cooking spray
½ pound lean ground beef
1 medium onion, chopped
1 medium green pepper, chopped
2 cloves garlic, minced
1 can (15 ounces) tomato sauce
1 teaspoon Italian seasoning
1 teaspoon any salt-free herb
   seasoning
¼ teaspoon black pepper
2 cups sliced fresh mushrooms
2 cups (8 ounces) shredded part-skim
   mozzarella cheese

In medium bowl, blend egg and milk.
Add spaghetti; toss to coat. Spray
15×10-inch baking pan with vegetable
cooking spray. Spread spaghetti mixture
evenly into prepared pan. In large skillet
over medium heat, brown meat with
onion, green pepper and garlic, stirring
occasionally to separate meat; drain.
Add tomato sauce and seasonings;
simmer 5 minutes, stirring occasionally.
Spoon meat mixture evenly over
spaghetti mixture; top with mushrooms
and cheese. Bake at 350°F, 20 minutes.
Let stand 5 minutes before cutting to
serve. Refrigerate leftovers.

*Makes 6 to 8 servings*

**Note:** To reduce sodium, substitute no-
salt-added tomato sauce.

# Baked Mostaccioli

1 package (10 ounces) mostaccioli *or* other large macaroni, cooked and drained
½ pound Italian sausage, casing removed
2 cups sliced fresh mushrooms
½ cup chopped onion
1 teaspoon minced fresh garlic
1 can (15 ounces) HUNT'S® Tomato Sauce
1 can (14½ ounces) HUNT'S® Whole Tomatoes, cut up, undrained
1½ teaspoons brown sugar
2 teaspoons dried basil leaves, crushed
1 teaspoons dried oregano leaves, crushed
¼ teaspoon pepper
2 eggs, slightly beaten
1 carton (16 ounces) small curd cottage cheese
3 tablespoons grated Parmesan cheese

Crumble sausage into large skillet. Add mushrooms, onion and garlic. Cook until sausage is no longer pink and vegetables are tender, stirring occasionally to separate meat; drain. Stir in tomato sauce, tomatoes, brown sugar and seasonings. Combine 2 cups meat sauce and pasta; mix lightly. Combine eggs and cottage cheese; mix until well blended. In 13×9-inch baking dish, layer pasta mixture, cottage cheese mixture and remaining sauce; sprinkle with Parmesan cheese. Bake, uncovered, at 350°F, 30 minutes or until hot and bubbly. *Makes 6 to 8 servings*

# Baked Rigatoni with Cheese

*An old-style family favorite.*

8 ounces rigatoni pasta, cooked and drained
½ pound Italian sausage
2 cups milk
2 tablespoons all-purpose flour
2½ cups (10 ounces) shredded mozzarella cheese
¼ cup (1 ounce) grated Parmesan cheese
1 teaspoon LAWRY'S® Garlic Salt
¾ teaspoon LAWRY'S® Seasoned Pepper
2 to 3 tablespoons plain dry bread crumbs *or* ¾ cup croutons

Crumble sausage into large skillet over medium heat. Brown 5 minutes, stirring occasionally to break up meat; drain. In small bowl, gradually add milk to flour, stirring until well blended. Add to sausage. Bring to a boil, stirring constantly. Stir in pasta, cheeses, Garlic Salt and Seasoned Pepper. Place in 1½-quart baking dish. Bake at 350°F, 25 minutes. Sprinkle with bread crumbs. Broil just until crumbs are lightly browned. *Makes 6 servings*

**Presentation:** Garnish with chopped fresh parsley. Serve with crusty Italian bread.

**Hint:** ¼ pound chopped cooked ham can be substituted for sausage.

# Spaghetti Rolls

1 package (8 ounces) manicotti shells, cooked and drained
1½ pounds ground beef
1 tablespoon vegetable oil
1 tablespoon onion powder
1 teaspoon salt
½ teaspoon pepper
2 cups spaghetti sauce, divided
1 cup (4 ounces) shredded pizza flavored cheese blend *or* mozzarella cheese

Preheat oven to 350°F. Brown meat in oil in large skillet over medium-high heat, stirring occasionally to separate meat; drain. Add onion powder, salt and pepper; mix well. Stir in 1 cup spaghetti sauce; cool and set aside.

Reserve ½ cup meat mixture. Combine remaining meat mixture and cheese in large bowl; stuff into manicotti. Arrange in greased 13×9-inch baking dish. Combine remaining spaghetti sauce and reserved meat mixture in small bowl; mix well. Pour over manicotti. Cover with foil. Bake 20 to 30 minutes or until hot. Garnish as desired.

*Makes 4 servings*

*Favorite recipe from* **North Dakota Beef Comminssion**

# Easy Macaroni and Cheese

1 can (46 ounces) COLLEGE INN® Chicken *or* Beef Broth
1 package (12 ounces) spiral macaroni
½ cup BLUE BONNET® Margarine, divided
¼ cup all-purpose flour
2 cups (8 ounces) shredded Cheddar cheese
30 RITZ® Crackers, coarsely crushed

Pour broth into large heavy saucepan. Bring to a boil. Add macaroni; cook according to package directions, omitting salt. Drain, reserving 2 cups broth. (If necessary, add enough water to reserved broth to measure 2 cups.) Set aside.

In medium saucepan over medium-high heat, melt ¼ cup margarine. Blend in flour. Gradually add reserved broth, stirring constantly, until mixture comes to a boil and thickens. Cook and stir 2 minutes. Add cheese; stir until melted. Combine cheese sauce and macaroni in 2-quart casserole; mix lightly to coat. Melt remaining ¼ cup margarine; stir in cracker crumbs. Sprinkle over macaroni mixture. Bake at 400°F, 30 minutes or until hot and bubbly.

*Makes 6 to 8 servings*

# Creamy Crab Alfredo

6 ounces fettuccine, cooked and drained
2 tablespoons butter *or* margarine
4 teaspoons all-purpose flour
1¼ cups half-and-half
¼ cup (1 ounce) grated Parmesan cheese
2 packages (8 ounces *each*) LOUIS KEMP® CRAB DELIGHTS® Flakes *or* Chunks
1 tablespoon chopped fresh parsley

• Melt butter in saucepan over medium heat; stir in flour. Gradually add half-and-half, stirring constantly until thickened.

• Add Parmesan cheese; cook and stir until smooth. Stir in surimi seafood; continue cooking 3 minutes, stirring occasionally.

• Add sauce to hot fettuccine; toss lightly to coat. Sprinkle with parsley. Serve immediately. *Makes 4 servings*

*Spaghetti Rolls*

# Northern Italian Chicken and Mushrooms

*An easy, tasty main dish that's ideal for an after-work family meal.*

2 cups egg noodles, cooked and
   drained
3 tablespoons PROGRESSO® Olive
   Oil
1 pound boneless skinless chicken
   breast halves
1 cup sliced mushrooms
1 small onion, sliced and separated
   into rings
1 can (19 ounces) PROGRESSO®
   Chicken Vegetable Soup
½ cup sour cream
2 teaspoons cornstarch

*Northern Italian Chicken and Mushrooms*

1. In large skillet, heat olive oil over medium heat. Add chicken; cook 15 minutes or until browned on both sides and no longer pink in center.

2. Remove chicken from skillet. Add mushrooms and onion to skillet; cook and stir 5 minutes or until tender. (Add additional oil if necessary to prevent sticking.)

3. Return chicken to skillet. Pour soup over chicken; cover. Simmer 5 minutes.

4. Stir sour cream and cornstarch into soup mixture, rearranging chicken as necessary. Heat thoroughly until soup mixture is thickened, stirring occasionally.

5. Serve over hot noodles.

*Makes 4 servings*

**Prep time:** 15 minutes
**Cook time:** 30 minutes

**Microwave:** Reduce olive oil to 1 tablespooon. In 1½-quart microwave-safe casserole, pour 1 tablespoon olive oil, tilting casserole to evenly coat bottom. Place chicken in single layer in casserole, turning to coat with oil; cover. Microwave on HIGH (100% power) 5 minutes or until chicken is no longer pink in center, turning chicken over after 2½ minutes. Stir in mushrooms and onion; cover. Microwave on HIGH 1 minute. Add soup; cover. Microwave on HIGH 5 minutes, stirring after 3 minutes. In small dish, combine sour cream and cornstarch; stir into soup mixture. Cover. Microwave on MEDIUM (50% power) 5 minutes or until soup mixture is thickened, stirring after 3 minutes. Serve over hot noodles.

## Sunburst Stir-Fry

**4 ounces thin spaghetti, cooked and drained**
**1 can (20 ounces) DOLE® Pineapple Chunks in Juice, undrained**
**2 boneless skinless chicken breast halves**
**2 tablespoons vegetable oil**
**2 large cloves garlic, minced**
**2 tablespoons minced ginger root** *or* **1 teaspoon ground ginger**
**2 medium DOLE® Carrots, sliced**
**1 DOLE® Green Bell Pepper, slivered**
**3 DOLE® Green Onions with tops, cut into 1-inch pieces**

**Sauce:**

**1 tablespoon cornstarch**
**⅓ cup reserved pineapple juice**
**⅓ cup soy sauce**
**1 tablespoon sesame oil**

• Drain pineapple; reserve ⅓ cup juice for sauce.

• Cut chicken into bite-size pieces. In large skillet or wok, heat oil over medium-high heat. Add chicken, garlic and ginger; stir-fry 2 minutes. Add pineapple, carrots and green pepper. Cover; steam 2 to 3 minutes until vegetables are crisp-tender. Add hot spaghetti; toss lightly.

• Combine ingredients for sauce, mixing until well blended. Add to skillet along with onions; toss until ingredients are thoroughly mixed and heated through.
*Makes 4 servings*

**Prep time:** 15 minutes
**Cook time:** 10 minutes

*Ham Pasta Primavera*

## Ham Pasta Primavera

**10 ounces spaghetti, cooked and drained**
**3 tablespoons unsalted margarine** *or* **butter, divided**
**1 cup pea pods, cut crosswise in half**
**½ cup shredded carrots**
**3 green onions with tops, sliced**
**1 small red pepper, cut into strips**
**¾ cup evaporated skim milk**
**3 cups (12 ounces) ARMOUR® Lower Salt Ham, cut into small cubes**

Melt 1 tablespoon margarine in medium skillet over medium-high heat. Add vegetables; cook and stir until tender. Add remaining 2 tablespoons margarine, milk and ham. Cook 3 to 4 minutes or until mixture thickens slightly. Serve over hot spaghetti. Garnish with fresh basil leaves and freshly ground pepper, if desired.
*Makes 4 to 6 servings*

# Rigatoni with Four Cheeses

12 ounces rigatoni, cooked and drained
3 cups milk
1 tablespoon chopped carrot
1 tablespoon chopped celery
1 tablespoon chopped onion
1 tablespoon fresh parsley sprigs
½ bay leaf
¼ teaspoon black peppercorns
¼ teaspoon hot pepper sauce
   Dash of ground nutmeg
¼ cup butter
¼ cup all-purpose flour
½ cup grated Wisconsin Parmesan
   cheese
¼ cup grated Wisconsin Romano
   cheese
1½ cups (6 ounces) shredded Wisconsin
   Cheddar cheese
1½ cups (6 ounces) shredded Wisconsin
   Mozzarella cheese
¼ teaspoon chili powder

Preheat oven to 350°F. Combine milk, carrot, celery, onion, parsley, bay leaf, peppercorns, hot pepper sauce and nutmeg in medium saucepan. Bring to a boil over medium-high heat. Reduce heat to low; simmer 10 minutes, stirring occasionally. Strain, reserving milk.

Add butter to saucepan; melt over medium heat. Stir in flour. Gradually stir in reserved milk. Cook, stirring constantly, until thickened. Remove from heat. Stir in Parmesan and Romano cheeses. Combine pasta and sauce; toss gently. Combine Cheddar and Mozzarella cheeses. Place ½ of pasta mixture in buttered 2-quart casserole; cover with layers of cheese mixture and remaining pasta mixture. Sprinkle with chili powder. Bake 25 minutes or until hot and bubbly. Garnish as desired.

*Makes 6 servings*

*Favorite recipe from* **Wisconsin Milk Marketing Board**
© *1992*

# Chicken Stroganoff

2 pounds boneless chicken breasts,
   skinned and cut into thin strips
½ cup all-purpose flour
1½ teaspoons salt
⅛ teaspoon pepper
⅓ cup CRISCO® Shortening
½ cup finely chopped onion
2 cups chicken broth
   Noodles
   Butter
3 tablespoons CRISCO® Shortening,
   divided
8 ounces fresh mushrooms, cleaned
   and sliced
¾ cup sour cream
3 tablespoons tomato paste
1 teaspoon Worcestershire sauce

Coat chicken evenly with mixture of flour, salt and pepper.

Melt ⅓ cup CRISCO® in large heavy skillet. Add chicken and onion; cook and stir until chicken is evenly browned on all sides and no longer pink in center. Add broth; cover. Simmer 20 minutes or until chicken is tender. Remove from heat. Meanwhile, cook noodles according to package directions; drain. Add butter to taste; toss lightly to coat. Keep warm.

Melt 3 tablespoons CRISCO® in small skillet over medium heat. Add mushrooms; cook and stir until lightly browned and tender. Add to chicken mixture.

Combine sour cream, tomato paste and Worcestershire sauce; add in small amounts to chicken mixture, stirring until well combined.

Return to heat. Cook and stir over low heat until thoroughly heated. Serve over hot noodles.

*Makes 8 servings*

*Rigatoni with Four Cheeses*

# Dijon Chicken Pasta

1 pound Spaghetti *or* your favorite
  medium pasta shape, cooked and
  drained
1½ cups heavy cream
3 tablespoons Dijon-style mustard
2½ cups chopped cooked chicken
2 cups sliced mushrooms
2 cups chopped fresh spinach
  Salt and freshly ground pepper

In large skillet, heat cream over medium
heat, stirring frequently. Stir in mustard
until well blended. Add chicken and
mushrooms; heat thoroughly. Add pasta
and spinach; toss lightly to coat. Season
with salt and pepper to taste.

*Makes 6 to 8 servings*

*Favorite recipe from* **National Pasta Association**

*Fettuccine Italiano*

# Fettuccine Italiano

8 ounces fettuccine, cooked and
  drained
⅓ cup MIRACLE WHIP® Light
  Reduced Calorie Salad Dressing
1 clove garlic, minced
½ cup milk
5 crisply cooked bacon slices,
  crumbled
⅓ cup (1½ ounces) KRAFT® 100%
  Grated Parmesan Cheese
¼ cup chopped fresh parsley

• Combine salad dressing and garlic in
small saucepan. Gradually stir in milk;
heat thoroughly, stirring occasionally.

• Toss with hot fettuccine until well
coated. Add remaining ingredients; mix
lightly.                    *Makes 5 servings*

**Prep time:** 25 minutes

**Variations:**
Substitute spaghetti for fettuccine.

Substitute MIRACLE WHIP® Salad
Dressing for Reduced Calorie Salad
Dressing.

**Microwave:** • Cook fettuccine as
directed on package; drain. • Combine
salad dressing and garlic in 2-quart
microwave-safe bowl; gradually add
milk. • Microwave on HIGH 1½ to 2
minutes or until thoroughly heated,
stirring after 1 minute. *(Do not boil.)*
• Add hot fettuccine; toss until well
coated. Continue as directed.

*String Pie*

Preheat oven to 350°F. Brown beef with onion and green pepper in large skillet over medium-high heat, stirring occasionally to separate meat; drain. Stir in spaghetti sauce. Combine eggs, spaghetti, Parmesan cheese and butter in large bowl; mix well. Place in 13×9-inch baking dish; cover with layers of cottage cheese and spaghetti sauce mixture. Sprinkle with mozzarella cheese. Bake 20 minutes or until cheese is melted and mixture is thoroughly heated.          *Makes 6 to 8 servings*

*Favorite recipe from* **North Dakota Beef Commission**

## String Pie

8 ounces spaghetti, cooked and
    drained
1 pound ground beef
½ cup chopped onion
¼ cup chopped green pepper
1 jar (15½ ounces) spaghetti sauce
2 eggs, slightly beaten
⅓ cup (1½ ounces) grated Parmesan
    cheese
2 teaspoons butter
1 cup cottage cheese
½ cup (2 ounces) shredded mozzarella
    cheese

## Classic Macaroni & Cheese

2 cups elbow macaroni
3 tablespoons butter *or* margarine
¼ cup chopped onion, optional
2 tablespoons all-purpose flour
½ teaspoon salt
⅛ teaspoon pepper
2 cups milk
2 cups (8 ounces) SARGENTO®
    Classic Supreme Shredded *or*
    Fancy Supreme Shredded
    Cheddar Cheese, divided

Cook macaroni according to package directions; drain. Meanwhile, in medium saucepan, melt butter. Add onion; cook and stir until tender, about 5 minutes. Stir in flour, salt and pepper. Add milk; cook, stirring occasionally, until thickened. Remove from heat. Add 1½ cups Cheddar cheese; stir until melted. Add to macaroni in large bowl; mix lightly. Place in 1½-quart casserole; top with remaining ½ cup cheese. Bake at 350°F, 30 minutes or until mixture is hot and bubbly and cheese is golden brown.
                    *Makes 6 servings*

*Ham & Macaroni Twists*

## Prehistoric Pasta Stir-Fry

2 cups MUELLER'S® Super Shapes
   Dinosaur pasta (*or* any other
   Super Shapes)
3 tablespoons MAZOLA® Corn Oil,
   divided
12 frozen chicken nuggets, thawed
1 small onion, chopped
2 medium carrots, thinly sliced
1 rib celery, thinly sliced
1 small red pepper, chopped
1 cup prepared sweet and sour sauce
1 to 2 tablespoons cider vinegar

Cook pasta according to package
directions; drain. Meanwhile, in large
skillet, heat 2 tablespoons oil over
medium-high heat. Add chicken
nuggets; stir-fry 5 minutes. Remove from
skillet. Add remaining 1 tablespoon oil,
onion, carrots, celery and red pepper to
skillet; stir-fry 3 minutes. Return chicken
to skillet. Add sweet and sour sauce and
vinegar. Cook 2 minutes or until
thoroughly heated, stirring constantly.
Spoon over hot pasta; mix lightly.
*Makes 4 servings*

## Ham & Macaroni Twists

2 cups rotini *or* elbow macaroni,
   cooked in unsalted water and
   drained
1½ cups (8 ounces) cubed cooked ham
1 can (2.8 ounces) DURKEE® French
   Fried Onions, divided
1 package (10 ounces) frozen broccoli
   spears,* thawed and drained
1 can (10¾ ounces) condensed cream
   of celery soup
1 cup milk
1 cup (4 ounces) shredded Cheddar
   cheese, divided
¼ teaspoon DURKEE® Garlic Powder
¼ teaspoon DURKEE® Ground Black
   Pepper

Preheat oven to 350°F. In 12×8-inch
baking dish, combine hot macaroni,
ham and ½ can French Fried Onions.
Divide broccoli spears into six small
bunches. Arrange bunches of spears
down center of dish, alternating
direction of flowerets. In small bowl,
combine soup, milk, ½ cup cheese and
seasonings; pour over macaroni mixture
and broccoli. Cover. Bake 30 minutes or
until thoroughly heated. Top with
remaining cheese. Sprinkle onions down
center of cheese. Continue baking,
uncovered, 5 minutes or until onions are
golden brown.    *Makes 4 to 6 servings*

*1 small head fresh broccoli (about ½
pound) may be substituted for frozen
spears; divide into spears. Cook 3 to 4
minutes before using.

**Microwave:** In 12×8-inch microwave-
safe dish, assemble recipe as directed;
cover. Microwave on HIGH 8 minutes or
until broccoli is done, rotating dish after
4 minutes. Top with remaining cheese
and onions as directed. Microwave,
uncovered, 1 minute or until cheese
melts. Let stand 5 minutes.

# Pastitsio
## (Greek Macaroni Bake)

**Pasta layer:**

1 package (7 ounces) *or* 2 cups
   CREAMETTES® Elbow Macaroni,
   cooked and drained
2 eggs, slightly beaten
1/3 cup (1½ ounces) grated Parmesan
   cheese
1 tablespoon margarine *or* butter,
   melted

**Meat layer:**

1 pound lean ground beef
1/2 cup finely chopped onion
1 clove garlic, minced
1 can (8 ounces) tomato sauce
1/4 teaspoon ground allspice
1/4 teaspoon ground cinnamon
1/4 teaspoon ground nutmeg
2 teaspoons WYLER'S® or STEERO®
   Beef-Flavor Instant Bouillon *or*
   2 Beef-Flavor Bouillon Cubes
1/8 teaspoon pepper

**Cream Sauce:**

3 tablespoons margarine *or* butter
2 tablespoons all-purpose flour
1 teaspoon WYLER'S® or STEERO®
   Chicken-Flavor Instant Bouillon
   *or* 1 Chicken-Flavor Bouillon
   Cube
1/8 teaspoon pepper
2 cups BORDEN® or MEADOW
   GOLD® Milk
1/4 cup (1 ounce) grated Parmesan
   cheese

Preheat oven to 325°F. In large bowl, combine eggs, macaroni, 1/3 cup Parmesan cheese and 1 tablespoon melted margarine. Spoon evenly into greased 13×9-inch baking dish.

In large skillet over medium heat, brown meat with onion and garlic, stirring occasionally to separate meat; drain. Stir in tomato sauce, spices, *beef-flavor* bouillon and pepper; simmer 10 minutes, stirring occasionally. Spoon over macaroni mixture.

In medium saucepan, melt 3 tablespoons margarine over medium heat; stir in flour, *chicken-flavor* bouillon and pepper. Gradually stir in milk. Cook and stir until slightly thickened (mixture should coat spoon). Remove from heat. Stir in 1/4 cup Parmesan cheese. Spoon evenly over meat layer; cover. Bake 30 minutes or until hot and bubbly. Garnish as desired. Refrigerate leftovers.
*Makes 8 servings*

# Jambalaya with Shells

8 ounces medium Shells, cooked and
   drained
3 cups chopped cooked chicken
1/2 pound link sausage, sliced
2 medium onions, chopped
1 medium green pepper, chopped
1 cup chopped celery
2 cloves garlic, minced
3 cups chicken stock *or* broth
1 can (28 ounces) crushed tomatoes,
   undrained
1 tablespoon Worcestershire sauce
1 teaspoon salt
1/2 teaspoon dried thyme leaves,
   crushed
1/4 teaspoon cayenne pepper
1 bay leaf
2 green onions with tops, sliced

In large saucepan over medium heat, combine chicken, sausage, vegetables and garlic; cook until sausage is browned, stirring occasionally. Stir in chicken stock, tomatoes, Worcestershire sauce, seasonings and bay leaf. Bring to a boil. Reduce heat to low; simmer, uncovered, 20 minutes, stirring occasionally. Remove bay leaf. Stir in hot pasta; simmer 5 minutes, stirring occasionally. Top with green onions.
*Makes 8 to 10 servings*

*Favorite recipe from* **National Pasta Association**

# Tacos in Pasta Shells

18 jumbo pasta shells, cooked and
    drained
1¼ pounds ground beef
  1 package (3 ounces) cream cheese
    with chives, cubed and softened
  1 teaspoon salt
  1 teaspoon chili powder
  2 tablespoons butter, melted
  1 cup prepared taco sauce
  1 cup (4 ounces) shredded Cheddar
    cheese
  1 cup (4 ounces) shredded Monterey
    Jack cheese
1½ cups crushed tortilla chips
  1 cup dairy sour cream
  3 green onions with tops, chopped

Preheat oven to 350°F. Brown meat in
large skillet over medium-high heat,
stirring to separate meat; drain. Reduce
heat to medium-low. Add cream cheese,
salt and chili powder; simmer 5 minutes,
stirring occasionally.

Combine shells with butter; toss lightly
to coat. Fill shells with meat mixture.
Arrange in buttered 13×9-inch baking
dish. Pour taco sauce over each shell;
cover with foil. Bake 15 minutes.
Uncover; top with Cheddar cheese,
Monterey Jack cheese and chips.
Continue baking 15 minutes or until hot
and bubbly. Top with sour cream and
onions. Garnish as desired.

*Makes 4 to 6 servings*

*Favorite recipe from* **Southeast United Dairy**
**Association, Inc.**

# Chicken Vegetable Tetrazzini

*Welcome back this easy old-time favorite.*

  4 ounces spaghetti, cooked and
    drained
3½ tablespoons IMPERIAL® Margarine,
    divided
  1 pound boneless skinless chicken
    breasts, cut into ½-inch strips
  1 cup fresh mushrooms, quartered
  1 red pepper, julienne-cut into ½-inch
    pieces
1½ tablespoons all-purpose flour
  ¾ teaspoon LAWRY'S® Garlic Powder
    with Parsley
  ¾ teaspoon LAWRY'S® Seasoned Salt
  ½ teaspoon LAWRY'S® Seasoned
    Pepper
  ¾ cup *plus* 2 tablespoons milk
  1 package (10 ounces) frozen peas,
    thawed

In large skillet over medium heat, melt 1
tablespoon margarine. Add chicken;
cook and stir until no longer pink in
center. Remove from skillet; keep warm.
Melt remaining 2½ tablespoons
margarine in same skillet. Add
mushrooms and red pepper; cook and
stir until tender. Remove with slotted
spoon; set aside. Add flour and
seasonings to skillet; stir until mixture
forms a paste. Gradually add milk,
stirring until well blended. Bring to a
boil. Reduce heat to low; simmer 1
minute, stirring constantly. Stir in peas,
chicken, vegetables and hot spaghetti.
Heat thoroughly, stirring occasionally.

*Makes 4 servings*

**Presentation:** Serve with crusty Italian
or French bread and fresh fruit for
dessert.

**Hint:** Fettuccine can be substituted for
spaghetti.

*Tacos in Pasta Shells*

# Five-Way Cincinnati Chili

1½ pounds ground beef
1 medium onion, finely chopped
2 cloves garlic, minced
1 can (28 ounces) Italian plum
   tomatoes, undrained
1 cup water
1 tablespoon unsweetened cocoa
2 tablespoons chili powder
1 teaspoon *each* salt, dry mustard,
   ground cumin and paprika
¼ teaspoon *each* ground red and black
   pepper
⅛ teaspoon *each* ground allspice,
   cardamom, cinnamon and cloves
8 ounces vermicelli *or* thin spaghetti,
   cooked and drained
1 can (15¼ ounces) red kidney beans,
   heated
1 small onion, finely chopped
1 cup (4 ounces) shredded Cheddar
   cheese

Brown ground beef with chopped medium onion and garlic in Dutch oven over medium-high heat, stirring occasionally to separate meat; drain. Stir in tomatoes, water, cocoa, seasonings and spices. Bring to a boil. Reduce heat to low; simmer, uncovered, 45 minutes. stirring occasionally.

Top individual servings of hot vermicelli with beans, meat sauce, finely chopped onion and cheese.    *Makes 6 servings*

**Prep time:** 15 minutes
**Cook time:** 1 hour

**Four-Way Cincinnati Chili:** Omit kidney beans. Top vermicelli with meat sauce, chopped small onion and cheese.

**Three-Way Cincinnati Chili:** Omit one small onion, chopped. Top vermicelli with meat sauce and cheese.

*Favorite recipe from* **National Live Stock and Meat Board**

*Five-Way Cincinnati Chili*

## Turkey Noodle Toss

4 ounces fine egg noodles, cooked and
    drained
2 eggs
½ cup milk
⅓ cup mayonnaise
1 tablespoon lemon juice
1 tablespoon instant minced onion
1½ teaspoons dill weed
¾ teaspoon salt
1 package (10 ounces) frozen cut
    asparagus, thawed and drained
4 hard-cooked eggs,* chopped
1 cup chopped cooked turkey
½ cup (2 ounces) shredded mozzarella,
    Monterey Jack *or* Swiss cheese

Preheat oven to 350°F. In large bowl,
beat together two eggs and milk. Blend
in mayonnaise. Stir in lemon juice,
onion, dill weed and salt. Add all
remaining ingredients; mix lightly. Pour
into greased 8-inch square baking dish;
cover with foil.

Bake 35 to 40 minutes, until knife
inserted near center comes out clean.
Let stand, covered, 10 minutes before
serving. *Makes 6 servings*

**\*To hard-cook eggs:** Place eggs in single
layer in small saucepan. Add enough tap
water to come at least 1 inch above eggs;
cover. Bring just to a boil. Turn off heat.
If necessary, remove pan from burner to
prevent further boiling. Let eggs stand,
covered, in the hot water 15 to 17
minutes for large eggs. (Adjust time up
or down by about 3 minutes for each
size larger or smaller.) Immediately run
cold water over eggs or put them in ice
water until completely cooled. To
remove shell, crack it by tapping gently
all over. Roll egg between hands to
loosen shell, then peel, starting at large
end. Hold egg under running cold water
or dip into bowl of water to help ease off
shell.

*Favorite recipe from* **American Egg Board**

*Ham & Cheese Thriller*

## Ham & Cheese Thriller

2 cups MUELLER'S® Super Shapes
    Monsters pasta (*or* any other
    Super Shapes), cooked and
    drained
3 tablespoons butter *or* margarine, cut
    into pieces
1 cup frozen peas, thawed
½ cup chopped ham
½ cup (2 ounces) grated Parmesan
    cheese
½ cup milk
1 chicken-flavor bouillon cube

**Microwave:** In 2-quart microwave-safe
dish, combine butter, peas, ham, cheese,
milk and bouillon cube. Microwave on
HIGH (100%) 5 minutes, stirring every 2
minutes. Stir in hot pasta. Microwave on
HIGH (100%) 1 minute. Let stand 2
minutes. *Makes about 4 servings*

*Quick Chicken Cacciatore*

## Quick Chicken Cacciatore

4 skinless boneless chicken breast
    halves (about 1 pound)
Salt and pepper
All-purpose flour
4 tablespoons olive oil, divided
2 cloves garlic, minced
1 jar (26 ounces) CLASSICO® Di
    Napoli (Tomato & Basil) *or* Di
    Sicilia (Ripe Olives &
    Mushrooms) Pasta Sauce
1 small green pepper, cut into strips
1 small red pepper, cut into strips
2 slices Provolone cheese, cut in half
1 package (7 ounces) *or* 2 cups
    CREAMETTES® Elbow Macaroni,
    cooked and drained
Chopped fresh parsley

Season chicken with salt and pepper; coat with flour. In large skillet, heat 3 tablespoons oil over medium heat. Add chicken and garlic; cook until chicken is no longer pink in center. Remove chicken from skillet. Add pasta sauce to skillet; top with chicken. Bring to a boil; reduce heat to low. Cover and simmer 15 minutes. Add peppers; simmer an additional 5 minutes. Uncover; top each chicken breast with cheese. Combine hot macaroni with remaining 1 tablespoon oil and parsley. Serve with chicken and sauce. Refrigerate leftovers.

*Makes 4 servings*

## Three-Cheese Macaroni

1½ cups elbow macaroni, cooked and
    drained
3 tablespoons butter *or* margarine
3 tablespoons all-purpose flour
½ teaspoon salt
    Dash pepper
3 cups milk
1½ cups (6 ounces) SARGENTO®
    Classic Supreme Shredded *or*
    Fancy Supreme Shredded
    Cheddar Cheese
1 cup (4 ounces) SARGENTO® Fancy
    Supreme Shredded Swiss Cheese
¼ cup (1 ounce) SARGENTO® Grated
    Cheese*

In medium saucepan over medium heat, melt butter. Stir in flour, salt and pepper. Gradually stir in milk; cook and stir until thick and bubbly. Remove from heat. Add Cheddar and Swiss cheeses; stir until melted. Stir in grated cheese. Add to macaroni in large bowl; mix lightly. Spoon into lightly greased 2-quart casserole. Sprinkle with additional grated cheese, if desired. Bake, uncovered, at 350°F, 30 to 40 minutes or until top begins to brown.

*Makes 8 servings*

*SARGENTO® Parmesan, Parmesan and Romano *or* Italian-Style Grated Cheese can be used.

# Spicy Spaghetti Pie

8 ounces Spaghetti, cooked and
   drained
1 egg
½ cup milk
½ pound ground pork
½ pound ground beef
1 medium onion, chopped
1 medium green pepper, chopped
1 jalapeño pepper, minced
1 large clove garlic, minced
1 can (16 ounces) tomato sauce
1 tablespoon chili powder
1 teaspoon ground cumin
½ teaspoon dried oregano leaves,
   crushed
½ teaspoon salt
¼ teaspoon freshly ground black
   pepper
1 cup (4 ounces) shredded Monterey
   Jack cheese
1 cup (4 ounces) shredded Cheddar
   cheese

Beat egg and milk in large bowl. Add
hot spaghetti; toss lightly to coat.
Spread evenly into 13×9-inch casserole
dish sprayed with vegetable spray. In
large skillet over medium heat, brown
meats with onion, green pepper,
jalapeño pepper and garlic, stirring
occasionally to separate meat; stir in
tomato sauce and seasonings. Reduce
heat to low; simmer 5 minutes, stirring
occasionally. Spread meat mixture over
spaghetti mixture. Sprinkle with
cheeses. Bake at 425°F, 15 minutes or
until cheese is melted and mixture is hot
and bubbly. Let stand 5 minutes before
cutting to serve.    *Makes 4 to 6 servings*

*Favorite recipe from* **National Pasta Association**

# Smoked Turkey Fettuccine

2 cups (10 ounces) bite-size cubes
   BUTTERBALL® Slice 'N Serve
   Hickory Smoked Breast of Turkey
8 ounces spinach fettuccine, cooked
   and drained
3 tablespoons butter *or* margarine
3 tablespoons all-purpose flour
¼ teaspoon salt
   Dash ground white pepper
1 cup milk
1 cup chicken broth *or* bouillon
1 jar (2.5 ounces) sliced mushrooms,
   drained
¼ cup (1 ounce) grated Parmesan
   cheese

Melt butter in medium saucepan over
medium heat. Stir in flour, salt and
pepper. Gradually add milk and broth.
Cook until thickened, stirring
frequently. Stir in turkey, mushrooms
and cheese. Continue cooking until
mixture is thoroughly heated, stirring
occasionally. Serve over hot fettuccine.
*Makes 4 to 5 servings*

**Microwave:** Microwave butter in 2-quart
microwave-safe casserole on HIGH
(100%) 45 seconds or until melted. Stir in
flour, salt and pepper. Gradually stir in
milk and broth. Microwave on HIGH 3
minutes; stir. Microwave on HIGH 3 to 4
minutes or until thickened, stirring
every minute. Add turkey, mushrooms
and cheese. Microwave on HIGH 1½ to 2
minutes or until mixture is thoroughly
heated, stirring every minute. Serve over
hot fettuccine.

# Vegetable & Cheese Pot Pie

2 tablespoons butter *or* margarine
½ cup sliced green onions with tops
1¾ cups water
1 package LIPTON® Noodles &
    Sauce—Chicken Flavor
1 package (1 pound) frozen mixed
    vegetables, partially thawed
1 cup (4 ounces) shredded mozzarella
    cheese
1 teaspoon prepared mustard
½ cup milk
1 tablespoon all-purpose flour
    Salt and pepper
    Pastry for 9-inch single-crust pie
1 egg yolk
1 tablespoon water

Preheat oven to 425°F. In large saucepan, melt butter over medium heat. Add onions; cook and stir 3 minutes or until tender. Add 1¾ cups water. Bring to a boil. Stir in noodles & chicken flavor sauce and vegetables; simmer 7 minutes or until noodles are almost tender, stirring occasionally. Stir in cheese, mustard and milk blended with flour. Cook 2 minutes or until thickened, stirring frequently. Season with salt and pepper to taste.

Spoon into greased 1-quart round casserole or soufflé dish; top with pastry. Press pastry around edge of dish to seal. Trim excess pastry; flute edge. (Use extra pastry to make decorative shapes, if desired.) Beat egg yolk with 1 tablespoon water; brush over pastry. With tip of knife, make small slits in pastry. Bake 12 minutes or until crust is golden brown.     *Makes about 4 servings*

**Variation:** Stir in 1 cup chopped cooked turkey, chicken or ham with the salt and pepper. Increase baking time to 20 minutes.

# Pasta "Pizza"

2 cups corkscrew macaroni, cooked
    and drained
3 eggs, slightly beaten
½ cup milk
½ cup (2 ounces) shredded Wisconsin
    Cheddar cheese
¼ cup finely chopped onion
1 pound lean ground beef
1 can (15 ounces) tomato sauce
1 teaspoon dried basil leaves, crushed
1 teaspoon dried oregano leaves,
    crushed
½ teaspoon garlic salt
1 medium tomato, thinly sliced
1 green pepper, sliced into rings
1½ cups (6 ounces) shredded Wisconsin
    Mozzarella cheese

Combine eggs and milk. Add to hot macaroni; mix lightly to coat. Stir in Cheddar cheese and onion; mix well. Spread macaroni mixture onto bottom of well-buttered 14-inch pizza pan. Bake at 350°F, 25 minutes. Meanwhile, in large skillet over medium-high heat, brown meat, stirring occasionally to separate meat; drain. Stir in tomato sauce, basil, oregano and garlic salt. Spoon over macaroni crust. Arrange tomato slices and pepper rings on top. Sprinkle with Mozzarella cheese. Continue baking 15 minutes or until cheese is bubbly.
*Makes 8 servings*

**Prep time:** 50 minutes

*Favorite recipe from* **Wisconsin Milk Marketing Board**
*© 1992*

*Vegetable & Cheese Pot Pie*

*Pasta and Broccoli*

Chop broccoli; set aside. Heat oil in large skillet over medium-high heat. Add garlic; cook and stir until lightly browned. Add broccoli; cook and stir 3 to 4 minutes. Stir in American cheese, Parmesan cheese, butter, broth and wine. Reduce heat to low; simmer until mixture is thoroughly heated and cheese is melted, stirring occasionally.

Pour sauce over hot ziti in large bowl; toss gently to coat.

*Makes 6 to 8 servings*

*Favorite recipe from* **National Pasta Association**

## Pasta and Broccoli

 1 package (1 pound) ziti macaroni, cooked and drained
 1 bunch broccoli, steamed
 2 tablespoons olive oil
 1 clove garlic, minced
 ¾ cup (3 ounces) shredded process American *or* mozzarella cheese
 ½ cup (2 ounces) grated Parmesan cheese
 ¼ cup butter
 ¼ cup chicken broth
 3 tablespoons dry white wine

## Arizona Skillet Dinner

 2 tablespoons MAZOLA® Corn Oil
 1 medium onion, chopped
 1 medium green pepper, chopped
 2 cloves garlic, minced
 2 tablespoons chili powder
 ½ teaspoon ground cumin
 2 cans (14½ ounces *or* 16 ounces *each*) whole tomatoes, cut up, undrained
 1 can (16 ounces) kidney beans, drained and rinsed
 1 package (10 ounces) frozen corn kernels, thawed
 8 ounces MUELLER'S® Elbow Macaroni
 ½ cup (2 ounces) shredded Monterey Jack cheese with jalapeño pepper

In large skillet, heat corn oil over medium-high heat. Add onion, green pepper, garlic, chili powder and cumin; cook and stir 4 minutes or until vegetables are tender. Stir in tomatoes, kidney beans and corn. Bring to a boil. Reduce heat to low; simmer, 15 minutes, stirring occasionally. Meanwhile, cook macaroni according to package directions; drain. Add to tomato mixture; mix lightly. Sprinkle with cheese. *Makes 8 servings*

## Vegetable Pasta with Cheese

1 package (12 ounces) uncooked
   mostaccioli
2 cups DOLE® Broccoli florettes
2 cups DOLE® Cauliflower florettes
1 cup sliced DOLE® Carrots
1 cup *each* shredded mozzarella,
   Monterey Jack and fontina
   cheese*
⅓ cup (1½ ounces) grated Parmesan
   cheese, divided
3 tablespoons margarine, melted

• Cook pasta according to package
directions, adding vegetables during last
2 minutes of cooking; drain.

• Combine pasta mixture in large bowl
with mozzarella, Monterey Jack, fontina,
½ of Parmesan cheese and margarine;
mix lightly. Spoon into large casserole
dish.

• Sprinkle top with remaining Parmesan
cheese.

• Bake at 450°F, 5 minutes or until
cheese melts.       *Makes 6 servings*

*Cheese may be shredded in food
processor.

## All American Noodles 'n Cheese

3 tablespoons butter *or* margarine,
   divided
½ cup chopped onion
1 cup milk
¾ cup water
1 package LIPTON® Noodles &
   Sauce—Butter
6 slices (1 ounce *each*) American
   cheese,* chopped
½ teaspoon Worcestershire sauce
¼ teaspoon dry mustard
   Pepper
¼ cup plain dry bread crumbs

In medium saucepan, melt 2
tablespoons butter over medium heat.
Add onion; cook and stir until tender.
Add milk and water. Bring to a boil. Stir
in noodles & butter sauce. Simmer 8
minutes or until noodles are tender,
stirring occasionally. Stir in cheese,
Worcestershire sauce and mustard.
Season with pepper to taste. Spoon into
greased 1-quart casserole. Melt
remaining 1 tablespoon butter. Add
bread crumbs; mix well. Sprinkle over
casserole. Broil until bread crumbs are
golden brown. Let stand 5 minutes.
       *Makes about 4 servings*

**\*Substitution:** Use 1½ cups (6 ounces)
shredded American cheese.

**Microwave:** In glass measuring cup,
place bread crumbs and 1 tablespoon
butter. Microwave, uncovered, on HIGH
(Full Power) 1 minute; stir and set aside.
In 2-quart microwave-safe casserole,
place remaining 2 tablespoons butter
and onion. Microwave, uncovered, 2
minutes. Stir in milk, water and noodles
& butter sauce . Microwave 11 minutes
or until noodles are tender, stirring after
6 minutes. Stir in cheese, Worcestershire
sauce, mustard and pepper. Top with
bread crumb mixture.

*Vegetable Pasta with Cheese*

# Fettuccine with Garden Herb Sauce

1 tablespoon vegetable oil
2 pounds pork shoulder blade steaks
1 can (14½ ounces) cut up peeled tomatoes, undrained
1 can (15 ounces) tomato sauce
1 medium onion, quartered, sliced
2 cloves garlic, minced
1½ teaspoons sugar
1 tablespoon chopped fresh oregano leaves
1 tablespoon chopped fresh basil leaves
½ teaspoon salt
⅛ teaspoon pepper
1½ pounds fettuccine, mostaccioli *or* rigatoni
2 tablespoons chopped fresh parsley
1 package (8 ounces) fresh mushrooms, sliced

Heat oil in large skillet over medium-high heat. Add pork steaks; cook until browned and no longer pink in center. Pour off drippings. Add all remaining ingredients *except* fettuccine, parsley and mushrooms; cover. Simmer 1 to 1½ hours, until pork is very tender. Cook fettuccine according to package directions; drain. Remove pork from sauce; cut into small pieces. Return to sauce. Add parsley and mushrooms. Cook and stir over medium heat 5 minutes. Serve over hot fettuccine.

*Makes 6 servings*

**Prep time:** 20 minutes
**Cook time:** 90 minutes

*Favorite recipe from* **National Pork Producers Council**

# Pasta e Fagioli
## (Pasta and Beans)

1 cup ziti pasta, cooked and drained
2 tablespoons PROGRESSO® Olive Oil
½ cup chopped onion
⅓ cup chopped green pepper
⅓ cup chopped red pepper
¼ cup chopped celery
3 cloves garlic, minced
1 can (28 ounces) PROGRESSO® Peeled Tomatoes Italian Style, cut up, undrained
1 teaspoon Italian seasoning
½ teaspoon dried basil leaves, crushed
¼ teaspoon salt
¼ teaspoon ground black pepper
1 can (15 ounces) PROGRESSO® Cannellini Beans, drained
¼ cup (1 ounce) PROGRESSO® Grated Parmesan Cheese

1. In large skillet, heat olive oil over medium-high heat. Add onion, green and red peppers, celery and garlic; cook and stir 6 to 8 minutes or until tender.

2. Stir in tomatoes and seasonings; simmer 20 minutes, stirring occasionally.

3. Add pasta and beans; heat thoroughly, stirring occasionally.

4. Stir in Parmesan cheese.

*Makes 4 servings*

**Prep time:** 25 minutes
**Cook time:** 25 minutes

**Microwave:** In 2-quart microwave-safe casserole, combine olive oil, onion, green and red peppers, celery and garlic; cover. Microwave on HIGH (100% power) 5 minutes, stirring every 2 minutes. Stir in tomatoes and seasonings; cover. Microwave on HIGH 15 minutes, stirring every 6 minutes. Stir in pasta and beans. Microwave on HIGH 3 minutes. Stir in Parmesan cheese.

## Hearty Beef Stew with Noodles

2 tablespoons vegetable oil
1 teaspoon minced fresh garlic
1 pound boneless sirloin steak, cut
    into ½-inch cubes
3 cups water
½ cup dry red wine
4 medium new potatoes, quartered
1 large carrot, thinly sliced
1 cup sliced mushrooms
1 cup sliced celery
1 large onion, cut into wedges
1 tablespoon tomato paste
¼ teaspoon dried thyme leaves,
    crushed
1 bay leaf
1 package LIPTON® Noodles &
    Sauce—Beef Flavor
1 tablespoon finely chopped fresh
    parsley
    Salt and pepper

Heat oil in 3-quart saucepan over medium heat. Add garlic; cook and stir 30 seconds. Add steak; cook 2 minutes or until browned, stirring frequently. Stir in water, wine, potatoes, carrot, mushrooms, celery, onion, tomato paste, thyme and bay leaf. Bring to a boil; simmer, stirring occasionally, 30 minutes or until steak is almost tender. Stir in noodles & beef flavor sauce; simmer 10 minutes or until noodles are tender, stirring occasionally. Stir in parsley. Season with salt and pepper to taste. Remove bay leaf.

*Makes about 4 (2-cup) servings*

*Hearty Beef Stew with Noodles*

## Spaghetti with Cream Sauce

8 ounces spaghetti, cooked and
    drained
2 cups mushroom slices
1 cup halved zucchini slices
1 clove garlic, minced
2 tablespoons PARKAY® Margarine
⅓ cup half-and-half
½ pound VELVEETA® Pasteurized
    Process Cheese Spread, cubed

• Cook and stir vegetables and garlic in margarine in large skillet until zucchini is crisp-tender. Reduce heat to low.

• Add half-and-half and process cheese spread; stir until process cheese spread is melted. Toss with hot spaghetti.

*Makes 6 servings*

**Prep time:** 15 minutes
**Cook time:** 10 minutes

## Southwest Spaghetti

*Can't decide between Mexican or Italian food tonight? Try this easy combination.*

8 ounces spaghetti, cooked and
    drained
1 package (1.5 ounces) LAWRY'S®
    Original Style Spaghetti Sauce
    Spices & Seasonings
1 can (6 ounces) tomato paste
1 bottle (12 ounces) salsa
½ cup water
1 can (4 ounces) diced green chiles,
    undrained

In medium saucepan over medium-high heat, combine Original Style Spaghetti Sauce Spices & Seasonings, tomato paste, salsa, water and green chiles; blend well. Bring to a boil. Reduce heat to low; simmer, uncovered, 15 minutes, stirring occasionally. Serve over hot spaghetti. *Makes 4 servings*

**Presentation:** Garnish with shredded Cheddar cheese, avocado slices and sliced ripe olives. Serve with a tossed green salad.

## Mediterranean Pasta

Hot cooked thin spaghetti
1 roll (16 ounces) ECKRICH® Country
    Sausage
1 tablespoon olive oil
2 medium onions, thinly sliced
1 small clove garlic, minced
2 medium zucchini, thinly sliced
½ teaspoon dried basil leaves, crushed
¼ teaspoon dried oregano leaves,
    crushed
¼ teaspoon salt
    Dash ground black pepper
2 large tomatoes, seeded, cut into large
    pieces
    Grated Parmesan cheese, optional

Break sausage into pieces. Cook in large skillet over medium heat until lightly browned, stirring occasionally to separate meat; drain. Set aside. Add oil to skillet; heat. Add onions and garlic; cook and stir until tender. Stir in zucchini, basil, oregano, salt and pepper; cook 5 minutes. Stir in sausage and tomatoes. Cover; simmer 10 minutes, stirring occasionally. Serve over hot spaghetti. Sprinkle with Parmesan cheese. *Makes 4 to 5 servings*

## Tuna-Stuffed Shells

12 jumbo shell macaroni, cooked and
    drained
 1 egg, slightly beaten
 1 can (6½ ounces) tuna, drained and
    flaked
⅔ cup ricotta cheese
½ cup HEINZ® Seafood Cocktail Sauce
⅓ cup chopped red pepper
¼ cup sliced green onions with tops
¼ cup finely chopped celery
 2 tablespoons plain dry bread crumbs
 2 tablespoons grated Parmesan cheese
⅛ to ¼ teaspoon hot pepper sauce
 2 tablespoons water
½ cup (2 ounces) shredded mozzarella
    cheese

Combine egg, tuna, ricotta, cocktail sauce, vegetables, bread crumbs, Parmesan cheese and hot pepper sauce; mix well. Stuff into shells. Arrange shells in 1½-quart baking dish. Add water to dish; cover tightly with foil. Bake at 375°F, 35 minutes. Uncover; top with mozzarella cheese. Continue baking, uncovered, 2 minutes or until cheese is melted. Let stand 5 minutes. Serve with additional cocktail sauce, if desired.

*Makes 4 servings*

*Southwest Spaghetti*

*Lite Pad Thai*

## Lite Pad Thai

8 ounces linguine
½ pound skinless boneless chicken breast
¾ cup no-salt-added tomato juice
3 tablespoons KIKKOMAN® Lite Soy Sauce
1 tablespoon vinegar
2 teaspoons sugar
¾ teaspoon cornstarch
3 tablespoons vegetable oil, divided
8 ounces fresh bean sprouts, rinsed and drained
½ cup sliced green onions with tops
2 cloves garlic, minced
½ pound cooked baby shrimp, rinsed and drained
1 tablespoon minced fresh cilantro
Lime wedges

Cook linguine according to package directions, omitting salt; drain. Cut chicken into thin strips. Combine tomato juice, lite soy sauce, vinegar, sugar and cornstarch; set aside. Heat 1 tablespoon oil in hot wok or large skillet over high heat. Add chicken; stir-fry 1 minute. Remove from wok. Heat remaining 2 tablespoons oil in wok. Add bean sprouts, onions and garlic; stir-fry 1 minute. Stir in linguine; cook 2 minutes or until thoroughly heated. Add chicken, shrimp, cilantro and tomato juice mixture. Cook and stir until sauce boils and thickens. Serve with lime wedges. Garnish with additional cilantro, if desired. *Makes 4 servings*

## Chile Cheese Macaroni

8 ounces elbow macaroni, cooked and drained
2 cups (8 ounces) shredded process American cheese
2 cans (4 ounces *each*) *or* 1 can (7 ounces) ORTEGA® Diced Green Chiles, undrained
¼ cup milk
⅛ teaspoon ground black pepper
¼ cup chopped fresh parsley, optional

In large bowl, combine macaroni, process cheese, chiles, milk and pepper. Spoon into greased 1½-quart casserole; cover. Bake at 350°F, 45 minutes or until hot and bubbly. Garnish with parsley.
*Makes 4 (1-cup) servings*

# Fettuccine with Tomatoes and Zucchini

6 ounces fettuccine, cooked and
  drained
½ pound ground beef
½ onion, chopped
1 can (14½ ounces) DEL MONTE®
  Original Style Stewed Tomatoes
1 can (8 ounces) DEL MONTE®
  Tomato Sauce
1 medium carrot, cut into julienne
  strips
1 teaspoon dried tarragon leaves,
  crushed
1 medium zucchini, cubed
  Chopped fresh parsley, optional

In large skillet over medium heat, brown meat with onion, stirring occasionally to separate meat; drain. Add stewed tomatoes, tomato sauce, carrots and tarragon. Simmer, uncovered, 8 minutes, stirring occasionally. Stir in zucchini; cover. Simmer an additional 7 minutes or until zucchini is tender, stirring occasionally. Just before serving, spoon sauce over hot pasta. Garnish with parsley. *Makes 4 to 6 servings*

**Prep time:** 6 minutes
**Cook time:** 20 minutes

**Hint:** Pasta may be cooked ahead and rinsed in cold water. It may then be frozen or refrigerated; reheat in boiling water or in microwave oven.

# Spaghetti with Ricotta

1 pound thin spaghetti, cooked and
  drained
8 tablespoons sweet butter, melted
2 cups POLLY-O® Ricotta Cheese
  Salt and pepper
1 tablespoon chopped fresh parsley
  Freshly grated Parmesan cheese

Combine hot spaghetti and butter; toss lightly to coat. Add ricotta; mix lightly. Season with salt and pepper to taste. Sprinkle with parsley and Parmesan cheese. Serve immediately.

*Makes 6 servings*

**Spaghetti with Four Cheeses:** Place 4 tablespoons melted butter and ¼ cup cream in warmed serving bowl. Cook and drain spaghetti; transfer to bowl. Add 1 cup shredded POLLY-O® Mozzarella Cheese, 1 cup POLLY-O® Ricotta Cheese, 1 cup chopped Gruyere cheese and ½ cup grated Parmesan cheese; mix lightly. Serve with additional Parmesan cheese, if desired.

*Fettuccine with Tomatoes and Zucchini*

## Tortellini with Three-Cheese Tuna Sauce

1 pound cheese-filled tortellini
1 tablespoon butter *or* margarine
2 green onions with tops, thinly sliced
1 clove garlic, minced
1 cup lowfat ricotta cheese
½ cup lowfat milk
1 can (6½ ounces) STARKIST® Tuna, drained and broken into chunks
½ cup (2 ounces) shredded lowfat mozzarella cheese
¼ cup (1 ounce) grated Parmesan *or* Romano cheese
2 tablespoons chopped fresh basil leaves *or* 2 teaspoons dried basil leaves, crushed
1 teaspoon grated lemon peel

In large saucepan, cook tortellini in boiling salted water according to package directions. When tortellini is nearly done, in another large saucepan, melt butter over medium heat. Add onions and garlic; cook and stir 2 minutes. Whisk in ricotta cheese and milk. Add tuna, cheeses, basil and lemon peel. Reduce heat to medium-low. Simmer until mixture is heated and cheeses are melted, stirring occasionally.

Drain pasta. Add to sauce; toss lightly to coat. Garnish with tomato wedges, if desired. Serve immediately.

*Makes 4 to 5 servings*

**Prep time:** 25 minutes

## Beef 'n Orzo Stuffed Peppers

1½ cups cooked orzo (rice-shaped pasta)
1 pound ground beef (80% lean)
4 large green peppers
⅔ cup tightly packed Italian parsley leaves
¼ cup *plus* 2 tablespoons grated Parmesan cheese, divided
2 tablespoons chopped walnuts
1½ teaspoons dried basil leaves, crushed
1 teaspoon salt, divided
1 clove garlic
¼ cup olive oil
1 medium tomato, seeded and chopped

Cut tops off peppers; discard. Remove seeds and membrane. Add peppers to boiling salted water; simmer 3 minutes. Invert onto paper towels to drain. Place parsley, ¼ cup Parmesan cheese, walnuts, basil, ½ teaspoon salt and garlic in food processor container with steel blade attached or in blender container; cover. Process until blended. With motor running, slowly pour in oil, processing until well blended.

Brown meat in large skillet, stirring occasionally to separate meat; drain. Stir in parsley mixture, orzo, tomato and remaining ½ teaspoon salt. Spoon an equal amount of beef mixture into each pepper. Bake at 350°F , 20 minutes. Sprinkle with remaining 2 tablespoons Parmesan cheese. *Makes 4 servings*

**Prep time:** 25 minutes
**Cook time:** 20 minutes

*Favorite recipe from **National Live Stock and Meat Board***

*Tortellini with Three-Cheese Tuna Sauce*

## Manicotti Villa Santa Maria
### (Cannelloni alla Villa Santa Maria)

1 package (8 ounces) CREAMETTE®
   Manicotti, cooked and drained
2 eggs, slightly beaten
1 container (15 *or* 16 ounces) ricotta
   cheese
1½ cups (6 ounces) shredded mozzarella
   cheese
4 ounces prosciutto *or* cooked ham,
   thinly sliced and finely chopped,
   optional
¼ cup finely chopped fresh parsley
⅛ teaspoon pepper
½ cup (2 ounces) grated Parmesan
   cheese, divided
1 jar (26 ounces) CLASSICO®
   D'Abruzzi (Beef & Pork) *or* Di
   Salerno (Sweet Peppers & Onions)
   Pasta Sauce

Preheat oven to 375°F. In large bowl,
combine eggs, ricotta, mozzarella,
prosciutto, parsley, pepper and ¼ cup
Parmesan cheese; mix well. Stuff
manicotti with cheese mixture; arrange
in 13×9-inch baking dish. Spoon pasta
sauce over manicotti; top with
remaining ¼ cup Parmesan cheese.
Cover. Bake 40 minutes or until hot.
Refrigerate leftovers.

*Makes 6 to 8 servings*

## East Meets West Spaghetti and Meat Balls

8 ounces spaghetti *or* vermicelli
½ pound mild Italian sausage, casing
   removed
½ pound ground beef
¼ cup chopped green onions with tops
1 clove garlic, minced
2 tablespoons dry sherry, divided
½ cup KIKKOMAN® Sweet & Sour
   Sauce
⅓ cup beef broth
1 tablespoon olive oil
½ (16-ounce) package frozen Italian-
   style vegetables, thawed and
   drained

Cook spaghetti according to package
directions, omitting salt. Drain and keep
warm. Meanwhile, combine sausage,
beef, onions, garlic and 1 tablespoon
sherry; mix well. Shape into sixteen
meatballs; set aside. Combine sweet
& sour sauce, beef broth and remaining
1 tablespoon sherry; set aside.

Heat oil in large skillet over medium
heat. Add meatballs. Brown on all sides;
drain. Pour sweet & sour sauce mixture
over meatballs; cover. Simmer 5 minutes.
Add vegetables; simmer, uncovered, an
additional 7 minutes or until vegetables
are cooked, stirring occasionally. Serve
over hot spaghetti.     *Makes 4 servings*

*East Meets West Spaghetti and Meat Balls*

## Smoked Sausage-Stuffed Pasta Shells

¾ pound ECKRICH® Smoked Sausage, finely chopped
18 large macaroni shells, cooked and drained
1 egg, slightly beaten
1 pound ricotta cheese
1½ cups (6 ounces) shredded mozzarella cheese
½ cup chopped fresh parsley
¼ cup (1 ounce) grated Parmesan cheese
½ teaspoon dried basil leaves, crushed
½ teaspoon dried oregano leaves, crushed
1 jar (15 ounces) prepared spaghetti sauce with mushrooms and onions
⅓ cup water

Preheat oven to 375°F. Combine egg and ricotta cheese in medium bowl. Add mozzarella cheese, parsley, Parmesan cheese, basil and oregano; mix well. Stir in sausage. Combine spaghetti sauce and water in small bowl. Spoon ¾ cup sauce into 13×9-inch baking dish, spreading to cover bottom of dish. Fill shells with sausage-cheese mixture; arrange in dish. Top with remaining sauce. Bake 35 minutes or until shells are heated through and cheese is melted.

*Makes 9 servings (2 shells each)*

*Smoked Sausage-Stuffed Pasta Shells*

## PACE® Macaroni and Cheese

*"Comfort food" with contemporary Texas style, this lively casserole is the cherished childhood favorite, spiced to suit sophisticated "grown up" tastes.*

8 ounces elbow macaroni, cooked and drained (about 2 cups uncooked)
2 tablespoons butter *or* margarine
3 tablespoons all-purpose flour
2 cups milk
½ cup PACE® Picante Sauce
¾ teaspoon ground cumin
½ teaspoon salt
2 cups (8 ounces) shredded sharp Cheddar cheese, divided
½ cup chopped green pepper, optional

Melt butter in 2-quart saucepan over medium heat. Stir in flour; cook until mixture is smooth and bubbly. Remove from heat; gradually stir in milk. Stir in picante sauce, cumin and salt. Bring to a boil; simmer, until thickened, stirring constantly. Remove from heat. Add 1¾ cups cheese and green pepper; stir until cheese is melted. Add macaroni; mix well. Pour into greased 1½-quart baking dish; top with remaining ¼ cup cheese. Cover. Bake at 350°F, 15 minutes; uncover. Continue baking 5 minutes. Serve with additional picante sauce, if desired. *Makes 4 to 6 servings*

# GOOD ENOUGH FOR GUESTS

## Fettuccine Alfredo with Shiitake Mushrooms

1 tablespoon olive *or* vegetable oil
2 medium cloves garlic, minced
1 cup sliced shiitake *or* white mushrooms
2 tablespoons dry white wine
1 tablespoon finely chopped fresh basil leaves*
1½ cups milk
1 cup canned crushed tomatoes
½ cup water
2 tablespoons butter *or* margarine
1 package LIPTON® Noodles & Sauce —Alfredo
Dash pepper

In medium skillet, heat oil over medium heat. Add garlic; cook and stir 30 seconds. Add mushrooms, wine and basil; cook and stir 2 minutes or until mushrooms are tender. Stir in remaining ingredients. Bring to a boil; simmer 8 minutes or until noodles are tender, stirring occasionally. Garnish with additional basil leaves and cherry tomatoes, if desired.

*Makes about 2 main-dish or 4 appetizer servings*

**\*Substitution:** Use ½ teaspoon dried basil leaves, crushed.

## Veal Scallopine

1 tablespoon all-purpose flour
½ teaspoon salt
Dash pepper
4 veal cutlets (about 1 pound)
¼ cup CRISCO® Shortening
½ onion, thinly sliced
1 can (14½ ounces) tomatoes, cut up, undrained
1 can (4 ounces) mushrooms, undrained
1 tablespoon chopped fresh parsley
1 tablespoon capers, drained
¼ teaspoon garlic salt
¼ teaspoon dried oregano leaves, crushed
Hot buttered noodles

Combine flour, salt and pepper; coat veal lightly with mixture. In medium skillet, brown veal slowly in hot CRISCO®. Remove veal from skillet. Add onion; cook and stir until tender. Add veal, tomatoes, mushrooms, parsley, capers, garlic salt and oregano. Cover; simmer until veal is tender, 20 to 30 minutes, stirring occasionally. Place veal over noodles; top with sauce.

*Makes 4 servings*

*Fettuccine Alfredo with Shiitake Mushrooms*

*Velvet Shrimp*

## Velvet Shrimp

Hot cooked pasta
3 tablespoons unsalted butter
½ cup finely chopped green onions
    with tops
1 tablespoon *plus* 1 teaspoon CHEF
    PAUL PRUDHOMME'S® Seafood
    Magic®, divided
½ teaspoon minced fresh garlic
1 pound deveined shelled medium to
    large shrimp
2 cups heavy cream, divided
2 tablespoons water, optional
1 cup (4 ounces) shredded Muenster
    cheese

Melt butter in 10-inch skillet over high heat. When it comes to a hard sizzle, add onions and 1 tablespoon Seafood Magic®. Cook and stir 1 to 2 minutes. Add garlic and shrimp; cook and stir 2 minutes. Stir in 1 cup cream and remaining 1 teaspoon Seafood Magic®. Stir and scrape any browned bits off sides and bottom of skillet. Cook about 1 minute; stir in remaining 1 cup cream. Cook 1 minute or just until shrimp are plump and pink; remove shrimp from sauce with slotted spoon. Set aside.

Still over high heat, whisk sauce in skillet until it comes to a boil. Reduce heat to low. Simmer 2 to 3 minutes. Stir in water, if desired, and cheese. Simmer an additional minute or until cheese is melted. Return shrimp to skillet; stir to coat. Serve over hot pasta.

*Makes 4 servings*

## Smoked Salmon and Olive Pasta

2 cups heavy cream
3 medium cloves garlic
¼ teaspoon pepper
1 teaspoon finely chopped lemon zest
    (yellow part of peel)
1 cup pitted California ripe olives,
    chopped
½ cup dry white wine
12 ounces fusilli *or* other corkscrew-
    type pasta
6 ounces smoked salmon, thinly sliced
    and cut into short strips
Salt

Combine cream and garlic in large skillet over medium heat; heat thoroughly, stirring frequently. Stir in pepper, lemon zest, olives and wine; bring to a boil. Reduce heat to low; simmer 10 minutes to blend flavors and reduce volume a little, stirring occasionally. Meanwhile, cook pasta according to package directions; drain. Remove garlic from sauce; discard garlic. Add pasta and salmon to sauce; toss lightly to coat. Season with salt to taste. Top with freshly ground black pepper and chopped fresh parsley, if desired. Serve immediately. *Makes 4 servings*

*Favorite recipe from **California Olive Industry***

## Beef 'n Eggplant Stir-Fry

1 beef flank steak (1 to 1¼ pounds)
4 tablespoons dry red wine, divided
½ teaspoon dried basil leaves, crushed
½ teaspoon dried oregano leaves, crushed
½ teaspoon salt
¼ teaspoon black pepper
4 to 5 tablespoons olive oil, divided
1 eggplant (approximately 1 pound), peeled, cut into 2×¼-inch strips
2 cloves garlic, minced
1 large red pepper, cut into thin strips
1 tablespoon cornstarch
¾ cup beef broth
2 cups hot cooked and drained spinach linguine
1 tablespoon grated Parmesan cheese

Partially freeze beef flank steak to firm. Cut steak in half lengthwise; slice each half diagonally across the grain into thin slices (knife should be almost parallel to cutting surface). Combine 1 tablespoon wine, basil, oregano, salt and black pepper; toss with meat. Heat 3 tablespoons oil in wok or large nonstick skillet. Add eggplant and garlic; stir-fry 8 to 10 minutes until eggplant is transparent. Add red pepper; stir-fry 2 minutes. Remove from skillet; reserve. Stir-fry beef strips (⅓ at a time) in remaining oil 2 to 3 minutes. Remove from skillet; reserve. Combine cornstarch with beef broth. Stir into drippings in wok with remaining 3 tablespoons wine. Cook until thickened, stirring occasionally. Stir in reserved beef strips and vegetables; heat thoroughly, stirring occasionally. Combine hot linguine with Parmesan cheese; toss lightly. Top with beef mixture. *Makes 4 servings*

**Prep time:** 35 minutes
**Cook time:** 25 to 30 minutes

*Favorite recipe from **National Live Stock and Meat Board***

## Turkey Rolls Di Napoli

3 tablespoons olive oil, divided
1 green bell pepper, cut into strips
1 red bell pepper, cut into strips
1 clove garlic, minced
6 fresh turkey breast slices (4 ounces *each*), pounded and lightly seasoned with salt and black pepper
3 ounces Swiss cheese, cut into 12 strips
1 jar (26 ounces) CLASSICO® Di Napoli (Tomato & Basil) Pasta Sauce
½ (1-pound) package CREAMETTE® Linguine, cooked and drained

In large skillet, heat 2 tablespoons oil over medium-high heat. Add bell peppers and garlic; cook and stir until tender. Remove from skillet. On each turkey cutlet, place one green and one red pepper strip and two cheese strips. Roll tightly; secure with wooden picks. Heat remaining 1 tablespoon oil. Add turkey rolls; brown on all sides. Add pasta sauce and remaining bell peppers. Reduce heat to low; cover. Simmer 10 minutes or until turkey is no longer pink in center. Remove picks; serve over hot pasta. Refrigerate leftovers.
*Makes 4 to 6 servings*

*Beef 'n Eggplant Stir-Fry*

## Sunday Super Stuffed Shells

1 package (12 ounces) jumbo pasta shells, cooked and drained
2 tablespoons olive oil
3 cloves fresh garlic
¾ pound ground veal
¾ pound ground pork
2 eggs, slightly beaten
1 package (10 ounces) frozen chopped spinach, cooked, drained and squeezed dry
1 cup fresh parsley sprigs, finely chopped
1 cup fresh bread crumbs
3 cloves fresh garlic, minced
3 tablespoons grated Parmesan cheese
Salt
3 cups spaghetti sauce, divided

Preheat oven to 375°F. Heat oil in large skillet over medium heat. Add 3 whole cloves garlic; cook and stir until lightly browned. Discard garlic. Add veal and pork to skillet; cook until browned, stirring to separate meat. Drain. Cool.

Combine eggs, spinach, parsley, bread crumbs, minced garlic and cheese in large bowl; mix well. Season with salt. Add meat mixture; blend well. Spoon into shells.

Spread about 1 cup spaghetti sauce onto bottom of greased 12×8-inch baking dish. Arrange shells in dish; top with remaining sauce. Cover with foil. Bake 35 to 45 minutes or until hot and bubbly. Serve with sautéed zucchini slices, if desired. Garnish as desired.

*Makes 9 to 12 servings*

*Favorite recipe from* **The Fresh Garlic Association**

## Pesto Chicken Almond Manicotti

8 ounces Manicotti, cooked and drained
3 eggs, slightly beaten
2 containers (12 ounces *each*) ricotta cheese
1¼ cups freshly grated Parmesan cheese, divided
½ cup heavy cream
2½ cups chopped cooked chicken
¾ cup chopped toasted almonds
1 package (10 ounces) frozen chopped spinach, thawed and drained
1 tablespoon dried basil leaves, crushed
¾ teaspoon freshly ground black pepper
3 cups tomato sauce

Mix together eggs, ricotta cheese, ¾ cup Parmesan cheese and cream. Stir in all remaining ingredients *except* tomato sauce and manicotti. Spoon mixture into manicotti shells; divide shells between 13×9-inch baking dish and 9-inch square baking dish. Cover shells with tomato sauce; sprinkle with remaining ½ cup Parmesan cheese. Cover. Bake at 350°F, 20 minutes. Remove cover; continue baking 15 minutes or until cheese is golden brown.

*Makes 6 to 8 servings*

*Favorite recipe from* **National Pasta Association**

*Sunday Super Stuffed Shells*

*Shrimp Noodle Supreme*

## Shrimp Noodle Supreme

1 package (8 ounces) spinach noodles, cooked and drained
1 package (3 ounces) cream cheese, cubed and softened
½ cup butter, softened
1½ pounds medium shrimp, peeled and deveined
Salt and pepper
1 can (10¾ ounces) condensed cream of mushroom soup
1 cup dairy sour cream
½ cup half-and-half
½ cup mayonnaise
1 tablespoon chopped fresh chives
1 tablespoon chopped fresh parsley
½ teaspoon Dijon-style mustard
¾ cup (3 ounces) shredded sharp Cheddar cheese

Preheat oven to 325°F. Combine cream cheese and hot noodles; mix lightly to coat. Spread noodle mixture onto bottom of greased 13×9-inch baking dish. Melt butter in large skillet over medium-high heat. Add shrimp; cook and stir until shrimp turn pink and are tender, about 5 minutes. Season with salt and pepper to taste. Spoon over noodle mixture.

Combine soup, sour cream, half-and-half, mayonnaise, chives, parsley and mustard in another medium bowl. Spread over shrimp. Sprinkle with Cheddar cheese. Bake 25 minutes or until hot and cheese is melted. Garnish as desired.          *Makes 6 servings*

*Favorite recipe from Southeast United Dairy Industry Association, Inc.*

## Nokkelost Pasta Soufflé

8 ounces fettuccine noodles, cooked and drained
1⅔ cups scalded milk
½ cup butter *or* margarine
1½ cups shredded Nokkelost cheese
1 cup finely chopped ham
½ teaspoon salt
⅛ teaspoon pepper
6 large eggs, separated

Combine hot fettuccine with milk, butter, cheese, ham, salt and pepper; toss lightly to coat. Cool 10 minutes. Blend in egg yolks. Beat egg whites in small bowl until stiff but not dry; fold into noodle mixture. Spoon into ungreased 2½-quart soufflé dish. Bake at 350°F, 40 minutes or until puffed and golden brown. Serve immediately.

*Makes 6 servings*

*Favorite recipe from Norseland Foods, Inc.*

## Tortellini Primavera

**8 to 9 ounces cheese-filled tortellini, cooked and drained**
**1 cup sliced mushrooms**
**½ cup chopped onion**
**1 clove garlic, minced**
**2 tablespoons PARKAY® Margarine**
**1 package (10 ounces) BIRDS EYE® Chopped Spinach, thawed, well drained**
**1 container (8 ounces) PHILADELPHIA BRAND® Soft Cream Cheese**
**1 medium tomato, chopped**
**¼ cup milk**
**¼ cup (1 ounce) KRAFT® 100% Grated Parmesan Cheese**
**1 teaspoon Italian seasoning**
**¼ teaspoon *each* salt and pepper**

Cook and stir mushrooms, onion and garlic in margarine in large skillet. Add all remaining ingredients *except* tortellini; mix well. Cook until mixture just begins to boil, stirring occasionally. Add hot tortellini; cook until thoroughly heated, stirring occasionally.

*Makes 4 servings*

**Prep time:** 10 minutes
**Cook time:** 10 minutes

## Pasta with Spinach-Cheese Sauce

**¼ cup FILIPPO BERIO® Extra-Virgin Flavorful Olive Oil, divided**
**1 medium onion, chopped**
**1 clove garlic, chopped**
**3 cups chopped fresh spinach, washed and well drained**
**1 cup lowfat ricotta *or* cottage cheese**
**½ cup chopped fresh parsley**
**1 teaspoon dried basil leaves, crushed**
**1 teaspoon lemon juice**
**¼ teaspoon black pepper**
**¼ teaspoon ground nutmeg**
**12 ounces uncooked spaghetti**

1. Heat 3 tablespoons olive oil in large skillet over medium heat. Add onion and garlic; cook and stir until tender.

2. Add spinach; cook 3 to 5 minutes or until spinach wilts.

3. Place spinach mixture, cheese, parsley, basil, lemon juice, pepper and nutmeg in blender container; cover. Blend until smooth. Leave in blender, covered, to keep sauce warm.

4. Cook pasta according to package directions. *(Do not overcook)*. Drain pasta, reserving ¼ cup water. In large bowl, toss pasta with remaining 1 tablespoon olive oil.

5. Add reserved ¼ cup water to sauce in blender. Blend; serve over pasta.

*Makes 4 servings*

*Tortellini Primavera*

## Veal Sauce Lucia

*A hearty Italian sauce to serve with any kind of pasta.*

8 ounces linguine *or* other pasta of
　　your choice, cooked and drained
2 tablespoons vegetable oil
1½ pounds veal stew meat, cut into
　　bite-size cubes
1 medium onion, chopped
1 medium carrot, shredded
¾ teaspoon dried basil leaves, crushed
¾ teaspoon LAWRY'S® Garlic Powder
　　with Parsley
1 package (1.5 ounces) LAWRY'S®
　　Extra Rich & Thick Spaghetti
　　Sauce Spices & Seasonings
1¾ cups water
1 can (6 ounces) tomato paste
½ cup frozen peas

In Dutch oven, heat oil over medium
heat. Add veal; cook until browned,
stirring occasionally. Drain. Add onion,
carrot, basil and Garlic Powder with
Parsley; cook and stir 5 minutes. Stir in
Extra Rich & Thick Spaghetti Sauce
Spices & Seasonings, water and tomato
paste. Bring to a boil. Reduce heat to
low; cover. Simmer 30 minutes, stirring
occasionally. Stir in peas; heat 5 minutes.
Serve over hot pasta.

*Makes 4 servings*

**Presentation:** Serve with a Caesar salad
and garlic bread.

*Crabmeat with Herbs and Pasta*

## Crabmeat with Herbs and Pasta

4 ounces vermicelli, cooked and
　　drained
⅓ cup olive oil
3 tablespoons butter *or* margarine
1 small onion, finely chopped
1 carrot, shredded
1 clove garlic, minced
6 ounces drained and flaked crabmeat
¼ cup chopped fresh basil leaves *or*
　　1 teaspoon dried basil leaves,
　　crushed
2 tablespoons chopped fresh parsley
1 tablespoon lemon juice
½ cup chopped pine nuts, optional
½ teaspoon salt

Heat oil and butter in large skillet over medium-high heat. Add onion, carrot and garlic; cook and stir until tender. Reduce heat to medium. Stir in crabmeat, basil, parsley and lemon juice; simmer 4 minutes, stirring constantly. Stir in pine nuts and salt. Pour sauce over hot vermicelli in large bowl; toss gently to coat. Garnish as desired.

*Makes 4 servings*

*Favorite recipe from New Jersey Department of Agriculture*

# Pasta with White Clam Sauce

1 can (10½ ounces) minced clams, undrained
1½ cups water
1 tablespoon olive oil
1 package LIPTON® Pasta & Sauce—Creamy Garlic
1 tablespoon finely chopped fresh parsley
1 tablespoon grated Parmesan cheese
Pepper to taste

Drain clams, reserving ¼ cup liquid. Combine reserved liquid, water and oil in medium saucepan. Bring to a boil over medium heat. Stir in pasta & creamy garlic sauce; simmer, stirring occasionally, 11 minutes or until pasta is tender. Stir in clams, parsley, cheese and pepper; heat thoroughly, stirring occasionally. Garnish with additional chopped parsley, if desired.

*Makes about 4 servings*

**Microwave:** Increase water to 1¾ cups. In 1½-quart microwave-safe casserole, combine reserved clam liquid, water, oil and pasta & creamy garlic sauce. Microwave, uncovered, on HIGH (Full Power) 13 minutes or until pasta is tender, stirring after 7 minutes. Stir in clams, parsley, cheese and pepper. Microwave 1 minute. Garnish as above.

# Chicken and Spinach Manicotti

*Manicotti filled with the earthy flavors of Italy is baked as a casserole. A pastry bag with a large plain tip is an easy way to stuff manicotti.*

1 package (8 ounces; 14 count) manicotti shells, cooked and drained
1½ cups shredded cooked chicken
1 container (15 ounces) ricotta cheese
1 package (10 ounces) frozen chopped spinach, cooked according to package directions
1¼ cups half-and-half, divided
½ cup PROGRESSO® Plain Bread Crumbs
1 teaspoon garlic powder
½ teaspoon dried basil leaves, crushed
½ teaspoon dried oregano leaves, crushed
½ teaspoon salt
¼ teaspoon ground black pepper
1 jar (14 ounces) PROGRESSO® Marinara Sauce
1½ cups (6 ounces) shredded mozzarella cheese

1. Preheat oven to 350°F.

2. In large bowl, combine chicken, ricotta cheese, spinach, ½ cup half-and-half, bread crumbs, garlic powder, basil, oregano, salt and pepper; mix well.

3. Stuff chicken mixture into manicotti; place in 13×9-inch baking dish.

4. Combine marinara sauce and remaining ¾ cup half-and-half; pour over manicotti. Top with mozzarella cheese.

5. Bake 30 minutes or until thoroughly heated. *Makes 7 servings*

**Prep time:** 30 minutes
**Baking time:** 30 minutes

# Saucy Mediterranean Frittata

**Sauce:**

  1 can (8 ounces) tomato sauce
  1 teaspoon minced dried onion
  ¼ teaspoon *each* dried basil and
    oregano leaves, crushed
  ¼ teaspoon pepper
  ⅛ teaspoon minced fresh garlic

**Frittata:**

  ⅓ cup cooked orzo
  1 tablespoon olive oil
  ⅓ cup chopped onion
  1 medium tomato, chopped
  1 teaspoon dried basil leaves, crushed
  ¼ teaspoon dried oregano leaves,
    crushed
  ⅓ cup chopped pitted ripe olives
  8 eggs
  ½ teaspoon salt
  2 tablespoons butter
  ½ cup (2 ounces) shredded mozzarella
    cheese

Combine all sauce ingredients in small saucepan. Bring to a boil over medium-high heat. Reduce heat to low; simmer 5 minutes, stirring frequently. Set aside; keep warm.

For frittata, heat oil in ovenproof 10-inch skillet over medium-high heat. Add onion; cook and stir until tender. Add tomato, basil and oregano; cook and stir 3 minutes. Stir in orzo and olives. Remove from skillet; set aside. Beat eggs and salt in medium bowl. Stir in tomato mixture. Melt butter in skillet. Add egg mixture; sprinkle with cheese. Cook over low heat 8 to 10 minutes or until set. Broil 1 to 2 minutes, until top is browned. Serve with sauce. Garnish as desired. Cut into wedges to serve.

*Makes 4 to 6 servings*

*Favorite recipe from **Kansas Poultry Association***

# Herbed Seafood Linguine

*A light, colorful easy-to-prepare pasta for seafood lovers.*

  6 ounces linguine, cooked and drained
  1 can (10½ ounces) PROGRESSO® Red
    Clam Spaghetti Sauce
  ¼ pound sole, cut into small pieces
  3 ounces (about ½ cup) imitation
    crabmeat
  2 ounces (8 to 10) peeled and deveined
    medium shrimp
  ⅓ cup chopped onion
  ¼ cup chopped green pepper
  1 clove garlic, minced
  ⅛ teaspoon dried basil leaves, crushed
  ⅛ teaspoon dried oregano leaves,
    crushed
  2 tablespoons PROGRESSO® Grated
    Parmesan Cheese

1. In medium saucepan over medium-high heat, combine red clam sauce, sole, crabmeat, shrimp, onion, green pepper, garlic, basil and oregano.

2. Bring to a boil. Reduce heat to low; simmer until sole flakes easily with fork and shrimp are tender.

3. Serve clam sauce mixture over hot linguine; sprinkle with Parmesan cheese.

*Makes 4 servings*

**Prep time:** 10 minutes
**Cook time:** 10 minutes

**Microwave:** In 2-quart microwave-safe casserole, combine red clam sauce, sole, crabmeat, shrimp, onion, green pepper, garlic, basil and oregano; cover. Microwave on HIGH (100% power) 4 to 5 minutes or until fish flakes easily with fork and shrimp are tender, stirring after 2 minutes. Serve over hot linguine; sprinkle with Parmesan cheese.

*Saucy Mediterranean Frittata*

## Shrimp in Angel Hair Pasta Casserole

1 tablespoon butter
2 eggs, slightly beaten
1 cup half-and-half
1 cup plain yogurt
½ cup (2 ounces) shredded Swiss
    cheese
⅓ cup crumbled feta cheese
⅓ cup chopped fresh parsley
¼ cup chopped fresh basil leaves *or*
    1 teaspoon dried basil leaves,
    crushed
1 teaspoon dried oregano leaves,
    crushed
1 package (9 ounces) uncooked fresh
    angel hair pasta
1 jar (16 ounces) mild, thick and
    chunky salsa
1 pound medium shrimp, peeled and
    deveined
½ cup (2 ounces) shredded Monterey
    Jack cheese

*Shrimp in Angel Hair Pasta Casserole*

Preheat oven to 350°F. With 1 tablespoon butter, grease 12×8-inch baking dish. Combine eggs, half-and-half, yogurt, Swiss cheese, feta cheese, parsley, basil and oregano in medium bowl; mix well. Place ½ of pasta in prepared dish; cover with layers of salsa and ½ of shrimp. Top with remaining pasta. Spread egg mixture over pasta; cover with remaining shrimp. Sprinkle Monterey Jack cheese over top. Bake 30 minutes or until hot and bubbly. Let stand 10 minutes before cutting to serve. Garnish as desired.     *Makes 6 servings*

*Favorite recipe from **Southeast United Dairy Industry Association, Inc.***

## Linguine Louisiana Style

12 ounces Linguine *or* your favorite
    long pasta shape, cooked and
    drained
2 ounces finely chopped cooked lean
    ham *or* Canadian-style bacon
1 clove garlic, minced
½ cup chopped onion
2 tablespoons dry white wine
8 ounces stewed tomatoes
½ cup chopped red and green pepper
½ cup finely chopped celery
1 tablespoon spicy tomato juice
½ teaspoon ground allspice, optional
½ teaspoon ground cloves, optional
    Hot pepper sauce to taste
1 cup crabmeat *or* tiny shrimp, cooked

Spray large nonstick skillet with cooking spray. Add ham and garlic; cook and stir until lightly browned. Stir in onion and wine. Cook 1 minute. Add all remaining ingredients *except* pasta and crabmeat; heat thoroughly, stirring occasionally. Serve over hot pasta; top with crabmeat.     *Makes 4 servings*

*Favorite recipe from **National Pasta Association***

*Fettuccine with Mussels*

## Creamy Orzo with Prosciutto

*This savory pasta can be served as a hearty side dish or as a main course for a light supper or luncheon.*

1 package (1 pound) orzo, cooked and drained
2 tablespoons PARKAY® Margarine
2 cloves garlic, minced
1 package (8 ounces) PHILADELPHIA BRAND® Cream Cheese, cubed
½ cup chicken broth
    Dash turmeric
1 package (10 ounces) BIRDS EYE® Deluxe Tender Tiny Peas, thawed and drained
3 ounces thinly sliced prosciutto, cut into julienne strips
    Salt and pepper

• Melt margarine in large saucepan over low heat. Add garlic; cook and stir until tender. Add cream cheese, broth and turmeric; stir until cream cheese is melted.

• Stir in orzo, peas and prosciutto; heat thoroughly, stirring occasionally. Season with salt and pepper to taste. Serve with grated Parmesan cheese, if desired.

*Makes 8 to 10 servings*

**Prep time:** 25 minutes
**Tip:** Recipe can be doubled for a main-dish meal.

## Fettuccine with Mussels

*If fresh mussels aren't available in your store, use canned clams instead.*

4 ounces fettuccine, cooked and drained
1 can (10½ ounces) PROGRESSO® White Clam Spaghetti Sauce
½ pound mussels in shells, cleaned
¼ cup (1 ounce) PROGRESSO® Grated Parmesan Cheese, divided
¼ teaspoon seafood seasoning
¼ teaspoon Italian seasoning

1. In medium saucepan over medium heat, combine white clam sauce, mussels, 2 tablespoons Parmesan cheese and seasonings. Bring to a boil. Reduce heat to low; simmer until mussels pop open. (Discard any mussels that remain closed.)

2. Serve clam sauce mixture sauce over hot fettuccine. Sprinkle with remaining 2 tablespoons Parmesan cheese.

*Makes 4 servings*

**Prep time:** 15 minutes
**Cook time:** 10 minutes

## Pasta Delight

12 ounces penne pasta, cooked and
   drained
 1 tablespoon olive oil
 1 medium zucchini, sliced
 2 tablespoons chopped shallots
 2 cloves garlic, minced
 1 medium tomato, chopped
 2 tablespoons chopped fresh basil
   leaves *or* ½ teaspoon dried basil
   leaves, crushed
 2 tablespoons grated Parmesan cheese

Heat oil in large skillet over medium-
high heat. Add zucchini; cook and stir
until crisp-tender. Reduce heat to
medium. Add shallots and garlic; cook 1
minute. Add tomato; cook and stir 45
seconds. Stir in basil and cheese. Pour
vegetable mixture over hot pasta in
large bowl; toss gently to coat.

*Makes 4 to 6 servings*

*Favorite recipe from* **National Pasta Association**

## Tangy Asparagus Linguine

 5 ounces linguine
 2 tablespoons reduced-calorie
   margarine
¼ cup finely chopped onion
 3 cloves garlic, minced
 8 ounces fresh asparagus, peeled and
   sliced diagonally into ½-inch
   pieces
 2 tablespoons dry white wine
 2 tablespoons fresh lemon juice
   Freshly ground black pepper
¼ cup (1 ounce) SARGENTO® Grated
   Parmesan Cheese
¾ cup (3 ounces) SARGENTO®
   Preferred Light Fancy Shredded
   Mozzarella Cheese

Chop and measure all ingredients before
beginning. Bring water to a boil. Add
pasta; cook to al dente (firm to the bite).
Drain. Meanwhile, melt margarine over
medium heat in large skillet. Add onion
and garlic; cook and stir until tender.
Add asparagus; cook and stir 2 minutes.
Add wine and lemon juice; simmer 1
minute. Season with pepper to taste.
Remove from heat. Add to hot pasta in
large bowl with Parmesan cheese; toss
lightly to coat. Remove to serving
platter; top with mozzarella cheese.
Garnish with strips of lemon zest, if
desired. Serve immediately.

*Makes 4 servings*

## Chicken Roman Style
### (Pollo alla Romana)

¼ cup olive oil
2½ to 3 pounds chicken pieces
 3 ounces prosciutto *or* cooked ham,
   thinly sliced and cut into strips
 1 jar (26 ounces) CLASSICO® Di
   Roma Arrabbiata (Spicy Red
   Pepper) *or* Di Salerno (Sweet
   Peppers & Onions) Pasta Sauce
¼ cup dry white wine
½ (1-pound) package CREAMETTE®
   Fettuccini

In large skillet over medium-high heat,
heat oil. Add chicken; cook and stir until
browned on all sides. Remove chicken
from skillet; pour off oil. In same skillet,
cook prosciutto until lightly browned.
Reduce heat to low; stir in pasta sauce
and wine. Return chicken to skillet;
cover. Simmer 20 minutes or until
chicken is tender and no longer pink in
center, stirring occasionally. Meanwhile,
cook fettuccini according to package
directions. Serve chicken and sauce over
hot fettuccini. Refrigerate leftovers.

*Makes 4 to 6 servings*

*Pasta Delight*

## Chicken Diane

6 ounces pasta, cooked and drained
¾ cup (1½ sticks) unsalted butter, divided
1 tablespoon *plus* 2 teaspoons CHEF PAUL PRUDHOMME'S® Poultry Magic®
12 ounces boneless skinless chicken breasts, cut into strips
3 cups sliced mushrooms (about 8 ounces)
¼ cup chopped green onions with tops
3 tablespoons chopped fresh parsley
1 teaspoon minced fresh garlic
1 cup chicken broth *or* water

Beat 4 tablespoons butter in medium bowl until creamy. Stir in Poultry Magic®. Add chicken; mix lightly to coat. Heat large skillet over high heat until hot, about 4 minutes. Add chicken; cook and stir until browned on all sides and no longer pink in center. Add mushrooms; cook and stir 2 minutes. Add onions, parsley, garlic and broth. Cook 2 minutes or until sauce comes to a boil. Cut up remaining ½ cup butter. Add to sauce; stir until melted. Cook 3 minutes. Stir in hot pasta. Serve immediately.     *Makes 2 servings*

*Chicken Diane*

## Seafood Supreme Pasta Pie

6 ounces fine egg noodles, cooked and drained
2 eggs, slightly beaten
½ cup dairy sour cream
½ cup milk
¼ cup (1 ounce) grated Parmesan cheese
1 teaspoon dried tarragon leaves, crushed

Seafood Sauce:

4 tablespoons (½ stick) butter
4 ounces fresh mushrooms, sliced
¼ cup chopped green onions with tops
1 large clove garlic, minced
8 ounces small shrimp, shelled and cleaned
8 ounces bay scallops
1 can (6 ounces) crabmeat, drained
3 tablespoons all-purpose flour
½ teaspoon seasoned salt
¼ teaspoon pepper
1½ cups half-and-half
1 cup (4 ounces) finely shredded Swiss cheese, divided
1 cup dry white wine

Preheat oven to 350°F. In medium bowl, blend together eggs, sour cream, milk, Parmesan cheese and tarragon. Stir in noodles; spoon into buttered 9-inch pie plate. Cover with foil. Bake 35 to 45 minutes or until knife inserted near center comes out clean.

Meanwhile, melt butter in large skillet over medium heat. Add mushrooms, onions and garlic; cook and stir 2 minutes. Add seafood; cook and stir 3 minutes. Add flour, salt and pepper. Gradually stir in half-and-half and ½ cup Swiss cheese. Cook, stirring constantly, until mixture thickens. Stir in wine. To serve, cut pasta pie into wedges; serve with Seafood Sauce. Sprinkle individual servings with the remaining ½ cup Swiss cheese.
*Makes 6 to 8 servings*

*Favorite recipe from Southeast United Dairy Industry Association, Inc.*

## Penne with Artichokes

12 ounces penne, cooked and drained
1¼ cups water
  2 tablespoons lemon juice
  1 package (10 ounces) frozen
      artichokes
  2 tablespoons olive oil, divided
  5 cloves garlic
  2 ounces oil-packed sun-dried
      tomatoes, drained
  2 small dried hot red peppers, crushed
  2 tablespoons chopped fresh parsley
  ¼ teaspoon salt
  ¼ teaspoon black pepper
  ¾ cup fresh bread crumbs
  1 tablespoon minced fresh garlic
  1 tablespoon grated Romano cheese

Pour water and lemon juice into medium saucepan. Bring to a boil over medium-high heat. Add artichokes. Reduce heat to low; simmer until artichokes are tender. Drain artichokes, reserving cooking liquid. Cool artichokes; cut into quarters.

Heat 1½ tablespoons oil in large skillet over medium-high heat. Add 5 whole cloves garlic; cook and stir until lightly browned. Reduce heat to low. Add artichokes and tomatoes; simmer 1 minute. Stir in reserved artichoke liquid, red peppers, parsley, salt and black pepper. Simmer 5 minutes, stirring occasionally.

Meanwhile, heat remaining ½ tablespoon oil in small skillet over medium heat. Add bread crumbs and minced garlic; cook and stir until lightly browned. Pour artichoke sauce over hot pasta in large bowl; toss gently to coat. Sprinkle with bread crumb mixture and cheese.          *Makes 4 to 6 servings*

*Favorite recipe from **National Pasta Association***

*Penne with Artichokes*

## HIDDEN VALLEY® Pasta

  1 package (1 ounce) HIDDEN
      VALLEY RANCH® Milk Recipe
      Original Ranch® Salad Dressing
      Mix
  ½ cup picante sauce
  4 large tomatoes, coarsely chopped
  ¼ cup olive *or* vegetable oil
  1 medium clove garlic, minced
  8 ounces Brie cheese, chilled
  8 ounces medium egg noodles

In large bowl, whisk together salad dressing mix and picante sauce. Stir in tomatoes, oil and garlic. Remove as much rind from Brie as possible and discard. Cut Brie into bite-size pieces; stir into tomato mixture. Cook noodles according to package directions; drain. Return noodles to same saucepan. Pour tomato-Brie sauce over noodles. Cook over medium heat, stirring constantly, until cheese melts. Serve immediately.
*Makes 4 servings*

*Stuffed Shells Bolognese*

## Stuffed Shells Bolognese

*An easy recipe to serve to guests or for a special family meal.*

**12 jumbo pasta shells, cooked and
drained
1 package (1.5 ounces) LAWRY'S®
Original Style Spaghetti Sauce
Spices & Seasonings
1 can (28 ounces) whole tomatoes, cut
up, undrained
2 tablespoons dry red wine
2 tablespoons IMPERIAL® Margarine
1 pound lean ground beef
½ cup chopped onions
½ cup chopped green pepper
½ cup shredded carrot
½ teaspoon LAWRY'S® Garlic Powder
with Parsley
1 cup (4 ounces) shredded mozzarella
cheese
¼ cup (1 ounce) grated Parmesan
cheese**

In medium saucepan over medium heat, combine Original Style Spaghetti Sauce Spices & Seasonings with tomatoes, wine and margarine; blend well. Bring to a boil; reduce heat to low. Simmer, uncovered, 25 minutes, stirring occasionally. In medium skillet, brown ground beef with onions, stirring occasionally to separate meat; drain. Add green pepper, carrot, Garlic Powder with Parsley and ½ cup prepared sauce; heat 5 minutes. Fill shells with meat mixture; place in 13×9-inch baking dish. Cover with remaining sauce; sprinkle with mozzarella and Parmesan cheeses. Bake at 350°F, 20 to 30 minutes or until cheeses are melted and sauce is bubbly.

*Makes 4 servings*

**Presentation:** Serve with fresh asparagus or a green salad and fruit sorbet for dessert.

# Sesame Baked Chicken with Fusilli

8 pounds chicken pieces
1 quart buttermilk
2½ cups plain dry bread crumbs
¾ cup *plus* 1 tablespoon sesame seed, lightly toasted, divided
⅓ cup (1½ ounces) grated Parmesan cheese
1 teaspoon salt
½ teaspoon white pepper
½ cup *plus* 3 tablespoons butter *or* margarine, divided
1½ tablespoons lemon juice
2 teaspoons minced fresh garlic
4½ cups water
1½ cups milk
3 packages LIPTON® Pasta & Sauce—Cheddar Broccoli
1 large tomato, chopped
⅓ cup sliced green onions with tops

In large glass baking dishes, place chicken pieces. Pour buttermilk over chicken; cover and marinate in refrigerator, turning occasionally, 6 hours or overnight. Remove chicken; discard marinade.

Preheat oven to 450°F. In shallow pan, combine bread crumbs, ¾ cup sesame seed, cheese, salt and pepper. Dip chicken into bread crumb mixture, coating well; place in two 13×9-inch baking dishes.

In small saucepan, melt ½ cup butter with lemon juice and garlic; drizzle over chicken. Bake 10 minutes. **Reduce oven temperature to 350°F.** Continue baking 1 hour or until chicken is no longer pink in center, basting occasionally with butter mixture.

Meanwhile, in large saucepan over medium heat, bring water, milk and remaining 3 tablespoons butter to a boil. Stir in pasta & Cheddar broccoli sauce; simmer, stirring occasionally, 11 minutes or until pasta is tender. Stir in tomato and onions. To serve, arrange pasta around chicken on platter; sprinkle with remaining 1 tablespoon sesame seed.

*Makes about 16 servings*

# Linguine with Creamy Clam Sauce

½ (1-pound) package CREAMETTE® Linguine, cooked and drained
2 cans (6½ ounces *each*) SNOW'S® or DOXSEE® Minced *or* Chopped Clams, undrained
¼ cup margarine *or* butter
1 cup sliced fresh mushrooms
¼ cup finely chopped onion
1 clove garlic, minced
2 tablespoons all-purpose flour
1 cup BORDEN® or MEADOW GOLD® Half-and-Half
2 teaspoons WYLER'S® or STEERO® Chicken-Flavor Instant Bouillon
¼ cup (1 ounce) grated Parmesan cheese
1 tablespoon dry sherry, optional
1 tablespoon chopped fresh parsley
¼ teaspoon pepper

Drain clams, reserving liquid. Melt margarine in medium saucepan over medium heat. Add mushrooms, onion and garlic; cook and stir until tender. Stir in flour. Gradually stir in reserved clam liquid, half-and-half and bouillon; cook and stir until thickened. Add clams, cheese, sherry, parsley and pepper; heat thoroughly, stirring occasionally. *(Do not boil.)* Serve over hot linguine. Refrigerate leftovers.

*Makes 4 servings*

# Marinated Lemon Chicken with Lemon-Pepper Noodles

⅓ cup olive *or* vegetable oil
⅓ cup lemon juice
1 medium onion, sliced
2 large cloves garlic, minced
1 tablespoon *plus* 1½ teaspoons grated lemon peel, divided
1 teaspoon dried parsley flakes
½ teaspoon dried oregano leaves, crushed
½ teaspoon salt
¼ teaspoon pepper
1½ pounds boneless skinless chicken breasts, halved
1 package LIPTON® Noodles & Sauce—Butter & Herb Pepper

In large shallow glass baking dish, combine oil, lemon juice, onion, garlic, 1 tablespoon lemon peel and seasonings. Add chicken; cover. Marinate in refrigerator, stirring occasionally, at least 1 hour; drain.

Grill or broil chicken with onion until chicken is no longer pink in center.

Meanwhile, prepare noodles & butter & herb sauce according to package directions. Stir in remaining 1½ teaspoons lemon peel. Season with additional pepper to taste, if desired. To serve, arrange chicken over noodles. Garnish as desired.

*Makes about 4 servings*

*Marinated Lemon Chicken with Lemon-Pepper Noodles*

# Turkey & Asparagus Rolls Campania

½ (1-pound) package CREAMETTE® Linguine, cooked and drained
4 fresh turkey breast slices (4 ounces *each*)
Salt and pepper
4 slices (2 ounces) Provolone cheese
4 slices (4 ounces) cooked ham *or* prosciutto
8 stalks fresh asparagus
1 tablespoon olive oil
1 clove garlic, minced
1 jar (26 ounces) CLASSICO® Di Napoli (Tomato & Basil) *or* Di Salerno (Sweet Peppers & Onions) Pasta Sauce

Pound turkey slices to flatten slightly; season with salt and pepper. On each turkey slice, place one cheese slice, one ham slice and two asparagus stalks. Roll up tightly; secure with wooden picks. In large skillet, heat oil over medium-high heat. Add garlic; cook and stir 1 minute. Add turkey rolls; cover with pasta sauce. Reduce heat to low; cover and simmer 20 minutes or until turkey is no longer pink in center. Remove picks; serve turkey rolls over hot pasta. Refrigerate leftovers. *Makes 4 servings*

*Saucy Shrimp over Chinese Noodles Cakes*

# Saucy Shrimp over Chinese Noodle Cakes

    **Chinese Noodle Cakes (recipe follows)**
  1 teaspoon ketchup
  2 tablespoons cornstarch, divided
1¼ cups water
  4 tablespoons KIKKOMAN® Soy Sauce, divided
  ½ pound medium shrimp, peeled and deveined
  2 tablespoons vegetable oil, divided
  1 clove garlic, minced
1½ teaspoons minced fresh ginger root
  1 green pepper, cut into chunks
  1 medium onion, cut into chunks
  2 stalks celery, cut diagonally into thin slices
  2 tomatoes, cut into chunks

Prepare Chinese Noodle Cakes. Combine ketchup, 1 tablespoon cornstarch, water and 3 tablespoons soy sauce; set aside. Blend remaining 1 tablespoon *each* cornstarch and soy sauce in small bowl; stir in shrimp until coated. Heat 1 tablespoon oil in wok or large skillet over high heat. Add shrimp mixture; stir-fry 1 minute. Remove shrimp from wok; set aside. Heat remaining 1 tablespoon oil in wok. Add garlic and ginger; stir-fry until fragrant. Add green pepper, onion and celery; stir-fry 4 minutes. Stir in soy sauce mixture, shrimp and tomatoes. Cook and stir until sauce boils and thickens. Cut Chinese Noodle Cakes into squares. Serve with shrimp mixture.

*Makes 6 servings*

**Chinese Noodle Cakes:** Cook 8 ounces capellini (angel hair pasta) according to package directions. Drain; rinse under cold water and drain thoroughly. Heat 1 tablespoon vegetable oil in large nonstick skillet over medium-high heat. Add ½ of capellini; spread slightly to cover bottom of skillet to form noodle cake. Cook 5 minutes, without stirring, or until golden on bottom. Lift cake with wide spatula. Add 1 tablespoon vegetable oil to skillet; turn cake over. Cook 5 minutes or until golden brown, shaking skillet occasionally to brown evenly; remove to rack and keep warm in 200°F oven. Repeat with remaining capellini.

# Seafood Primavera

1 package (8 ounces) linguine, cooked
    and drained
⅓ cup olive oil
1 medium onion, chopped
4 green onions with tops, chopped
3 cloves garlic, minced
3 carrots, cut into julienne strips
1 zucchini, cut into julienne strips
1 *each* small red and yellow pepper,
    cut into strips
3 ounces snow peas
⅓ cup sliced mushrooms
½ pound *each* peeled and deveined
    medium shrimp and scallops
⅔ cup clam juice
⅓ cup dry white wine
1 cup heavy cream
½ cup freshly grated Parmesan cheese
⅔ cup flaked crabmeat
2 tablespoons *each* lemon juice and
    chopped fresh parsley
¼ teaspoon *each* dried basil and
    oregano leaves, crushed
    Freshly ground black pepper to taste

Heat oil in large skillet over medium-
high heat. Add onions and garlic; cook
and stir until tender. Add remaining
vegetables. Reduce heat to medium-low;
cover. Simmer until tender, stirring
occasionally. Remove vegetable mixture
from skillet; set aside. Add scallops and
shrimp to skillet; cook and stir until
scallops are opaque and shrimp turn
pink. Remove from skillet, reserving
liquid in skillet. Add clam juice and
wine to skillet; bring to a boil. Stir in
cream and Parmesan. Reduce heat to
low; simmer 3 minutes or until slightly
thickened, stirring constantly.

Return vegetables and seafood to skillet.
Heat thoroughly, stirring occasionally.
Stir in all remaining ingredients *except*
linguine. Pour over hot linguine in large
bowl; toss gently to coat.

*Makes 6 servings*

# Spaghetti with Chicken and Wild Mushrooms

1 pound Spaghetti *or* your favorite
    long thin pasta
2 tablespoons butter *or* margarine
2 small shallots, finely chopped
4 ounces chanterelle, morel *or* shiitake
    mushrooms, finely chopped
4 ounces fresh button mushrooms,
    chopped
½ cup dry Madeira *or* sherry
⅔ cup light table cream
2 to 3 chicken breasts, cooked, cooled
    and diagonally sliced into 1-inch
    thin strips
½ teaspoon salt
¼ teaspoon freshly ground black
    pepper
4 sprigs parsley, finely chopped

Cook pasta according to package
directions; drain. While pasta is cooking,
melt butter in large nonstick skillet over
medium heat. Add shallots; cook and
stir until tender, about 5 minutes. Stir in
mushrooms and Madeira; simmer 5
minutes, stirring constantly, until liquid
is reduced by ⅓. Stir in cream; simmer,
stirring occasionally, until sauce
thickens. Stir in chicken; heat
thoroughly, stirring occasionally. Season
with salt and pepper. To serve, pour
chicken sauce over pasta; toss lightly to
coat. Garnish with parsley.

*Makes 6 to 8 servings*

*Favorite recipe from **National Pasta Association***

# Linguine with Clams and Scallops

¼ cup olive oil, divided
½ cup sliced green onions with tops
1 can (28 ounces) CONTADINA®
    Whole Peeled Tomatoes,
    undrained
½ teaspoon salt
¼ teaspoon red pepper flakes
1 pound linguine
1 pound scallops
3 cloves garlic, minced
½ cup dry white wine
2 tablespoons finely chopped fresh
    parsley
16 fresh clams

Heat 2 tablespoons oil in large saucepan over medium-high heat. Add onions; cook and stir until tender. Add tomatoes, salt and red pepper flakes. Bring to a boil. Reduce heat to low; simmer, uncovered, 20 minutes, stirring occasionally. Meanwhile, cook pasta according to package directions; drain. Add scallops to sauce; simmer an additional 5 minutes or until scallops are just tender. Heat remaining 2 tablespoons oil in 10-inch skillet over medium-high heat. Add garlic; cook and stir 2 to 3 minutes. Stir in wine and parsley. Bring to a boil. Add clams; simmer, covered, 5 to 8 minutes or until clams have opened. (Discard any clams that do not open.) Stir cooking liquid from clams into tomato mixture. Combine hot pasta with ½ of sauce in large bowl; toss lightly to coat. Place pasta on deep serving platter; top with remaining sauce. Arrange clams around edge of platter. *Makes 8 servings*

**Microwave:** Cook pasta according to package directions; drain. Meanwhile, combine onions, garlic and oil in 3-quart microwave-safe dish. Microwave on HIGH 2 minutes. Add tomatoes, wine, salt and red pepper flakes. Microwave 10 minutes, stirring after 5 minutes. Stir in scallops. Microwave 4 minutes or until scallops are just tender. Stir in parsley; set aside. Arrange 8 clams at a time in shallow microwave-safe dish; cover with vented plastic wrap or lid. Microwave 45 seconds. Remove all opened clams. Microwave any unopened clams, checking every 15 seconds. (Discard any clams that do not open within 2 minutes of cooking.) Serve as directed.

# Fettuccine Romano Aldana

6 ounces plain fettuccine, cooked and
    drained
6 ounces spinach fettuccine, cooked
    and drained
¾ cup butter, divided
8 ounces mushrooms, sliced
⅔ cup chopped green onions with tops
2½ cups heavy cream, divided
1½ cups (6 ounces) grated Wisconsin
    Romano cheese, divided
¼ teaspoon ground nutmeg
⅓ pound prosciutto ham slices,
    julienne cut
White pepper

Melt ¼ cup butter in large skillet over medium-high heat. Add mushrooms and onions; cook and stir until tender. Remove from skillet; set aside. Add remaining ½ cup butter to skillet; heat until lightly browned. Add 1 cup cream; bring to a boil. Reduce heat to low; simmer until slightly thickened, about 5 minutes. Add pasta, 1 cup cream, 1 cup cheese and nutmeg; mix lightly. Combine remaining cream and cheese with mushroom mixture and prosciutto. Pour over hot pasta mixture; toss lightly. Season with pepper to taste. *Makes 4 to 6 servings*

*Favorite recipe from* **Wisconsin Milk Marketing Board**
© 1992

*Shrimp Pasta Medley*

## Shrimp Pasta Medley

  8 ounces linguine, cooked and drained
  ¼ cup PARKAY® Margarine
  1 clove garlic, minced
12 ounces cleaned medium shrimp
  1 cup half-and-half
  1 cup pea pods, cut in half diagonally
  1 red bell pepper, cut into strips
  ¼ cup dry white wine
  ¼ teaspoon crushed red pepper flakes
  1 (4-ounce) KRAFT® 100% Parmesan
      Cheese wedge, shredded, divided

• Melt margarine in large skillet over medium heat. Add garlic; cook and stir until lightly browned.

• Add all remaining ingredients *except* cheese. Simmer 3 to 5 minutes or until shrimp turn pink.

• Pour sauce over hot linguine. Add ¾ cup cheese; toss to coat. Serve with remaining ¼ cup cheese.

*Makes 4 servings*

**Prep time:** 10 minutes
**Cook time:** 10 minutes

**Variation:** Substitute 1½ cups chopped cooked chicken for medium shrimp.

## Pasta Primavera with Chicken

8 ounces spaghetti, cooked and drained
1 package (1¼ pounds) PERDUE®
    Fit 'n Easy Fresh skinless and boneless chicken breasts
2 tablespoons vegetable oil, divided
4 green onions with tops, cut into julienne strips (about ½ cup)
2 cloves garlic, minced
1 pound asparagus, peeled and cut into 2-inch pieces, *or* 2 cups julienned zucchini
2 carrots, peeled and cut into julienne strips (about 1 cup)
½ cup low-sodium chicken broth *or* bouillon
½ cup dry white wine
¼ cup chopped fresh parsley
½ teaspoon dried oregano leaves, crushed
⅛ teaspoon ground pepper
⅓ cup freshly grated Parmesan cheese

Cut breast meat into thin strips. In large skillet, heat 1 tablespoon oil over medium-high heat. Add onions and garlic; cook and stir 1 minute. Add chicken; cook and stir 2 to 3 minutes or until chicken is no longer pink in center. Remove chicken mixture from skillet; set aside. Heat remaining 1 tablespoon oil over medium-high heat in skillet. Add asparagus and carrots; cook and stir 2 minutes. Stir in broth, wine, parsley, oregano and pepper. Reduce heat to low; simmer 1 to 2 minutes or until vegetables are crisp-tender, stirring occasionally.

Place hot spaghetti on large platter; top with chicken and vegetable mixtures. Sprinkle with cheese.

*Makes 6 servings*

## Spinach-Garlic Pasta with Garlic-Onion Sauce

**Spinach-Garlic Pasta:**

1½ cups all-purpose flour, divided
  2 eggs *plus* 4 yolks
  1 tablespoon olive oil
  8 ounces fresh spinach, blanched,
    squeezed dry and finely chopped
  6 large cloves garlic, minced
  ½ teaspoon salt

**Garlic-Onion Sauce:**

½ cup butter
  1 tablespoon olive oil
  1 pound Vidalia *or* other sweet
    onions, sliced
  ⅓ cup chopped fresh garlic (about
    12 large cloves)
  1 tablespoon honey, optional
  ¼ cup Marsala wine
    Grated Parmesan cheese, optional

For pasta, place 1 cup flour in large bowl. Make well in center; place eggs, yolks and 1 tablespoon oil in well. Add spinach, minced garlic and salt. Mix, working in more flour as needed. Knead until dough is smooth. Cover with plastic wrap. Let rest 15 to 30 minutes. Roll dough to desired thickness with pasta machine. Cut into desired width. Cook in boiling water 2 minutes; drain.

For sauce, heat butter and 1 tablespoon oil in large skillet over medium heat. Add onions and chopped garlic; cook and stir until tender. Stir in honey; reduce heat to low. Simmer, uncovered, 30 minutes stirring occasionally. Stir in wine; simmer an additional 5 to 10 minutes, stirring occasionally. Pour sauce over hot pasta; toss gently to coat. Serve with cheese. Garnish as desired.

*Makes 2 to 4 servings*

*Favorite recipe from* **The Fresh Garlic Association**

*Spinach-Garlic Pasta with Garlic-Onion Sauce*

## Vermicelli Frittata

8 ounces Vermicelli *or* your favorite
    long, thin pasta shape, cooked and
    drained
  3 tablespoons butter
  2 leeks, sliced into quarters
    lengthwise and chopped
  1 package (9 ounces) frozen artichoke
    hearts, cooked according to
    package directions and quartered
  ½ teaspoon dried sage leaves, crushed
  8 eggs *or* equivalent egg substitute
  1 cup (4 ounces) shredded Gruyere *or*
    Swiss cheese
  2 tablespoons chopped Italian parsley
    Salt and freshly ground pepper

In large skillet over medium heat, melt butter. Add leeks; cook and stir until tender, about 3 minutes. Add cooked artichoke hearts; cook and stir 2 minutes. Stir in sage.

In medium bowl, beat eggs lightly. Stir in vermicelli, Gruyere and parsley. Season with salt and pepper to taste. Add vegetables; stir lightly.

Heat 8-inch nonstick skillet, lightly sprayed with vegetable spray, over medium-high heat. Pour ⅓ of the egg mixture into skillet; cover. Cook 3 or 4 minutes until set and bottom is lightly browned. Slide frittata from skillet onto plate. Invert skillet over frittata and flip back into skillet. Cook, covered, 3 or 4 minutes. Remove to serving dish; keep warm. Repeat twice with remaining egg mixture. Cut into quarters; serve immediately. *Makes 6 servings*

**Variations:** Replace butter, leeks, artichoke hearts, parsley, sage and Gruyere with one of the following or make your own favorite combination:

— 1 cup mushrooms and 1 finely chopped shallot, cooked and stirred in 3 tablespoons butter, with 1 cup chopped Brie cheese.

— 1 finely chopped red delicious or other sweet apple, cooked and stirred until tender in 3 tablespoons butter, with 1 cup crumbled Blue cheese or shredded Cheddar cheese.

— 1 cup blanched chopped asparagus with 2 ounces chopped prosciutto or other cooked ham and 1 cup shredded white Cheddar cheese.

— 1 chopped tomato with 1 cup shredded Mozzarella cheese, ¼ cup grated Parmesan and 1 teaspoon dried basil leaves.

*Favorite recipe from* **National Pasta Association**

# Pesto Pasta

8 ounces radiatore pasta, cooked and drained
1 cup packed fresh basil leaves
1 package (3 ounces) KRAFT® 100% Shredded Parmesan Cheese *or* KRAFT® 100% Parmesan Cheese wedge, shredded, divided
⅓ cup olive oil
¼ cup pine nuts
1 clove garlic, minced
1 cup pitted ripe olive halves
1 cup chopped seeded tomatoes

• Place basil, ½ cup cheese, oil, pine nuts and garlic in covered food processor container with steel blade attached; process until smooth.

• Toss together basil mixture, hot pasta, olives and tomatoes in large bowl. Sprinkle with remaining ¼ cup cheese.
*Makes 4 servings*

**Prep/Cook time:** 20 minutes
**Variation:** Substitute 8 ounces of your favorite pasta for the radiatore pasta.

*Pesto Pasta*

## Fettuccine with Sun-Dried Tomato Cream

1 pound fettuccine, cooked and
   drained
2/3 cup sun-dried tomatoes
3 to 4 cloves garlic
1 container (8 ounces)
   PHILADELPHIA BRAND® Soft
   Cream Cheese
1/2 teaspoon dried oregano leaves,
   crushed
1/4 cup PARKAY® Margarine
1/4 cup sour cream
1/4 cup olive oil
   Salt and pepper
2 tablespoons chopped fresh parsley

• Cover tomatoes with boiling water; let stand 10 minutes. Drain.

• Place tomatoes and garlic in covered food processor or blender container; process until coarsely chopped. Add cream cheese and oregano; process until well blended.

• Melt margarine in medium saucepan; stir in cream cheese mixture and sour cream. Cook until thoroughly heated.

• Toss hot fettuccine with oil in large bowl.

• Add cream cheese mixture. Season with salt and pepper to taste. Sprinkle with chopped parsley. Serve immediately.     *Makes 8 to 10 servings*

**Prep time:** 30 minutes

## Sweet and Sour Scallops

8 ounces Rotini, Spirals *or* Twists,
   cooked and drained
2 tablespoons vegetable oil
   Dash sesame oil
2 shallots, finely chopped
1 clove garlic, minced, optional
1/4 yellow pepper, coarsely chopped
1/4 teaspoon grated fresh ginger
1 pound sea scallops, cut in half
1/4 teaspoon salt, optional
1 can (8 ounces) pineapple chunks,
   drained*
1/3 cup water*
1/4 cup light corn syrup
2 tablespoons wine vinegar
2 teaspoons light soy sauce
1 tablespoon cornstarch
3 tablespoons cold water

In large nonstick skillet, heat oils over medium heat. Add shallots, garlic, pepper and ginger; cook and stir until tender. Pat scallops dry on paper towels. Add scallops to skillet; cook and stir just until scallops are opaque, about 5 minutes. Season with salt, if desired. Remove skillet from heat. Stir in pineapple; set aside. Place 1/3 cup water, corn syrup, vinegar and soy sauce in medium saucepan over medium-high heat. Bring to a boil, stirring occasionally. Reduce heat to low; simmer, uncovered, 5 minutes. In small bowl, mix together cornstarch and 3 tablespoons cold water. Slowly stir into sauce. Simmer, stirring constantly, until slightly thickened. Stir sauce into scallop mixture. Heat until mixture is hot and bubbly. Serve over hot pasta.
*Makes 4 to 6 servings*

*You may substitute mixture of water and reserved pineapple juice from drained chunks to measure 1/3 cup, if desired.

*Favorite recipe of **National Pasta Association***

*Fettuccine with Sun-Dried Tomato Cream*

## Florentine-Stuffed Shells

**24 jumbo pasta shells for filling,
    cooked and drained**
**1 package (10 ounces) frozen chopped
    spinach, thawed**
**1 egg, slightly beaten**
**2 cups (15 ounces) SARGENTO®
    Ricotta Cheese***
**1½ cups (6 ounces) SARGENTO®
    Classic Supreme Shredded *or*
    Fancy Supreme Shredded
    Mozzarella Cheese**
**⅓ cup finely chopped onion**
**2 cloves garlic, minced**
**¼ teaspoon salt**
**⅛ teaspoon ground nutmeg**
**2 cups meatless spaghetti sauce**
**½ cup (2 ounces) SARGENTO® Grated
    Cheese****

Squeeze spinach to remove as much
moisture as possible. Combine egg,
spinach, Ricotta cheese, Mozzarella
cheese, onion, garlic, salt and nutmeg;
stir to blend well. Stuff shells with
Ricotta mixture, using about 2
tablespoons mixture for each shell. Place
in lightly greased 13×9-inch baking
dish. Pour spaghetti sauce over shells.
Sprinkle with grated cheese; cover. Bake
at 350°F, 30 to 40 minutes or until
thoroughly heated.      *Makes 8 servings*

*SARGENTO® Old Fashioned Ricotta,
Part Skim Ricotta or Light Ricotta can be
used.

**SARGENTO® Parmesan, Parmesan and
Romano or Italian-Style Grated Cheese
can be used.

*Florentine-Stuffed Shells*

## Sausage & Feta Strata

**8 ounces medium pasta shells, cooked
    and drained**
**1 pound Italian sausage**
**2 tablespoons vegetable oil**
**1 cup sliced green onions with tops**
**3 cloves garlic, minced**
**1 cup water**
**1 can (6 ounces) CONTADINA®
    Tomato Paste**
**⅔ cup dry red wine**
**¾ teaspoon fennel seed**
**½ teaspoon dried rosemary leaves,
    crushed**
**2 cups (8 ounces) crumbled feta cheese
    *or* ricotta cheese**
**2 cups sliced zucchini (about
    2 medium zucchini)**

Brown sausage in oil in 10-inch skillet over medium heat; drain on paper towels, reserving drippings in skillet. Add onions and garlic to reserved drippings. Cook and stir 3 minutes. Stir in water, tomato paste, wine, fennel and rosemary. Bring to a boil. Reduce heat to low; simmer 6 minutes, stirring occasionally. Spoon ½ of pasta into greased 2-quart baking dish; top with layers of ½ *each* of sauce and cheese. Place zucchini over cheese. Repeat layers of pasta, sauce and cheese. Arrange sausage on top to resemble pinwheel. Bake at 350°F, 35 to 40 minutes or until hot and bubbly.  *Makes 8 servings*

## Cheesy Chicken Roll-Ups

6 lasagna noodles, cooked, drained and each cut lengthwise into halves
¼ cup butter
1 medium onion, finely chopped
4 ounces fresh mushrooms, sliced
3 chicken breast halves, skinned, boned and cut into bite-size pieces
¾ cup dry white wine
½ teaspoon dried tarragon leaves, crushed
½ teaspoon salt
½ teaspoon pepper
1 package (8 ounces) cream cheese, cubed and softened
½ cup heavy cream
½ cup dairy sour cream
1½ cups (6 ounces) shredded Swiss cheese, divided
1 cup (4 ounces) shredded Muenster cheese, divided
3 tablespoons toasted sliced almonds
Chopped fresh parsley, optional

Preheat oven to 325°F. Melt butter in large skillet over medium-high heat. Add onion and mushrooms; cook and stir until tender. Add chicken, wine, tarragon, salt and pepper; bring to a boil. Reduce heat to low; simmer 10 minutes, stirring occasionally.

Curl each lasagna noodle half into a circle; place in 13×9-inch baking dish. Using slotted spoon, fill center of lasagna rings with chicken. To wine mixture remaining in skillet, add cream cheese, heavy cream, sour cream, ¾ cup Swiss cheese and ½ cup Muenster cheese. Heat until cheeses melt, stirring frequently. *(Do not boil.)* Pour over lasagna rings. Sprinkle remaining cheeses and almonds on top. Bake 35 minutes or until hot and bubbly; sprinkle with parsley. Garnish as desired.  *Makes 6 servings*

*Favorite recipe from **Southeast United Dairy Industry Association, Inc.***

*Cheesy Chicken Roll-Ups*

*Picante Pesto Linguine*

## Chicken Marsala

8 ounces linguine, cooked and drained
¼ cup all-purpose flour
½ teaspoon salt
¼ teaspoon pepper
4 boneless skinless chicken breasts
2 tablespoons WESSON® Vegetable Oil
2 cups sliced fresh mushrooms
½ teaspoon minced fresh garlic
1 can (14½ ounces) HUNT'S® Whole Tomatoes, cut up, undrained
1 can (8 ounces) HUNT'S® Tomato Sauce
⅓ cup Marsala wine
½ teaspoon dried basil leaves, crushed
Grated Parmesan cheese, optional

In large plastic bag, combine flour, salt and pepper. Add chicken; shake to coat thoroughly. Heat oil in large skillet over medium heat. Add chicken. Cook 5 minutes on each side or until browned on both sides and no longer pink in center; remove from skillet. Set aside. In same skillet, cook and stir mushrooms and garlic 2 to 3 minutes. Stir in tomatoes, tomato sauce, wine and basil. Reduce heat to low; simmer, uncovered, 5 minutes, stirring occasionally. Return chicken to skillet; spoon sauce over chicken. Simmer, uncovered, an additional 5 minutes, turning chicken once during cooking. Serve over hot linguine. Sprinkle with Parmesan cheese, if desired.     *Makes 4 servings*

## Picante Pesto Linguine

1 pound linguine *or* other favorite pasta, cooked and drained
1⅔ cups firmly packed fresh spinach leaves
¾ cup PACE® Picante Sauce, divided
⅔ cup (about 3 ounces) grated Parmesan cheese
½ cup pecans, coarsely chopped
⅓ cup vegetable oil
1 clove garlic, minced

Combine spinach, ¼ cup picante sauce, cheese, pecans, oil and garlic in food processor or blender container; cover. Process until smooth. Transfer to small bowl; stir in remaining ½ cup picante sauce. Combine spinach mixture with hot pasta in large bowl; mix lightly. Sprinkle with additional chopped pecans and serve with additional picante sauce, if desired.
*Makes 4 to 6 servings*

# Microwave Shrimp Pasta Primavera

8 ounces of your favorite pasta shape, cooked and drained
1 can (13¾ ounces) chicken broth
2 tablespoons cornstarch
2 tablespoons vegetable oil
1 large onion, cut into thin wedges
1 large clove garlic, minced
2 medium carrots, julienned
1 medium red bell pepper, julienned
½ cup snow peas, cut in half diagonally
2 tablespoons lemon juice
2 teaspoons dried basil leaves *or*
    2 tablespoons chopped fresh basil leaves
⅛ teaspoon crushed red pepper flakes, optional
¾ pound medium shrimp, peeled and deveined

In small bowl, gradually add broth to cornstarch, mixing until well blended. In 2-quart microwave-safe casserole or bowl, combine oil, onion, garlic, carrots, red bell pepper, snow peas, lemon juice, basil and crushed red pepper; cover. Microwave on HIGH 3 minutes or until vegetables are crisp-tender, stirring after 2 minutes. Stir cornstarch mixture; add to vegetables, stirring to coat. Cover. Microwave 5 minutes or until slightly thickened, stirring after 3 minutes. Add shrimp; cover. Microwave on HIGH 2 minutes, stirring after 1 minute. Let stand 2 minutes. Spoon shrimp mixture over hot pasta; toss lightly to coat.

*Makes 4 servings*

*Favorite recipe from* **National Pasta Association**

# Pasta, Chicken & Broccoli Pesto Toss

4 ounces (about 2 cups) vegetable spiral pasta, cooked and drained
2 cups cubed, cooked chicken *or* turkey breast meat
2 cups small broccoli florets, cooked until crisp-tender and cooled
1½ cups (6 ounces) SARGENTO® Fancy Supreme Shredded Low Moisture Part-Skim Mozzarella Cheese
⅔ cup lightly packed fresh basil leaves
2 cloves garlic
1 cup mayonnaise
1 tablespoon lemon juice
½ teaspoon salt
½ cup (2 ounces) SARGENTO® Fancy Supreme Shredded Parmesan Cheese
½ cup pine nuts *or* coarsely chopped walnuts, toasted

Combine pasta, chicken, broccoli and mozzarella cheese in large bowl. Place basil and garlic in blender or food processor container; cover. Blend until finely chopped. Add mayonnaise, lemon juice and salt; blend thoroughly. Stir in Parmesan cheese. Add to pasta mixture; toss to coat. Stir in pine nuts. Serve immediately or cover and refrigerate. For maximum flavor, remove from refrigerator 30 minutes before serving; toss gently.

*Makes 8 servings*

# Spinach-Stuffed Manicotti

8 manicotti shells, cooked and drained
1½ teaspoons olive oil
1 teaspoon minced fresh garlic
1½ cups canned *or* fresh tomatoes, chopped
1 teaspoon dried rosemary leaves, crushed
1 teaspoon dried sage leaves, crushed
1 teaspoon dried oregano leaves, crushed
1 teaspoon dried thyme leaves, crushed
1 package (10 ounces) frozen spinach, cooked, drained and squeezed dry
4 ounces ricotta cheese
1 slice whole wheat bread, torn into coarse crumbs
2 egg whites, slightly beaten

Preheat oven to 350°F. Heat oil in small saucepan over medium heat. Add garlic; cook and stir until lightly browned. Stir in tomatoes, rosemary, sage, oregano and thyme. Reduce heat to low; simmer 10 minutes, stirring occasionally.

Combine spinach, cheese and bread crumbs in medium bowl. Fold in egg whites. Stuff manicotti with spinach mixture. Spoon ⅓ of sauce into 13×9-inch baking dish. Arrange manicotti over sauce; cover with remaining sauce. Cover with foil. Bake 30 minutes or until hot and bubbly. Garnish as desired.

*Makes 4 servings*

*Favorite recipe* **National Pasta Association**

# Seafood over Angel Hair Pasta

8 ounces angel hair pasta (capellini), cooked and drained
¼ cup WISH-BONE® Italian Dressing
¼ cup chopped shallots *or* onions
1 cup thinly sliced carrots
1 cup thinly sliced snow peas (about 4 ounces)
1 cup chicken broth
¼ cup sherry
½ pound medium shrimp, peeled and deveined (with tails on)
½ pound sea scallops
8 mussels, well scrubbed
¼ cup whipping *or* heavy cream
2 tablespoons all-purpose flour
Salt and pepper

In 12-inch skillet, heat Italian dressing over medium-high heat. Add shallots; cook and stir 2 minutes. Add carrots and snow peas; cook and stir 2 minutes. Add broth, then sherry. Bring to a boil; add shrimp, scallops and mussels. Simmer, uncovered, 3 minutes or until seafood is done and mussel shells open. (Discard any unopened shells.) Stir in cream blended with flour. Cook over medium heat, stirring occasionally, 2 minutes or until sauce is slightly thickened. Season with salt and pepper to taste. Serve over hot pasta. Sprinkle with freshly ground pepper, if desired.

*Makes about 4 main-dish servings*

• Also terrific with WISH-BONE® Robusto Italian, Blended Italian or Lite Classic Dijon Vinaigrette Dressing.

*Spinach-Stuffed Manicotti*

*Turkey-Stuffed Pasta Italiano*

## Turkey-Stuffed Pasta Italiano

1 pound ground California Turkey
1 cup finely chopped onion
1 cup shredded peeled eggplant
2 cloves garlic, minced
  Salt and black pepper
1 can (28 ounces) tomatoes, undrained
1 can (8 ounces) tomato sauce
1 cup red wine *or* water
1 teaspoon garlic salt
1 teaspoon dried oregano leaves,
  crushed
1 teaspoon dried basil leaves, crushed
½ teaspoon dried tarragon leaves,
  crushed
½ teaspoon crushed red pepper
1 package (12 ounces) jumbo pasta
  shells
½ cup (2 ounces) grated Parmesan
  cheese
¾ cup (3 ounces) shredded mozzarella
  cheese

In large non-stick skillet over medium heat, brown turkey with onion, eggplant and garlic, stirring occasionally to separate meat; drain. Season with salt and black pepper to taste; set aside. In small saucepan over low heat, combine tomatoes, tomato sauce, wine and seasonings. Bring to a boil. Reduce heat to low; simmer 15 minutes, stirring occasionally. Meanwhile, cook pasta shells according to package directions; drain. In large bowl, combine turkey mixture, Parmesan cheese and ½ of the tomato sauce mixture; spoon into shells. Place in 13×9-inch baking dish. Spoon remaining sauce mixture over shells; sprinkle with mozzarella cheese. Bake at 350°F, 30 minutes or until hot and bubbly.          *Makes 8 to 10 servings*

**Note:** Shells can be stuffed ahead of time, covered and refrigerated. Top with sauce and mozzarella cheese just before baking. Increase baking time 8 to 10 minutes.

*Favorite recipe from* **California Poultry Industry Federation**

## Cajun Shrimp Fettuccine

4 to 6 ounces fettuccine, cooked and
  drained
½ pound medium shrimp, shelled and
  deveined
2 slices bacon, finely chopped
2 cloves garlic, minced
⅛ to ¼ teaspoon ground red pepper, *or*
  to taste
1 can (14½ ounces) DEL MONTE®
  Cajun *or* Original Style Stewed
  Tomatoes*
1 can (8 ounces) DEL MONTE®
  Tomato Sauce
1 green pepper, cut into thin strips

Cut shrimp in half lengthwise; set aside. In large skillet, cook bacon over medium-high heat until crisp; drain. Add garlic and ground red pepper; cook and stir 1 minute. Stir in tomatoes and tomato sauce. Reduce heat to medium; simmer, uncovered, 10 minutes, stirring occasionally. Add shrimp and green pepper; simmer an additional 2 to 3 minutes until shrimp are tender. Serve over hot fettuccine.        *Makes 4 servings*

**Prep time:** 10 minutes
**Cook time:** 20 minutes

*If using Original Style Tomatoes, add a pinch each of ground cinnamon, ground cloves and ground red pepper to tomato mixture; continue as directed.

**Hint:** After deveining shrimp, rinse thoroughly under cold water; drain.

*Scallops with Vermicelli*

# Scallops with Vermicelli

12 ounces vermicelli, cooked and
   drained
 1 pound bay scallops
 2 tablespoons fresh lemon juice
 2 tablespoons chopped fresh parsley
 2 tablespoons olive oil
 2 tablespoons butter, divided
 1 onion, chopped
 1 clove garlic, minced
1½ cups canned Italian tomatoes, cut
   up, undrained
 2 tablespoons chopped fresh basil
   leaves *or* ½ teaspoon dried basil
   leaves, crushed
 ¼ teaspoon dried oregano leaves,
   crushed
 ¼ teaspoon dried thyme leaves,
   crushed
 2 tablespoons heavy cream
   Dash ground nutmeg

Rinse scallops. Combine scallops, lemon juice and parsley in shallow glass dish. Cover; marinate in refrigerator while preparing sauce.

Heat oil and 1 tablespoon butter in large skillet over medium-high heat. Add onion and garlic; cook and stir until tender. Stir in tomatoes, basil, oregano and thyme. Reduce heat to low. Cover; simmer 30 minutes, stirring occasionally.

Drain scallops. Melt remaining 1 tablespoon butter in another large skillet over medium heat. Add scallops; cook and stir until scallops are opaque, about 2 minutes. Add cream, nutmeg and tomato mixture.

Pour sauce over hot vermicelli in large bowl; toss gently to coat. Garnish as desired.        *Makes 4 servings*

*Favorite recipe from **New Jersey Department of Agriculture***

**GOOD ENOUGH FOR GUESTS    181**

# Angel Hair Pasta Soufflé

Butter for pan
Plain dry bread crumbs

Sauce:

   2 tablespoons sweet butter
   2 tablespoons vegetable oil
   ½ pound ground veal
   1 large onion, chopped
   ½ cup dry white wine
   1 cup chicken broth
   1 tablespoon tomato paste
   ½ cup heavy cream

Souffle:

   1 pound angel hair pasta, cooked and
      drained
   2 eggs, slightly beaten
   1 cup POLLY-O® Ricotta Cheese
   2 slices prosciutto, finely chopped
   4 egg whites
   4 ounces POLLY-O® Mozzarella
      Cheese, sliced
   4 ounces POLLY-O® Smoked
      Mozzarella Cheese, sliced
   Grated Parmesan cheese

1. Preheat oven to 375°F. Butter 10-inch springform pan; sprinkle inside with bread crumbs.

2. Melt 2 tablespoons butter with oil in large skillet over medium heat. Add veal and onion; cook until veal is browned, stirring occasionally to separate meat. Add wine. Reduce heat to low; simmer until wine evaporates, stirring occasionally.

3. Gradually add broth to tomato paste, stirring until well blended; pour over meat. Cook, uncovered, 15 minutes or until sauce is reduced in volume. Stir in cream. Bring to a boil over medium heat; simmer 5 minutes. Remove from heat.

4. Combine two eggs, ricotta and prosciutto. Add to pasta; mix lightly. Add ¼ of the sauce; toss lightly to coat.

5. Beat egg whites until stiff; fold into pasta mixture.

6. Layer ½ of the pasta mixture in prepared dish; cover with mozzarella cheeses and ½ of the sauce. Sprinkle with Parmesan cheese. Repeat layers of pasta, sauce and Parmesan cheese. Bake 25 to 30 minutes until set. Let stand 10 minutes before removing from pan; cut into wedges. *Makes 6 to 8 servings*

# Greek Lamb Sauté with Mostaccioli

½ (1-pound) package CREAMETTE®
   Mostaccioli, cooked and drained
1 tablespoon olive *or* vegetable oil
1 medium green pepper, chopped
1 medium onion, chopped
1 medium eggplant, peeled, seeded
   and cut into 1-inch cubes
2 cloves garlic, minced
½ pound lean boneless lamb, cut into
   ¾-inch cubes
2 fresh tomatoes, peeled, seeded and
   chopped
¼ teaspoon ground nutmeg
¼ cup (1 ounce) grated Parmesan
   cheese

In large skillet, heat oil over medium-high heat. Add green pepper, onion, eggplant and garlic; cook and stir until crisp-tender. Add lamb; cook until tender, stirring occasionally. Stir in tomatoes and nutmeg; heat thoroughly. Add to hot mostaccioli with Parmesan cheese; toss lightly. Serve immediately. Refrigerate leftovers.

*Makes 6 to 8 servings*

*Sweet Apricots and Roasted Chicken in Pasta*

Cook pasta according to package directions. Meanwhile, in medium saucepan over medium heat, bring half-and-half to a boil, stirring frequently. Reduce heat to low; simmer 4 minutes. Add apricots, chicken, onions and butter; simmer an additional 2 minutes. Pour over hot drained pasta in large bowl; toss gently to coat. Season with salt and pepper to taste. Serve immediately. *Makes 4 servings*

*Favorite recipe from **California Apricot Advisory Board***

## Tortellini with Creamy Pesto

    2 cups loosely packed fresh basil
        leaves
    1 cup loosely packed fresh parsley
    1/3 cup WISH-BONE® Italian Dressing
    1/2 cup whipping *or* heavy cream
    1/4 cup (1 ounce) grated Parmesan
        cheese
    1/8 teaspoon pepper
    2 packages (15 ounces *each*) frozen
        tortellini, cooked and drained

In food processor or blender container, place basil and parsley; cover. Process until blended. While processing, gradually add Italian dressing, cream, cheese and pepper through feed cap until blended. Add to hot tortellini; toss lightly to coat. Serve with additional cheese and season with salt and additional pepper to taste, if desired. Garnish with toasted pine nuts, if desired. *Makes about 6 servings*

**Variation:** Substitute 1 package (1 pound) fettuccine noodles for tortellini. Increase grated Parmesan cheese to 1/2 cup.

• Also terrific with WISH-BONE® Robusto Italian, Blended Italian or Lite Italian Dressing.

## Sweet Apricots and Roasted Chicken in Pasta

    1 package (10 ounces) bow tie noodles
 1 1/2 cups half-and-half
    1 can (17 ounces) California apricot
        halves, drained and quartered
    6 ounces roasted chicken breast,
        chopped
    1/3 cup chopped green onions with tops
    2 tablespoons unsalted butter
        Salt and pepper

# An Early Spring Pasta

12 ounces Linguine, cooked and
    drained
1 cup Oriental Dressing (recipe
    follows)
8 ounces cooked turkey breast, cut
    into julienne strips
4 ounces carrots, cut into julienne
    strips
4 ounces asparagus, diagonally sliced
    into 1-inch pieces
4 ounces spinach, chopped

Bring Oriental Dressing to a boil in large
saucepan over high heat. Add turkey,
carrots, asparagus and spinach. Reduce
heat to medium; simmer 2 to 3 minutes.
Pour over hot linguine; toss gently.

*Makes 4 to 6 servings*

## Oriental Dressing

1 large onion, sliced
1¼ cups water, divided
¼ cup *each* soy sauce and rice vinegar
1 tablespoon *each* garlic and ginger
    root, minced
1 tablespoon *each* sesame oil and
    lemon juice
1½ teaspoons *each* sugar and pepper
1½ teaspoons hot pepper sauce
2 tablespoons cornstarch

Preheat oven to 400°F. Spread onions in
large baking pan. Bake 15 minutes or
until edges of onions are browned. Place
in food processor container; cover.
Process until smooth. Place onions and
all remaining ingredients *except* ¼ cup
water and cornstarch in saucepan. Bring
to a boil over medium-high heat.
Combine cornstarch and remaining ¼
cup water in small bowl. Add to onion
mixture. Bring to a boil, stirring
constantly. Reduce heat to low; simmer
2 to 3 minutes, stirring occasionally.

*Favorite recipe from **National Pasta Association***

# Chicken Ragout with Orzo

¾ cup (4 ounces) orzo, cooked and
    drained
1 tablespoon olive oil
⅔ cup chopped onion
1 can (4 ounces) mushrooms, drained
⅓ cup celery slices
⅓ cup finely chopped carrot
¼ pound Italian sausage, casing
    removed, crumbled
4 OSCAR MAYER® Bacon Slices,
    chopped
1½ pounds boneless skinless chicken
    breasts, cut into ½-inch pieces
1 bay leaf
1 large clove garlic, minced
¾ cup dry Marsala wine
1 can (14½ ounces) tomatoes, cut up,
    undrained
1 cup chicken broth
⅛ teaspoon ground cloves
1 container (8 ounces)
    PHILADELPHIA BRAND® Soft
    Cream Cheese with Olives &
    Pimento

• Heat oil in Dutch oven over medium-
high heat. Add onions, mushrooms,
celery, carrots, sausage and bacon; cook
and stir until vegetables are tender and
sausage is browned, about 5 minutes.

• Add chicken, bay leaf and garlic; cook,
stirring occasionally, 4 minutes.

• Add wine. Bring to a boil; reduce heat
to low. Simmer 10 to 15 minutes or until
only slight amount of liquid remains.

• Stir in tomatoes, broth and cloves.
Bring to a boil over medium-high heat;
reduce heat to low. Simmer 20 minutes
or until slightly thickened, stirring
occasionally. Remove from heat.

• Stir in cream cheese and orzo.

*Makes 6 servings*

**Prep time:** 30 minutes
**Cook time:** 40 minutes

*Fusilli Pizzaiola*

Heat oil in large skillet over medium-high heat. Add mushrooms, bell peppers, onions, garlic and shallots; cook and stir until tender. Stir in tomatoes, basil, oregano and crushed red pepper. Season with salt and pepper to taste. Bring to a boil. Reduce heat to low; simmer 20 minutes, stirring occasionally. Meanwhile, cook pasta according to package directions; drain. Place hot pasta on serving plates; top with sauce. Sprinkle with parsley.

*Makes 6 to 8 servings*

*Favorite recipe from* **National Pasta Association**

## Fusilli Pizzaiola

¼ cup olive oil
8 ounces mushrooms, sliced
1 large red bell pepper, chopped
1 large green bell pepper, chopped
1 large yellow bell pepper, chopped
10 green onions with tops, chopped
1 large onion, chopped
8 cloves garlic, coarsely chopped
3 large shallots, chopped
4 cups canned *or* fresh tomatoes, chopped
½ cup chopped fresh basil leaves *or* 2 teaspoons dried basil leaves, crushed
2 tablespoons chopped fresh oregano leaves *or* 1 teaspoon dried oregano leaves, crushed
   Dash crushed red pepper
   Salt and pepper
1 package (1 pound) Fusilli *or* Spaghetti
2 tablespoons chopped fresh parsley, optional

## Pasta Primavera

8 ounces fettuccine noodles, cooked and drained
½ cup WISH-BONE® Italian Dressing
¼ cup finely chopped green onions with tops
2 medium tomatoes, chopped
4 cups Assorted Fresh Vegetables*
¼ cup dry white wine
1 tablespoon finely chopped fresh basil leaves, optional
¾ teaspoon salt
⅛ teaspoon pepper

In large skillet over medium heat, combine Italian dressing and onions; cook and stir 1 minute. Add tomatoes and Assorted Fresh Vegetables; cook, stirring occasionally, 5 minutes or until vegetables are crisp-tender. Stir in wine, basil, salt and pepper; cook 2 minutes. Add to hot fettuccine; toss lightly to coat. Sprinkle with grated Parmesan cheese, if desired.

*Makes about 4 main-dish servings*

**\*Assorted Fresh Vegetables:** Use any combination of the following to equal 4 cups: asparagus cut into 2-inch pieces; broccoli florets; sliced carrots, zucchini or yellow squash.

• Also terrific with WISH-BONE® Robusto Italian, Blended Italian or Lite Italian Dressing.

## Shrimp Fettuccine

8 ounces fettuccine, cooked and
    drained
1½ cups prepared HIDDEN VALLEY
    RANCH® Original Ranch® Salad
    Dressing
¼ cup sour cream
¼ cup (1 ounce) grated Parmesan
    cheese
½ pound peeled and deveined shrimp,
    cooked
½ cup cooked peas

In small bowl, combine salad dressing,
sour cream and Parmesan cheese. In
large bowl, toss hot fettuccine with
dressing mixture, shrimp and peas.
Divide equally among 4 plates. Sprinkle
with additional Parmesan cheese, if
desired. *Makes 4 servings*

## Pasta Tossed with Blue Cheese Sauce

*A quick, yet elegant recipe using
leftover ham.*

8 ounces fettuccine, cooked and
    drained
2 tablespoons PARKAY® Margarine
1 cup coarsely chopped leeks
1 cup coarsely chopped pecans
1½ cups ham strips
¼ cup Madeira wine *or* chicken broth
1 clove garlic, minced
1 container (8 ounces)
    PHILADELPHIA BRAND® Soft
    Cream Cheese
2 tablespoons milk
½ cup (2 ounces) KRAFT® Blue Cheese
    Crumbles

• Melt margarine in medium skillet over
medium-high heat. Add leeks and
pecans; cook and stir until leeks are
tender. Add ham; heat thoroughly.

• Cook wine and garlic in medium
saucepan over low heat 1 minute. Add
cream cheese and milk; stir until cream
cheese is melted. Remove from heat; stir
in blue cheese.

• Toss all ingredients together. Serve
immediately. *Makes 4 servings*

**Prep time:** 15 minutes
**Cook time:** 15 minutes
**Variation:** Substitute OSCAR MAYER®
Smoked Cooked Ham Slices, cut into
strips, for ham strips.
**Microwave:** Place margarine, leeks and
pecans in 1-quart casserole. Cover with
plastic wrap; vent. • Microwave on
HIGH 3 to 5 minutes or until leeks are
tender, stirring after 2 minutes. Stir in
ham. • Microwave on HIGH 2 to 3
minutes or until thoroughly heated.
• Microwave wine and garlic in 1-quart
bowl on HIGH 1 to 2 minutes or until
hot. Stir in cream cheese and milk.
• Microwave on HIGH 2 to 3 minutes or
until cream cheese is melted, stirring
every minute. Stir in blue cheese. Toss
all ingredients together. Serve
immediately.

*Shrimp Fettuccine*

## Shrimp Primavera on Pasta

8 ounces fettuccine
2 tablespoons CRISCO® Shortening
2 cloves garlic, minced
½ pound peeled and deveined medium shrimp (defrosted and drained if frozen)
2 cups thinly sliced zucchini
1 cup sliced fresh mushrooms
½ cup sliced green onions with tops
½ teaspoon dried basil leaves, crushed
¼ teaspoon salt
⅛ teaspoon black pepper
1 cup cherry tomatoes, halved
¼ red or green pepper, cut into narrow strips about 2 inches long
½ cup sour cream

1. Cook fettuccine in boiling salted water according to package directions. (1 tablespoon CRISCO® may be added to cooking water to help keep fettuccine from sticking together.)

2. While fettuccine cooks, melt 2 tablespoons CRISCO® in large skillet over medium-high heat. Add garlic; cook and stir 1 minute or until lightly browned.

3. Add shrimp, zucchini, mushrooms, onions and seasonings; stir-fry 5 minutes or until zucchini is crisp-tender and shrimp turn pink. Add tomatoes and red pepper strips. Cook and stir 2 minutes.

4. Drain fettuccine, rinse with hot water and drain again. Add sour cream; toss lightly to coat. Place on large warm platter; top with shrimp mixture. Serve immediately. Season with additional salt and pepper to taste, if desired.

*Makes 4 servings*

## Linguine with Red Seafood Sauce

12 ounces linguine, cooked and drained
3 tablespoons olive or vegetable oil
1 large onion, finely chopped (about 1 cup)
2 cloves garlic, minced
½ cup dry white wine
2 cups (16 ounces) canned, bottled or homemade meatless spaghetti sauce
2 tablespoons chopped fresh parsley
1 bay leaf, crumbled
2 teaspoons dried basil leaves, crushed
¾ teaspoon TABASCO® pepper sauce
½ teaspoon salt
¾ pound shelled and deveined medium shrimp (thawed if frozen)
¾ pound sea scallops, quartered

In 4-quart heavy saucepan or Dutch oven, heat oil over medium-high heat. Add onion and garlic; cook and stir until tender. Stir in wine. Reduce heat to low; simmer until reduced to 3 tablespoons. Stir in spaghetti sauce, parsley, bay leaf, basil, TABASCO® sauce and salt. Bring to a boil over medium-high heat; reduce heat to low. Simmer, covered, 10 minutes, stirring occasionally. Add shrimp and scallops; cover. Simmer 4 to 5 minutes, until seafood is just barely firm. Add to hot linguine in large serving bowl; toss lightly to coat. Serve immediately. *Makes 4 servings*

*Sweet Garlic with Chicken Pasta*

Heat oil in large skillet over medium-high heat. Add garlic; cook and stir until lightly browned. Add mushrooms, tomatoes, green onions and crushed red pepper; cook and stir 2 minutes. Add broth; simmer mixture to reduce slightly. Add chicken, noodles and ½ of the cilantro; heat thoroughly, stirring occasionally. Sprinkle with remaining cilantro.     *Makes 6 to 8 servings*

*Favorite recipe from **National Pasta Association***

## Pasta & Veal Naples Style

½ (1-pound) package CREAMETTE®
   Linguine, cooked and drained
2 eggs
2 tablespoons water
½ teaspoon garlic salt
8 thin veal cutlets (about 1 pound)
2 cups plain dry bread crumbs
½ cup butter *or* margarine
2 tablespoons olive oil
1 jar (26 ounces) CLASSICO® Di
   Napoli (Tomato & Basil) *or* Di
   Parma (Four Cheese) *or* Di Sicilia
   (Ripe Olives & Mushrooms) Pasta
   Sauce
Grated Parmesan cheese *or* shredded
   mozzarella cheese

In medium bowl, beat eggs, water and garlic salt until well blended. Dip veal into crumbs then into egg mixture; dip into crumbs second time. In large skillet, over medium heat, melt butter with oil. Add veal; cook until browned on both sides and no longer pink in center. In medium saucepan, heat pasta sauce. Arrange veal on hot linguine; top with pasta sauce. Garnish with cheese. Refrigerate leftovers.

*Makes 4 servings*

## Sweet Garlic with Chicken Pasta

1 package (1 pound) bow tie noodles,
   cooked and drained
5½ tablespoons olive oil
8 cloves garlic, minced
1½ pounds shiitake mushrooms, sliced
2 cups fresh plum tomatoes, finely
   chopped
1 cup chopped green onions with tops
1 teaspoon crushed red pepper
2 cups chicken broth
1½ pounds chicken breasts, grilled,
   skinned, boned and finely
   chopped
4 ounces cilantro, chopped, divided

# PASTA POTPOURRI

## Spicy Ravioli and Cheese

*This spicy pasta dish is perfect for those who like their sauce with a little heat.*

1 package (8 or 9 ounces) fresh *or* frozen ravioli, cooked and drained
1 medium red pepper, thinly sliced
1 medium green pepper, thinly sliced
1 medium yellow pepper, thinly sliced
1 tablespoon olive *or* vegetable oil
½ teaspoon LAWRY'S® Seasoned Salt
¼ teaspoon LAWRY'S® Garlic Powder with Parsley
¼ teaspoon sugar
1½ cups chunky salsa, divided
4 ounces mozzarella cheese, thinly sliced
2 green onions with tops, sliced

Place peppers in shallow baking dish; sprinkle with oil, Seasoned Salt, Garlic Powder with Parsley and sugar. Broil 15 minutes or until peppers are tender and browned, turning once.

Pour ½ of salsa into 8-inch square baking dish. Cover with alternating layers of peppers, ravioli, cheese and onions. Top with remaining salsa; cover with foil. Bake at 350°F, 15 to 20 minutes or until thoroughly heated and cheese is melted.          *Makes 4 to 6 servings*

**Presentation:** Serve as either a side dish or as a main dish.

**Hint:** You may also prepare this recipe in individual casseroles.

## Broccoli Three-Cheese Bake

7 ounces MUELLER'S® Pasta Curls™, cooked and drained
2 tablespoons MAZOLA® Margarine
1 large onion, chopped
2 cloves garlic, minced,
1 package (10 ounces) frozen chopped broccoli, thawed and drained
1 container (15 ounces) part-skim ricotta cheese
1½ cups (6 ounces) shredded part-skim mozzarella cheese, divided
¼ cup (1 ounce) grated Parmesan cheese
½ teaspoon salt
½ teaspoon dried basil leaves, crushed
¼ teaspoon dried oregano leaves, crushed
3 eggs
½ cup skim milk

In large skillet, melt margarine over medium heat. Add onion and garlic; cook and stir 8 minutes or until tender. Remove from heat. In 8-inch square baking dish, combine onion mixture, pasta, broccoli, ricotta, 1 cup mozzarella, Parmesan, salt, basil and oregano; mix well. In small bowl, beat eggs and milk until blended; pour over pasta mixture. Sprinkle remaining mozzarella over top. Bake at 350°F, 30 to 35 minutes, until thoroughly heated.          *Makes 6 servings*

*Spicy Ravioli and Cheese*

## Beef-Filled Macaroni Shells

1 package (12 ounces) large *or* jumbo
    macaroni shells
1½ pounds ground beef
⅓ cup finely chopped onion
¾ cup ketchup
1 tablespoon prepared mustard
¾ teaspoon chili powder
¾ teaspoon garlic salt
    CRISCO® Shortening for deep
    frying

1. Cook macaroni shells according to package directions, using maximum cooking time. Drain; rinse with cold water. Arrange on paper towels to dry.

2. While shells are cooking, brown ground beef with onion in large skillet over medium heat; drain. Stir in ketchup, mustard, chili powder and garlic salt. Heat thoroughly, stirring occasionally.

3. Heat CRISCO® to 365°F in deep saucepan or deep fryer.

4. Add several shells at a time; fry 2 minutes or until golden, turning once during frying. Drain on paper towels.

5. As shells are fried, spoon about 1 tablespoon warm filling into each fried shell. Garnish with sweet pickle slices, if desired. Serve warm.

*Makes 3 to 5 dozen appetizers*
*(depending on size of shells used)*

**Make ahead:** Fill shells as directed; cool. Cover and refrigerate. When ready to serve, preheat oven to 400°F. Arrange shells on baking sheet. Bake, uncovered, 5 minutes or until thoroughly heated.

*Pasta with Sunflower Kernels*

## Pasta with Sunflower Kernels

8 ounces tomato, spinach *or* plain
    spaghetti, cooked and drained
½ cup sunflower oil
3 parsley sprigs, chopped
3 cloves garlic, minced
1 teaspoon grated lemon peel
½ teaspoon salt
½ teaspoon pepper
⅔ cup (about 3 ounces) grated
    Parmesan cheese
½ cup roasted sunflower kernels

Heat sunflower oil in small skillet over medium-high heat. Add parsley, garlic and lemon peel; cook and stir 1 minute. Add salt and pepper. Pour over hot pasta. Add Parmesan cheese and sunflower kernels; toss lightly.

*Makes 4 servings*

Favorite recipe from **National Sunflower Association**

# Santa Fe Pasta

**2 cups (8 ounces) mostaccioli noodles,
    cooked and drained**
**¾ pound VELVEETA® Pasteurized
    Process Cheese Spread, divided**
**2 tablespoons milk**
**1 can (8¾ ounces) whole kernel corn,
    drained**
**1 can (8 ounces) kidney beans, drained**
**1 can (4 ounces) chopped green
    chilies, drained**
**½ teaspoon chili powder**
**1 cup corn chips**

• Heat oven to 350°F.

• Cube ½ pound process cheese spread.
Combine with milk in large saucepan;
stir over low heat until process cheese
spread is melted.

• Add corn, beans, noodles, chilies and
chili powder; mix lightly. Spoon mixture
into 1½-quart casserole.

• Bake 20 minutes. Top with chips and
remaining process cheese spread, sliced.
Continue baking until process cheese
spread begins to melt.

*Makes 6 servings*

**Prep time:** 15 minutes
**Baking time:** 25 minutes

**Microwave:** • Cube ½ pound process
cheese spread. Combine with milk in 2-
quart microwave-safe bowl. Microwave
on HIGH 2 to 3 minutes or until process
cheese spread is melted, stirring after 2
minutes. • Stir in corn, beans, noodles,
chilies and chili powder; microwave on
HIGH 5 minutes, stirring every 2 minutes.
Top with chips and remaining process
cheese spread, sliced. • Microwave on
HIGH 2 minutes or until process cheese
spread begins to melt.

# Cheesy Orzo Bake

**⅔ cup chopped whole natural almonds,
    divided**
**1 cup cooked orzo (rice-shaped pasta)**
**2 tablespoons butter**
**2 cups chopped onions**
**2 large cloves garlic, minced**
**1 can (14½ ounces) stewed tomatoes**
**¾ cup milk**
**2 eggs, slightly beaten**
**⅓ cup (1½ ounces) grated Romano *or*
    Parmesan cheese**
**2 teaspoons dried basil leaves, crushed**
**1 teaspoon dried oregano leaves,
    crushed**
**2 cups (8 ounces) shredded Monterey
    Jack cheese, divided**

Spread almonds in single layer in
shallow baking pan. Bake at 350°F, 8 to
12 minutes or until lightly toasted,
stirring every 2 minutes. (*Or* spread
almonds in single layer on microwave-
safe plate or shallow glass baking dish.
Microwave on HIGH 3 to 5 minutes or
until lightly toasted, stirring every
minute.) Cool completely.

Melt butter in large ovenproof skillet
over medium-high heat. Add onion and
garlic; cook and stir until tender. Stir in
all remaining ingredients *except* ⅓ cup
almonds and ½ cup Monterey Jack
cheese. Bake at 375°F, 1 hour. Top with
reserved cheese and almonds. Continue
baking 5 minutes or until cheese is
melted and mixture is hot and bubbly.

*Makes 6 to 8 servings*

*Favorite recipe from **Almond Board of California***

*Fresh Tomato Pasta Andrew*

## Fresh Tomato Pasta Andrew

**4 ounces angel hair pasta, vermicelli**
   ***or* other thin pasta, cooked and**
   **drained**
**1 pound fresh tomatoes, cut into**
   **wedges**
**1 cup packed fresh basil leaves**
**2 cloves garlic**
**2 tablespoons olive oil**
**8 ounces Camenzola cheese *or***
   **6 ounces ripe Brie *plus* 2 ounces**
   **Stilton cheese, each cut into small**
   **pieces**
   **Salt and white pepper to taste**
   **Grated Parmesan cheese**

Place tomatoes, basil, garlic and oil in
food processor or blender container;
cover. Pulse on and off until ingredients
are coarsely chopped, but not smooth.
Combine tomato mixture and
Camenzola cheese in large bowl. Season
with salt and pepper to taste. Add pasta;
toss gently until cheese melts. Serve
with Parmesan cheese. Garnish as
desired.        *Makes 4 side-dish servings*
                *or 2 main-dish servings*

*Favorite recipe from **California Tomato Board***

## Seasoned Wontons

*Wonderful Oriental dumplings you can
prepare at home.*

**1 pound ground turkey *or* pork**
**6 green onions with tops, thinly**
   **sliced, divided**
**1 tablespoon soy sauce**
**¾ teaspoon LAWRY'S® Seasoned**
   **Pepper**
**½ teaspoon LAWRY'S® Garlic Powder**
   **with Parsley**
**¼ to ½ teaspoon hot pepper sauce**
**1 package (about 4 dozen) wonton**
   **skins**
**½ cup peanut *or* vegetable oil**
**1 tablespoon sesame seeds**
**½ teaspoon ground ginger**

In medium bowl, combine turkey, ¼ cup
green onions, soy sauce, Seasoned
Pepper, Garlic Powder with Parsley and
hot pepper sauce; blend well. In large
saucepan, bring 2 quarts water to a boil.
For each wonton, place 1 tablespoon
meat mixture in center of one wonton
skin. Wet edges with warm water. Top
with second wonton skin; press edges
together gently to seal. Repeat with
remaining meat mixture and wonton
skins. Cook wontons in boiling water in
batches, 8 to 10 minutes for each batch.
Remove with slotted spoon; place in ice
water at least 20 seconds. Drain and pat
dry completely. Refrigerate wontons at
least 10 minutes. In large skillet, heat oil
over high heat. Add cold, dried wontons;
cook until crisp and golden on both
sides. Remove and keep warm. Wipe out
excess oil from skillet. Add sesame
seeds, ginger and remaining green
onions to skillet; cook and stir over
medium heat until sesame seeds are
golden brown. Place wontons in serving
dish; sprinkle with sesame seed mixture.
                *Makes about 2 dozen*

**Presentation:** Serve with hot mustard,
sweet and sour sauce or plum sauce.

# Linguine Primavera

1 pound linguine, cooked and drained
½ cup BLUE BONNET® Margarine
2 cups broccoli flowerettes
1 cup julienne carrot strips
1 clove garlic, minced
1 teaspoon Italian seasoning
⅛ teaspoon ground black pepper
1 large tomato, coarsely chopped
¼ cup GREY POUPON® Dijon *or*
    Country Dijon Mustard
    Grated Parmesan cheese, optional

In large skillet, melt margarine over medium heat. Add broccoli, carrots, garlic, Italian seasoning and pepper; cook and stir 3 minutes. Stir in tomato and mustard; cook 1 minute or until vegetables are crisp-tender. Add to hot linguine; toss lightly to coat. Serve immediately with Parmesan cheese, if desired.    *Makes 8 servings*

**Microwave:** In 2-quart microwave-safe casserole, place margarine, broccoli, carrots, garlic, Italian seasoning and pepper; cover. Microwave on HIGH (100% power) 4 minutes, stirring after 2 minutes. Add tomato and mustard; cover. Microwave on HIGH 2 to 3 minutes, stirring after 1½ minutes. Continue as directed.

# Sesame Peanut Noodles with Green Onions

1 tablespoon peanut *or* vegetable oil
1 teaspoon minced fresh garlic
¼ cup peanut butter
1 teaspoon soy sauce
2¼ cups water
1 package LIPTON® Noodles & Sauce—Chicken Flavor
½ cup sliced green onions with tops
2 tablespoons toasted sesame seeds, divided

Heat oil in medium saucepan over medium heat. Add garlic; cook and stir 30 seconds. Add peanut butter and soy sauce; stir until peanut butter is melted. Add water; bring to a boil. Stir in noodles & chicken flavor sauce. Simmer, stirring frequently, 10 minutes or until noodles are tender. Stir in green onions and 1 tablespoon sesame seeds. Sprinkle with remaining 1 tablespoon sesame seeds.    *Makes about 4 servings*

**Microwave:** In 1½-quart microwave-safe casserole, combine oil and garlic. Microwave, uncovered, on HIGH (Full Power) 20 seconds. Stir in peanut butter and soy sauce. Microwave 30 seconds or until peanut butter is melted; stir. Add water and noodles & chicken flavor sauce. Microwave 12 minutes or until noodles are tender, stirring after 6 minutes. Stir in green onions and 1 tablespoon sesame seeds. Sprinkle with remaining 1 tablespoon sesame seeds.

*Sesame Peanut Noodles with Green Onions*

# Tortellini Kabobs

2 tablespoons olive oil
1 large clove garlic, minced
1 can (15 ounces) CONTADINA® Tomato Sauce
2 tablespoons rinsed capers
2 tablespoons chopped fresh basil leaves
1 teaspoon Italian seasoning
¼ teaspoon red pepper flakes
6 cups of the following kabob ingredients: cooked, drained meat- or cheese-filled tortellini, cocktail franks, cooked shrimp, whole button mushrooms, bell pepper chunks, cooked broccoli, cauliflowerets, onion pieces

Heat oil in medium saucepan over medium-high heat. Add garlic; cook and stir until lightly browned. Stir in tomato sauce, capers, basil, Italian seasoning and red pepper flakes. Bring to a boil. Reduce heat to low; simmer 5 to 10 minutes, stirring occasionally.

Combine kabob ingredients in medium bowl; cover with tomato sauce mixture. Marinate in refrigerator 15 minutes or longer, if desired, stirring occasionally. Place on skewers. Broil 5 inches from heat source until heated through, turning once during cooking and brushing with any remaining tomato sauce mixture.

*Makes 12 appetizer servings*

# Garden Pasta and Beans

¾ cup (3 ounces) small shell pasta, cooked and drained
2 tablespoons PROGRESSO® Olive Oil
2 cloves garlic, minced
1½ cups cubed zucchini
1 cup chopped celery
1 can (28 ounces) PROGRESSO® Peeled Tomatoes Italian Style, cut up, undrained
1 can (19 ounces) PROGRESSO® Cannellini Beans
½ cup (2 ounces) PROGRESSO® Grated Parmesan Cheese

1. In large skillet, heat olive oil over medium-high heat. Add garlic; cook and stir 30 seconds. Add zucchini and celery; cook and stir until crisp-tender, about 5 minutes.

2. Add tomatoes. Reduce heat to low; simmer 10 minutes, stirring occasionally.

3. Add pasta and beans; heat thoroughly, stirring occasionally. Stir in Parmesan cheese.     *Makes 4 servings*

**Prep time:** 25 minutes

**Microwave:** In 2-quart microwave-safe container, combine olive oil, garlic, zucchini and celery. Microwave on HIGH (100% power) 3 minutes. Add tomatoes, omitting ¼ cup of the tomato liquid. Microwave on HIGH 4 minutes; stir. Microwave on MEDIUM (50% power) 5 minutes, stirring every 2 minutes. Stir in pasta and beans. Microwave on HIGH 2 minutes. Stir in Parmesan cheese.

*Tortellini Kabobs*

## Macaroni Cabbage Fry

2 cups macaroni, cooked and drained
1/4 cup (1/2 stick) butter
1 small head cabbage (about
    1 1/2 pounds), finely chopped
1 small onion, finely chopped
1 clove garlic, minced
    Salt and pepper
1 can (10 3/4 ounces) cream of chicken
    soup
1 cup sour cream
1 cup (4 ounces) shredded Cheddar
    cheese, divided

In large skillet, melt butter over
medium-high heat. Add cabbage, onion
and garlic. Cook and stir until cabbage is
tender. Add hot macaroni; mix lightly.
Season with salt and pepper to taste.
Stir in chicken soup, sour cream and 1/2
cup cheese. Reduce heat to low; simmer
5 minutes. Top with remaining 1/2 cup
shredded cheese just before serving.
*Makes 4 servings*

*Favorite recipe from* **Southeast United Dairy Industry Association, Inc.**

## Bow Tie Kabobs

4 ounces Bow Tie Pasta, cooked and
    drained
1 medium onion, coarsely chopped
1/4 cup coarsely chopped green pepper
1/4 cup coarsely chopped red pepper
28 bay scallops
1 cup lime juice
    Salt and freshly ground black
        pepper to taste
1/2 cup chicken broth

Place onion, green pepper, red pepper
and scallops in shallow dish. Add lime
juice, salt and pepper; cover. Refrigerate
overnight, stirring occasionally; drain.
Heat chicken broth in large skillet over
medium heat. Add scallops. Cook and
stir 2 minutes or until scallops turn
white; drain. Cool. To assemble kabobs,
alternate scallops, vegetables and pasta
on wooden picks. Serve as hors
d'oeuvres. *Makes about 2 dozen*

*Favorite recipe from* **National Pasta Association**

## Broccoli and Cauliflower Linguine

1/4 cup olive oil
2 cups broccoli flowerets
2 cups cauliflowerets
3 cloves garlic, minced
1 can (28 ounces) CONTADINA®
    Italian-Style Tomatoes, cut up,
    undrained
1 teaspoon salt
1 teaspoon dried basil leaves, crushed
1/4 teaspoon red pepper flakes
3 bay leaves
1/2 cup dry sherry
1 pound linguine
1/2 cup (2 ounces) grated Romano
    cheese
1/2 cup finely chopped fresh cilantro

Heat oil in large skillet over medium-
high heat. Add broccoli, cauliflower and
garlic; cook and stir until crisp-tender,
about 3 minutes. Add tomatoes, salt,
basil, red pepper flakes and bay leaves.
Bring to a boil. Reduce heat to low;
simmer, uncovered, 20 minutes, stirring
occasionally. Meanwhile, cook pasta
according to package directions; drain.
Add sherry to sauce; simmer an
additional 3 minutes. Remove bay
leaves. Toss hot pasta with sauce, cheese
and cilantro. *Makes 8 servings*

*Springtime Noodles Alfredo*

## Fiesta Pasta

6 ounces (about 2½ cups)
   MUELLER'S® Ruffle Trio, cooked
   6 minutes and drained
1½ cups (6 ounces) shredded Monterey
   Jack cheese with jalapeño peppers
1 can (7 ounces) corn with sweet
   peppers, undrained
1 cup sour cream
⅓ cup HELLMANN'S® or BEST
   FOODS® Real Mayonnaise

In large bowl, combine pasta, cheese, *undrained* corn, sour cream and real mayonnaise. Spoon into greased 2-quart casserole. Bake at 350°F, 25 minutes or until hot and bubbly.

*Makes 4 servings*

**Microwave:** In 2-quart microwave-safe casserole, combine pasta, cheese, *undrained* corn, sour cream and real mayonnaise. Microwave on HIGH (100%) 4 minutes; stir. Microwave 3 to 4 minutes or until hot and bubbly.

## Springtime Noodles Alfredo

2 tablespoons IMPERIAL® Margarine
2 medium carrots, sliced
1 medium zucchini *or* yellow squash,
   thinly sliced
1 medium clove garlic, minced
1⅓ cups water
1 cup milk
1 package LIPTON® Noodles &
   Sauce—Alfredo
½ cup frozen peas, thawed, optional
1 tablespoon chopped fresh dill
   Pepper

In 1½-quart microwave-safe casserole, combine margarine, carrots, zucchini and garlic. Microwave, uncovered, on HIGH (Full Power) 6 minutes or until vegetables are tender, stirring after 3 minutes. Remove vegetables from casserole; set aside. Into casserole, stir water, milk and noodles & Alfredo sauce. Microwave on HIGH 11 minutes or until noodles are tender, stirring after 6 minutes. Stir in vegetables and dill. Season with pepper to taste. Cover and let stand 2 minutes. Sprinkle with grated Parmesan cheese, if desired.

*Makes about 4 servings*

**Variation:** Substitute ½ teaspoon dried dill weed for 1 tablespoon fresh dill.

**Conventional:** In large skillet, melt margarine over medium-high heat. Add carrots, zucchini and garlic; cook and stir 3 minutes or until vegetables are tender. Remove vegetables from skillet; set aside. Into skillet, add water and milk. Bring to a boil. Stir in noodles & Alfredo sauce and dill. Reduce heat to medium; simmer, stirring occasionally, 7 minutes or until noodles are tender. Stir in vegetables. Season with pepper to taste. Heat thoroughly, stirring occasionally. Sprinkle with grated Parmesan cheese, if desired.

## Vegetables Fromage

1½ cups (6 ounces) bow noodles,
    cooked and drained
2 cups julienne-cut carrots
2 cups julienne-cut zucchini
1 medium green pepper, cut into strips
1 clove garlic, minced
3 tablespoons PARKAY® Margarine
½ pound VELVEETA® Pasteurized
    Process Cheese Spread, cubed
¼ cup half-and-half
1 teaspoon dried basil leaves, crushed

• Stir-fry carrots, zucchini, peppers and garlic in margarine in large skillet until crisp-tender. Reduce heat to low.

• Add process cheese spread, half-and-half and basil; stir until process cheese spread is melted. Add hot noodles; mix lightly. Heat thoroughly, stirring occasionally.          *Makes 4 to 6 servings*

**Prep time:** 20 minutes
**Cooking time:** 10 minutes
**Variations:**
Substitute milk for half-and-half.

Substitute corkscrew noodles for bow noodles.

Substitute 2 tablespoons chopped fresh basil leaves for 1 teaspoon dried basil leaves.

**Microwave:** • In 2-quart microwave-safe bowl, microwave carrots, zucchini, peppers, garlic and margarine on HIGH 3 to 4 minutes or until vegetables are crisp-tender. • Stir in process cheese spread, half-and-half and basil. Microwave on HIGH 2 minutes or until process cheese spread is melted. Add noodles; mix lightly.

*Vegetables Fromage*

## Pasta Snacks

Assorted pasta (such as bow ties,
    wheels and spirals)
CRISCO® or CRISCO PURITAN®
    Oil for deep frying
Seasoned salt

In large saucepan, cook pasta in boiling salted water until tender, yet firm, about 10 minutes. (If desired, keep the various shapes of pasta separate while cooking and frying.) Drain pasta thoroughly. Fry pasta, a few pieces at a time, in deep CRISCO® heated to 365°F, 2 minutes or until pasta is golden. Drain on paper towels. Immediately sprinkle generously with seasoned salt. Serve warm or cool.

## Lasagna Rollettes in Crab Meat Sauce

1 pound Lasagna Noodles, cooked and drained
6 tablespoons butter *or* margarine
½ cup dry vermouth *or* chicken bouillon
6 tablespoons all-purpose flour
1½ teaspoons salt
½ teaspoon white pepper
½ teaspoon ground nutmeg
2 cups milk
4 cups light cream, divided
4 egg yolks
3 cans (7¾ ounces *each*) crab meat, drained, boned and flaked
2 teaspoons lemon juice
½ cup finely chopped fresh parsley

Cheese Filling:
2 containers (15 ounces *each*) ricotta cheese
1 teaspoon salt
½ teaspoon white pepper
1 cup (4 ounces) shredded mozzarella cheese
¼ cup freshly grated Parmesan cheese
⅓ cup finely chopped celery
¼ cup finely chopped pimientos

Melt butter in large saucepan over medium heat. Add vermouth. Cook 3 or 4 minutes, until vermouth is reduced by half. Blend in flour, 1½ teaspoons salt, ½ teaspoon pepper and nutmeg. Gradually add milk and 2 cups cream; cook over medium heat, stirring constantly, until sauce thickens. Gradually add remaining 2 cups cream to egg yolks, mixing until well blended. Stir into sauce. Cook, stirring constantly, until sauce is thickened again. Stir in crab meat, lemon juice and parsley.

To prepare cheese filling, beat ricotta cheese until smooth. Stir in 1 teaspoon salt, ½ teaspoon pepper, mozzarella cheese, Parmesan cheese, celery and pimientos.

Spread about ¼ cup cheese filling onto each noodle. Fold each noodle over 1 inch and continue folding, making a roll. Cut each roll crosswise in half. Pour 2 cups sauce into each of two 13×9-inch baking dishes. Place lasagna rollettes in baking dishes; pour remaining sauce over rollettes. Bake, uncovered, at 350°F, 20 minutes.          *Makes about 4 dozen*

**Note:** For main-dish servings, leave lasagna rolls uncut. Place, seam side down, in baking dishes. *Makes 6 to 8 main-dish servings*

*Favorite recipe from* **National Pasta Association**

## Seasoned Pasta Pilaf

2 tablespoons margarine *or* butter
½ cup chopped onion
2 cloves garlic, minced
1 cup uncooked long grain rice
1 cup (4 ounces) uncooked CREAMETTE® Fideos or broken Vermicelli
2½ cups water
1 tablespoon WYLER'S® or STEERO® Chicken-Flavor Instant Bouillon *or* 3 Chicken-Flavor Bouillon Cubes
1½ teaspoons chili powder
½ teaspoon ground cumin

In large saucepan over medium-high heat, melt margarine. Add onion and garlic; cook and stir until tender. Add remaining ingredients; bring to a boil. Reduce heat to low; cover and simmer 15 to 20 minutes or until rice is tender and liquid is absorbed. Garnish as desired. Refrigerate leftovers.

*Makes 4 to 6 servings*

## Wisconsin Swiss Linguine Tart

½ cup butter, divided
2 cloves garlic, minced
30 thin French bread slices
3 tablespoons all-purpose flour
1 teaspoon salt
¼ teaspoon white pepper
   Dash ground nutmeg
2½ cups milk
¼ cup grated Wisconsin Parmesan
   cheese
2 eggs, slightly beaten
8 ounces fresh linguine, cooked and
   drained
2 cups (8 ounces) shredded Wisconsin
   Swiss cheese, divided
⅓ cup sliced green onions with tops
2 tablespoons minced fresh basil
   leaves *or* 1 teaspoon dried basil
   leaves, crushed
2 plum tomatoes, each cut lengthwise
   into eighths

Preheat oven to 400°F. Melt ¼ cup butter
in small saucepan over medium heat.
Add garlic; cook and stir 1 minute.
Brush 10-inch pie plate with butter
mixture. Line bottom and side of pie
plate with bread, allowing bread to
extend 1 inch over edge of dish. Brush
bread with remaining butter mixture.
Bake 5 minutes or until lightly browned.
**Reduce oven temperature to 350°F.**

Melt remaining butter in medium
saucepan over low heat. Stir in flour and
seasonings. Gradually stir in milk; cook,
stirring constantly, until thickened. Add
Parmesan cheese. Stir some of the sauce
into eggs; stir back into sauce. Set aside.
Combine linguine, 1¼ cups Swiss
cheese, onions and basil in large bowl.

Pour sauce over linguine mixture; toss to
coat. Pour into crust. Arrange tomatoes
on top; sprinkle with remaining ¾ cup
Swiss cheese. Bake at 350°F, 25 minutes
or until thoroughly heated; let stand 5
minutes before cutting to serve.

*Makes 8 servings*

*Favorite recipe from* **Wisconsin Milk Marketing Board**
© *1992*

## Vegetable Pasta with Spinach Pesto

2 cloves garlic
1 bunch DOLE® Spinach (about 2 cups
   torn spinach)
1 cup DOLE® Whole Natural
   Almonds, toasted
⅔ cup olive oil
¾ cup (3 ounces) grated Parmesan
   cheese
3 tablespoons dried basil leaves,
   crushed
1 package (8 ounces) fettuccine
2 cups DOLE® Broccoli florettes
2 cups slivered DOLE® Carrots

• To make pesto, combine garlic,
spinach, almonds, oil, Parmesan cheese
and basil in food processor or blender
container; cover. Process until spinach is
finely chopped.

• Cook pasta according to package
directions, adding broccoli and carrots
to pasta during last 2 minutes of
cooking; drain.

• In large bowl, combine hot pasta
mixture with spinach pesto; toss to coat.

*Makes 6 servings*

**Prep time:** 15 minutes
**Cook time:** 10 minutes

# Seafood Ravioli with Fresh Tomato Sauce

*PHILLY Soft Cream Cheese with Herb & Garlic combined with crab-flavored seafood makes a tasty filling for these unique ravioli appetizers.*

 1 container (8 ounces)
     PHILADELPHIA BRAND® Soft
     Cream Cheese with Herb & Garlic
 ¾ cup chopped LOUIS KEMP®
     CRAB DELIGHTS® Chunks,
     rinsed
 36 wonton wrappers
     Cold water
     Fresh Tomato Sauce (recipe follows)

• Stir together cream cheese and crab-flavored surimi seafood in medium bowl until well blended.

• For each ravioli, place 1 tablespoonful cream cheese mixture in center of one wonton wrapper. Brush edges with water. Place second wonton wrapper on top. Press edges together to seal, taking care to press out air. Repeat with remaining cream cheese mixture and wonton wrappers.

• For square-shaped ravioli, cut edges of wonton wrappers with pastry trimmer to form square. For round-shaped ravioli, place 3-inch round biscuit cutter on ravioli, making sure center of each cutter contains filling. Press down firmly, cutting through both wrappers, to trim edges. Repeat with remaining ravioli.

• Bring 1½ quarts water to a boil in large saucepan. Cook ravioli, a few at a time, 2 to 3 minutes or until they rise to surface. Remove with slotted spoon. Serve hot with Fresh Tomato Sauce.

*Makes 1½ dozen*

*Seafood Ravioli with Fresh Tomato Sauce*

## Fresh Tomato Sauce

 2 cloves garlic, minced
 2 tablespoons olive oil
 6 plum tomatoes, diced
 1 tablespoon red wine vinegar
 1 tablespoon chopped fresh parsley

• In medium saucepan over medium-high heat, cook and stir garlic in oil 1 minute. Add remaining ingredients. Reduce heat to low.

• Cook 2 to 3 minutes or until thoroughly heated, stirring occasionally. Cool to room temperature.

**Prep time:** 25 minutes
**Cooking time:** 3 minutes per batch
**Variation:** For triangle-shaped ravioli, prepare cream cheese mixture as directed. Place 2 teaspoons cream cheese mixture in center of each wonton wrapper; brush edges with water. Fold in half to form triangle. Press edges together to seal, taking care to press out air. Trim edges of wonton wrapper with pastry trimmer, if desired. Continue as directed. *Makes 3 dozen*

# Homemade Pasta Dough

*If pasta is to be served as a main dish, the rule is to use 1 egg to 3/4 cup flour per person. As a first course, a 4-egg pasta will serve 6 persons well.*

**1½ cups all-purpose flour
2 large eggs**

1. Place flour on pastry board; make well in center.

2. Break eggs into well; beat with fork. Draw in flour, a little at a time, using only enough flour to form soft dough. (Too much flour will make dough brittle or too hard.)

3. Start forming dough into a ball. Press and push dough with heel of your hand; turn, fold and press again. Knead until smooth and elastic, adding more flour when necessary. Dough should be firm but not hard.

4. Cover dough with a bowl. Let rest 30 minutes. Roll, shape or cut pasta as required by recipe. *Makes ¾ pound*

**Pasta Verde (Green Pasta):** Add ½ cup cooked, squeezed dry, finely chopped spinach to eggs; beat until well blended. Continue as directed.

**Processor-Method Pasta Dough:** • Place eggs in bowl of food processor fitted with metal blade; cover. Process 10 seconds. • Add 1 cup flour; process until well blended, gradually adding additional flour as needed until dough forms ball on blades. (If this doesn't happen and mixture resembles coarse meal, remove to pastry board and form ball with your hands.) • Cover dough on pastry board with a bowl. Let rest 30 minutes. Roll, shape or cut pasta as required by recipe.

**Note:** Pasta dough can be prepared ahead of time. Wrap well in plastic wrap and refrigerate overnight *or* freeze up to one month.

*Favorite recipe from **National Pasta Association***

# Capellini Orange Almondine

**1 pound Angel Hair Pasta (Capellini)** *or* **your favorite long, thin pasta shape, cooked and drained
½ cup** *plus* **1 tablespoon butter, divided
½ cup orange spreadable fruit** *or* **orange marmalade
1 cup slivered** *or* **chopped almonds, toasted
¼ cup half-and-half**

In small saucepan over medium heat, combine ½ cup butter and spreadable fruit; stir until smooth. Add to pasta; toss until well coated. Melt remaining 1 tablespoon butter in small skillet over medium-high heat. Add almonds; cook and stir until lightly toasted. Add to pasta mixture with half-and-half; toss lightly. Serve immediately.

*Makes 6 to 8 servings*

*Favorite recipe from **National Pasta Association***

# Noodles Alfredo

**8 ounces wide egg noodles** *or* **fettuccine, cooked and drained
¼ cup butter** *or* **margarine
½ cup half-and-half** *or* **light cream
1 cup (3 ounces) SARGENTO® Fancy Supreme Shredded Parmesan Cheese
1 tablespoon dried parsley flakes
¼ teaspoon salt
Dash pepper**

Melt butter in 1-quart saucepan over low heat. Stir in half-and-half, Parmesan cheese, parsley, salt and pepper until well blended. Pour over hot noodles; toss gently to coat. *Makes 6 servings*

## Vegetable-Pasta Stir-Fry

**2 tablespoons olive oil**
**6 cups cut-up vegetables (red pepper, carrots, zucchini, celery, peas)**
**1½ teaspoons DURKEE® Thyme Leaves *or* ¾ teaspoon ground thyme**
**¾ teaspoon DURKEE® Garlic Powder**
**½ teaspoon salt**
**¼ teaspoon DURKEE® Ground Black Pepper**
**1 cup cavetelli *or* small shell pasta, cooked and drained**
**½ cup chicken bouillon *or* broth**

In large skillet, heat oil over medium-high heat. Add vegetables and seasonings; cook and stir 5 minutes or until vegetables are crisp-tender. Add hot pasta and bouillon. Cook, stirring frequently, until most of liquid is absorbed, about 2 minutes. Serve with grated Parmesan cheese, if desired.

*Makes 6 servings*

## Oriental Noodles Stroganoff

**1½ cups water**
**½ cup milk**
**2 tablespoons butter *or* margarine**
**1 package LIPTON® Noodles & Sauce—Stroganoff**
**¼ teaspoon ground ginger**
**1 package (10 ounces) frozen green beans, partially thawed**
**¼ cup slivered almonds, toasted**

In medium saucepan, bring water, milk and butter to a boil. Stir in noodles & stroganoff sauce and ginger. Simmer over medium heat, stirring occasionally, 5 minutes. Stir in green beans and almonds. Simmer an additional 3 minutes or until noodles are tender.

*Makes about 4 servings*

*Sweet Peppered Pasta*

## Sweet Peppered Pasta

**7 ounces MUELLER'S® Pasta Ruffles, cooked and drained**
**3 tablespoons MAZOLA® Corn Oil**
**½ cup finely chopped onion**
**½ cup finely chopped red bell pepper**
**½ cup finely chopped yellow bell pepper**
**3 large cloves garlic, minced**
**⅓ cup water**
**2 tablespoons chopped fresh basil leaves**
**1 chicken-flavor bouillon cube**
**¼ teaspoon crushed red pepper**

In large skillet, heat corn oil over medium-high heat. Add onion, red and yellow bell peppers and garlic; cook and stir 4 minutes. Stir in water, basil, bouillon cube and crushed red pepper. Bring to a boil, stirring occasionally. Reduce heat to low; simmer 4 minutes, stirring occasionally. Spoon over hot pasta in large bowl; toss well to coat. Serve over assorted salad greens, if desired. *Makes 6 servings*

# Almond Crunch Macaroni Custard

**Custard:**
- ½ cup ring macaroni, cooked and drained
- 2 eggs
- 1 cup milk
- ½ cup packed brown sugar
- ¼ cup all-purpose flour
- ¼ cup butter, softened
- 1½ teaspoons almond extract

**Almond Topping:**
- ½ cup slivered almonds
- ⅓ cup packed brown sugar
- 2 tablespoons butter, softened
- 1 tablespoon milk

Preheat oven to 350°F. Combine all custard ingredients except pasta in blender container; cover. Blend on medium speed 2 minutes. Pour into large bowl. Add pasta; toss lightly. Spoon into greased and floured 8-inch square baking dish. Bake 40 to 45 minutes, until custard is set.

Combine all topping ingredients in small bowl; spread over hot custard. Broil 2 to 3 minutes or until topping is bubbly and golden brown.

*Makes 9 servings*

*Favorite recipe from* **North Dakota Wheat Commission**

# Toasted Ravioli

- Vegetable oil
- 24 meat- or cheese-filled ravioli, fresh or thawed if frozen
- 2 eggs, slightly beaten
- ¾ cup PROGRESSO® Italian Style Bread Crumbs

1. In heavy 1½-quart saucepan, heat 1 inch vegetable oil (approximately 2 cups) to 350°F.

2. Dip ravioli into eggs; coat with bread crumbs.

3. Deep fry ravioli, in small batches, 1 minute or until golden brown. Remove with slotted spoon; drain on paper towels.     *Makes 8 appetizer servings*

**Prep time:** 10 minutes
**Cooking time:** 5 minutes

*Almond Crunch Macaroni Custard*

*Two-Cheese Pasta*

In medium skillet, heat oil over medium-high heat. Add onion and red pepper; cook and stir until tender. Remove vegetables from skillet and set aside. In same skillet, gradually add milk to flour, stirring until well blended; bring just to a boil. Reduce heat to low; simmer 5 minutes. Gradually add cheeses, stirring constantly, until melted. Stir in Seasoned Salt and wine. Add to hot pasta with vegetables; toss lightly to coat.

*Makes 4 to 6 servings*

**Presentation:** Serve with crusty Italian bread.

**Hint:** If desired, 2 tablespoons water can be substituted for white wine.

## Two-Cheese Pasta

*For cheese lovers everywhere!*

8 ounces spiral multi-colored pasta, cooked and drained
1 tablespoon vegetable oil
½ cup chopped onion
1 red pepper, chopped
½ cup milk
1½ teaspoons all-purpose flour
1 cup (4 ounces) shredded fontina cheese
⅓ cup (2 ounces) crumbled Gorgonzola cheese
½ teaspoon LAWRY'S® Seasoned Salt
2 tablespoons dry white wine

## Spinach Tortellini with Roasted Red Peppers

2 packages (9 ounces *each*) fresh spinach tortellini, cooked and drained
1 jar (7 ounces) roasted red peppers *or* pimientos
2 tablespoons butter *or* olive oil
4 cloves garlic, minced
¼ cup chopped fresh basil leaves *or* 2 teaspoons dried basil leaves, crushed
½ cup chopped walnuts, toasted
1 cup prepared HIDDEN VALLEY RANCH® Original Ranch® Salad Dressing

Slice red peppers into strips; set aside. In large saucepan, melt butter over medium-high heat. Add garlic; cook and stir 2 minutes. Add red pepper, basil and hot tortellini; stir to coat. Add walnuts. Stir in enough salad dressing so mixture is creamy and tortellini are coated. Garnish with additional fresh basil leaves, if desired.

*Makes 4 to 6 servings*

## Cabbage and Noodles

2 cups egg noodles
¼ cup *plus* 1 tablespoon BUTTER
    FLAVOR CRISCO®, divided
⅓ cup chopped onion
3 cups coarsely shredded cabbage
    (about ¾ pound)
¼ teaspoon fennel seed
2 tablespoons chopped fresh parsley
½ teaspoon salt
¼ teaspoon pepper

Cook noodles according to package directions, adding 1 tablespoon BUTTER FLAVOR CRISCO® to cooking water; drain. Keep warm.

In large skillet, melt remaining ¼ cup BUTTER FLAVOR CRISCO® over medium heat. Add onion; cook and stir until crisp-tender. Add cabbage and fennel seed; cook and stir until cabbage is tender. Transfer mixture to medium serving bowl. Add hot noodles, parsley, salt and pepper; toss lightly to coat.

*Makes 4 to 6 servings*

## Cheesy Pasta Primavera

8 ounces fettuccine, cooked and
    drained
6 tablespoons butter, divided
1 cup diagonally-cut carrot slices
1 cup yellow summer squash slices
2 cups mushroom quarters
1 cup Chinese pea pod halves
¼ cup green onion slices with tops
1 tablespoon chopped fresh basil
    leaves *or* 1 teaspoon dried basil
    leaves, crushed
1 cup lowfat *or* cream-style cottage
    cheese
¼ cup (1 ounce) grated Wisconsin
    Parmesan cheese
Salt and pepper

Melt 4 tablespoons butter in large skillet over medium heat. Add carrots; cook and stir 5 minutes. Add squash; cook and stir 2 minutes. Add remaining vegetables; continue cooking until vegetables are tender, about 5 minutes, stirring occasionally. Stir in basil. Combine hot fettuccine and remaining 2 tablespoons butter; toss until butter is melted. Add cottage cheese and Parmesan cheese; toss to coat. Season with salt and pepper to taste. Place fettuccine mixture on serving platter; top with vegetable mixture.

*Makes 4 servings*

*Favorite recipe from* **Wisconsin Milk Marketing Board**
*© 1992*

## Linguine with Fresh Parsley Sauce

1 pound linguine
3 tablespoons KIKKOMAN® Lite Soy
    Sauce
1½ teaspoons lemon juice
½ cup olive oil, divided
½ cup raw sunflower seed, divided
2 cups packed fresh parsley leaves
1 green onion with top, cut into 1-inch
    pieces
1 medium clove garlic

Cook linguine according to package directions, omitting salt; drain. Meanwhile, combine lite soy sauce, lemon juice, ¼ cup olive oil, ¼ cup sunflower seed, parsley, onion and garlic in blender or food processor container. Cover; process until smooth. Gradually pour in remaining ¼ cup olive oil, continuing to process on low speed just until mixture is blended. Stir in remaining ¼ cup sunflower seed. Pour over hot linguine; toss to coat.

*Makes 4 to 6 servings*

## Breakfast Pasta "Pizza"

**Crust:**

2½ cups medium egg noodles, cooked and drained
1 teaspoon finely chopped onion
½ teaspoon broiled steak seasoning
1 egg
¼ cup milk
½ cup (2 ounces) shredded sharp Cheddar cheese

**Topping:**

¼ cup (½ stick) butter
1 can (4 ounces) sliced mushrooms, drained
½ can (8 ounces) sliced water chestnuts, drained and finely chopped
¼ cup chopped green pepper
1 teaspoon finely chopped onion
4 slices (½ to 1 ounce *each*) Swiss *or* Mozzarella cheese, cut into 4 strips each
2 eggs, slightly beaten
½ cup milk
6 slices bacon, cooked and crumbled
½ cup chopped ham, optional
1 cup (4 ounces) shredded sharp Cheddar cheese
Tomato slices
Mushroom slices
Green pepper strips

**Crust:** Preheat oven to 375°F. Combine all crust ingredients; mix well. Press into lightly greased 10- or 12-inch pizza pan.

**Topping:** Melt butter in small skillet over medium-high heat. Add mushrooms, water chestnuts, chopped green pepper and onion. Cook and stir until vegetables are tender; spoon over crust. Top with cheese strips. Combine eggs, milk, bacon, ham and shredded cheese; mix well. Pour over cheese strips. Bake 15 to 20 minutes, until egg mixture is set. Top with tomatoes, mushrooms and green pepper strips. Let stand 5 to 10 minutes before cutting to serve.

*Makes 6 to 8 servings*

**Microwave:** Assemble "pizza" on microwave-safe pizza pan or in shallow baking dish; cover. Microwave on HIGH 10 minutes or until egg mixture is set, turning pan after 5 minutes. Top with vegetables as directed.

*Favorite recipe from **Southeast United Dairy Industry Association, Inc.***

## Noodle Kugel

1 pound Egg Noodles, cooked and drained
1 package (8 ounces) cream cheese, softened
3 eggs
1½ cups cottage cheese
¾ cup sour cream
¼ cup honey
½ teaspoon vanilla
2 teaspoons ground cinnamon
Dash salt
2 apples, peeled, cored and sliced

**Brown Sugar Topping:**

¼ cup packed brown sugar
¼ cup wheat germ
1 cup fresh bread crumbs
2 teaspoons ground cinnamon
1 tablespoon cold butter

Combine cream cheese and eggs in medium bowl; beat until well blended. Add cottage cheese, sour cream, honey, vanilla, cinnamon and salt; beat until smooth. Add noodles and apples; mix lightly. Pour into well-buttered 1½-quart baking dish.

Combine all topping ingredients *except* butter; sprinkle over noodle mixture. Dot with butter. Bake at 375°F, 35 minutes. Let stand 10 minutes before serving. *Makes 6 to 8 servings*

*Favorite recipe from **National Pasta Association***

*Pumpkin Pasta Piccata*

## Pumpkin Pasta Piccata

4 cups half-and-half
½ cup margarine
1 pound spinach fettuccine
3 cups shredded peeled pumpkin
2 green onions with tops, finely
    chopped
½ cup chopped fresh parsley
¼ cup chopped fresh dill
2 tablespoons drained capers
1 tablespoon grated lemon peel
2 teaspoons Dijon-style mustard
¼ teaspoon pepper

Combine half-and-half and margarine in medium saucepan. Simmer over low heat until mixture is reduced by half, about 30 minutes, stirring occasionally. Meanwhile, cook pasta according to package directions; drain. Add all remaining ingredients *except* pasta to half-and-half mixture in saucepan. Simmer an additional 5 minutes, stirring constantly. Pour over hot pasta in large bowl; toss gently to coat. Garnish as desired. *Makes 8 servings*

## Penne alla Napolitana

12 ounces penne (*or* other small tubular
    pasta)
4 tablespoons virgin olive oil, divided
2 tablespoons minced fresh garlic
2 cups tomato sauce
1 cup pitted California ripe olives,
    sliced
¼ cup coarsely chopped fresh basil
    leaves
1 teaspoon red pepper flakes
½ cup cubed mozzarella cheese
    (¼-inch cubes)
½ cup (2 ounces) grated Parmesan
    cheese

Cook pasta according to package directions; drain. Add 1 tablespoon olive oil; toss lightly. Return pasta to pan; keep warm.

Heat remaining 3 tablespoons olive oil in medium skillet over medium-high heat. Add garlic; cook and stir until lightly browned. Stir in tomato sauce, olives, basil and red pepper. Heat thoroughly, stirring occasionally. Add cheeses; stir until mozzarella cheese begins to melt. Serve over hot pasta. Serve with additional grated Parmesan cheese, if desired. *Makes 4 servings*

*Favorite recipe from **California Olive Industry***

## Fruit 'n Nut Noodle Pudding

½ cup *plus* 1 tablespoon packed brown
    sugar, divided
¼ cup chopped almonds, toasted
2 eggs, slightly beaten
1½ cups milk
  1 tablespoon rum, optional
  ½ teaspoon ground cinnamon
  ¼ teaspoon ground nutmeg
  1 package LIPTON® Noodles &
    Sauce—Butter
  4 large plums,* pitted and thinly sliced

Preheat oven to 350°F.

In small bowl, combine 1 tablespoon
brown sugar with almonds; set aside.

In large bowl, with wire whisk,
thoroughly blend eggs, milk, rum,
remaining ½ cup brown sugar,
cinnamon and nutmeg. Stir in noodles
& butter sauce; let stand 15 minutes.
Pour into greased 9- or 10-inch deep-
dish pie plate. Top with plums and
almond mixture. Bake 30 minutes or
until slightly puffed and golden brown.
*Makes about 6 servings*

**\*Variation:** Substitute 2 large pears *or*
apples, cored and thinly sliced.

## Pasta with Fresh Tomatoes & Basil

2 tablespoons olive *or* vegetable oil
2 teaspoons minced fresh garlic
2 medium tomatoes, chopped
1 tablespoon finely chopped fresh
    basil leaves
1½ cups water
  ½ cup milk
  1 package LIPTON® Noodles
    & Sauce—Alfredo
  Pepper

In large skillet, heat oil over medium
heat. Add garlic; cook and stir 30
seconds. Add tomatoes and basil; cook,
stirring frequently, 3 minutes or until
tomatoes are softened. Add water and
milk; bring to a boil. Stir in noodles &
Alfredo sauce; simmer, stirring
occasionally, 9 minutes or until noodles
are tender. Season with pepper to taste.
Sprinkle with grated Parmesan cheese, if
desired. *Makes about 4 side-dish
or 2 main-dish servings*

**Variation:** Substitute 1 teaspoon dried
basil leaves, crushed, for 1 tablespoon
fresh basil leaves.

**Microwave:** In 1½-quart microwave-safe
casserole, combine oil and garlic.
Microwave, uncovered, on HIGH (Full
Power) 30 seconds. Add tomatoes and
basil. Microwave 3 minutes, stirring after
2 minutes. Stir in water, milk and
noodles & Alfredo sauce. Microwave 10
minutes or until noodles are tender; add
pepper. Let stand, covered, 5 minutes.
Sprinkle with grated Parmesan cheese, if
desired.

*Fruit 'n Nut Noodle Pudding*

## Stuffed Seafood Shells

16 jumbo pasta shells, cooked and
   drained
 1 can (6½ ounces) tuna, drained and
   flaked
 1 can (4½ ounces) medium shrimp,
   drained
½ cup pearl onions, cooked and sliced
½ cup chopped sweet pickles
½ cup sliced pimiento-stuffed olives
 1 jar (12 ounces) chili sauce
 2 tablespoons horseradish sauce
½ teaspoon Worcestershire sauce
   Hot pepper sauce
   Bibb lettuce leaves

Combine tuna, shrimp, onions, pickles
and olives in large bowl. Combine chili
sauce, horseradish sauce and
Worcestershire sauce in small bowl;
blend well. Season with hot pepper
sauce to taste. Pour over seafood
mixture; mix gently. Cover and
refrigerate at least 30 minutes. Fill
cooked shells with seafood mixture.
(Shells may be covered and refrigerated
several hours.) Serve on lettuce-covered
platter.    *Makes 8 appetizer servings*

*Favorite recipe from* **North Dakota Wheat Commission**

## Lemon Pasta with Asparagus

 1 pound DOLE® Asparagus
   Salt
   Grated peel and juice from 2 DOLE®
   Lemons
 8 ounces penne *or* shell pasta
 2 tablespoons margarine
 1 cup whipping cream
¼ cup (1 ounce) grated Parmesan
   cheese
¼ cup chopped fresh parsley
   Freshly ground pepper

***Stuffed Seafood Shells***

• Cut asparagus diagonally into 1-inch
pieces. Add to boiling water; let stand 1
to 2 minutes. Drain and set aside.

• Bring 2 quarts lightly-salted water to a
boil. Add lemon juice and pasta. Cook
pasta according to package directions;
drain.

• Melt margarine with cream in small
saucepan over low heat. Stir in lemon
peel and Parmesan cheese. Combine
sauce, asparagus, pasta and parsley; toss
to coat. Season with pepper to taste.
Serve immediately.

   *Makes 4 to 6 servings*

**Prep time:** 10 minutes
**Cook time:** 15 minutes

# Acknowledgments

*The publishers would like to thank the companies and organizations listed below for the use of their recipes in this publication.*

Almond Board of California
American Egg Board
Armour Swift-Eckrich
Bel Paese Sales Company
Best Foods, a Division of CPC International Inc.
Borden Kitchens, Borden, Inc.
California Apricot Advisory Board
California Artichoke Advisory Board
California Olive Industry
California Poultry Industry Federation
California Table Grape Commission
California Tomato Board
Canned Food Information Council
Chef Paul Prudhomme's Magic Seasoning Blends™
Contadina Foods, Inc., Nestlé Food Company
The Creamette Company
Del Monte Corporation
Dole Food Company, Inc.
Durkee-French Foods, A Division of Reckitt & Colman Inc.
Filippo Berio Olive Oil
The Fremont Company, Makers of Frank's & Snowfloss Kraut
The Fresh Garlic Association
Heinz U.S.A.
Hunt-Wesson, Inc.
The HVR Company
Jones Dairy Farm
Kansas Poultry Association

Kikkoman International Inc.
Kraft General Foods, Inc.
The Larsen Company
Lawry's® Foods, Inc.
Thomas J. Lipton Co.
McIlhenny Company
Nabisco Foods Group
National Live Stock and Meat Board
National Pasta Association
National Pork Producers Council
National Sunflower Association
New Jersey Department of Agriculture
Norseland Foods, Inc.
North Dakota Beef Commission
North Dakota Dairy Promotion Commission
North Dakota Wheat Commission
Oklahoma Agriculture Organizations
Oscar Mayer Foods Corporation
Pace Foods, Inc.
Perdue Farms
Pet Incorporated
Pollio Dairy Products
The Procter & Gamble Company, Inc.
Sargento Cheese Company, Inc.
Shade Pasta, Inc.
Southeast United Dairy Industry Association, Inc.
StarKist Seafood Company
Walnut Marketing Board
Wisconsin Milk Marketing Board

# Photo Credits

*The publishers would like to thank the companies and organizations listed below for the use of their photographs in this publication.*

Armour Swift-Eckrich
Best Foods, a Division of CPC International Inc.
Borden Kitchens, Borden, Inc.
California Apricot Advisory Board
California Olive Industry
California Poultry Industry Federation
Chef Paul Prudhomme's Magic Seasoning Blends™
Contadina Foods, Inc., Nestlé Food Company
The Creamette Company
Del Monte Corporation
Dole Food Company, Inc.
Durkee-French Foods, A Division of Reckitt & Colman Inc.
Hunt-Wesson, Inc.
The HVR Company
Jones Dairy Farm

Kikkoman International Inc.
Kraft General Foods, Inc.
The Larsen Company
Lawry's® Foods, Inc.
Thomas J. Lipton Co.
McIlhenny Company
Nabisco Foods Group
National Live Stock and Meat Board
National Sunflower Association
Oscar Mayer Foods Corporation
Pace Foods, Inc.
Pet Incorporated
Sargento Cheese Company, Inc.
StarKist Seafood Company
Walnut Marketing Board

# INDEX